Biblical Prophecy

INTERPRETATION
Resources for the Use of Scripture in the Church

INTERPRETATION

RESOURCES FOR THE USE OF SCRIPTURE IN THE CHURCH

Patrick D. Miller, *Series Editor*
Ellen F. Davis, *Associate Editor*
Richard B. Hays, *Associate Editor*
James L. Mays, *Consulting Editor*

OTHER AVAILABLE BOOKS IN THE SERIES

Ronald P. Byars, *The Sacraments in Biblical Perspective*
Jerome F. D. Creach, *Violence in Scripture*
Robert W. Jenson, *Canon and Creed*
Patrick D. Miller, *The Ten Commandments*

ELLEN F. DAVIS

Biblical Prophecy

Perspectives for Christian Theology,
Discipleship, and Ministry

INTERPRETATION *Resources for the Use of*
Scripture in the Church

WESTMINSTER
JOHN KNOX PRESS
LOUISVILLE · KENTUCKY

First edition
Published by Westminster John Knox Press
Louisville, Kentucky

14 15 16 17 18 19 20 21 22 23—10 9 8 7 6 5 4 3 2 1

Unless otherwise indicated, Scripture quotations are from the author's own translation.

Scripture quotations marked NRSV are from the New Revised Standard Version of the Bible, copyright © 1989 by the Division of Christian Education of the National Council of the Churches of Christ in the U.S.A., and are used by permission.

The quotation from *Audare/Audire* by Wilmer Mills is used with permission.

Book design by Drew Stevens
Cover design by designpointinc.com

Library of Congress Cataloging-in-Publication Data

Davis, Ellen F.
    Biblical prophecy : perspectives for Christian theology, discipleship, and ministry / Ellen F. Davis.—First edition.
        pages cm.—(Interpretation: resources for the use of scripture in the church)
    Includes bibliographical references and indexes.
    ISBN 978-0-664-23538-3 (alk. paper)
    1. Bible—Prophecies.   2. Bible—Criticism, interpretation, etc.   3. Prophecy—Christianity.   4. Eschatology.   5. Theology.   I. Title.
    BS647.3.D38 2014
    220.1′5—dc23

                                                                                2014009143

CONTENTS

SERIES FOREWORD

This series of volumes supplements Interpretation: A Bible Commentary for Teaching and Preaching. The commentary series offers an exposition of the books of the Bible written for those who teach, preach, and study the Bible in the community of faith. This new series is addressed to the same audience and serves a similar purpose, providing additional resources for the interpretation of Scripture, but now dealing with features, themes, and issues significant for the whole rather than with individual books.

The Bible is composed of separate books. Its composition naturally has led its interpreters to address particular books. But there are other ways to approach the interpretation of the Bible that respond to other characteristics and features of the Scriptures. These other entries to the task of interpretation provide contexts, overviews, and perspectives that complement the book-by-book approach and discern dimensions of the Scriptures that the commentary design may not adequately explore.

The Bible as used in the Christian community is not only a collection of books but also itself a book that has a unity and coherence important to its meaning. Some volumes in this new series will deal with this canonical wholeness and seek to provide a wider context for the interpretation of individual books as well as a comprehensive theological perspective that reading single books does not provide.

Other volumes in the series will examine particular texts, like the Ten Commandments, the Lord's Prayer, and the Sermon on the Mount, texts that have played such an important role in the faith and life of the Christian community that they constitute orienting foci for the understanding and use of Scripture.

A further concern of the series will be to consider important and often difficult topics, addressed at many different places in the books of the canon, that are of recurrent interest and concern to the church in its dependence on Scripture for faith and life. So the series will include volumes dealing with such topics as eschatology, women, wealth, and violence.

The books of the Bible are constituted from a variety of kinds of literature, such as narrative, laws, hymns and prayers, letters,

parables, and miracle stories. To recognize and discern the contribution and importance of all these different kinds of material enriches
and enlightens the use of Scripture. Volumes in the series will provide
help in the interpretation of Scripture's literary forms and genres.

The liturgy and practices of the gathered church are anchored
in Scripture, as with the sacraments observed and the creeds
recited. So another entry to the task of discerning the meaning and
significance of biblical texts explored in this series is the relation
between the liturgy of the church and the Scriptures.

Finally, there is certain ancient literature, such as the Apoc-
rypha and the noncanonical gospels, that constitutes an important
context to the interpretation of Scripture itself. Consequently, this
series will provide volumes that offer guidance in understanding
such writings and explore their significance for the interpretation
of the Protestant canon.

The volumes in this second series of Interpretation deal with
these important entries into the interpretation of the Bible. Together
with the commentaries, they compose a library of resources for
those who interpret Scripture as members of the community of
faith. Each of them can be used independently for its own significant addition to the resources for the study of Scripture. But all of
them intersect the commentaries in various ways and provide an
important context for their use. The authors of these volumes are
biblical scholars and theologians who are committed to the service
of interpreting the Scriptures in and for the church. The editors
and authors hope that the addition of this series to the commentaries will provide a major contribution to the vitality and richness of
biblical interpretation in the church.

The Editors

INTRODUCTION

With respect to prophecy, a strange and even disabling gap exists between the theological emphases of the Bible and the theological understanding of the church. Deliberately or not, the Bible in both Testaments is prophetically shaped, first and last. Abraham is the first person named as a prophet—and named thus by God (Gen. 20:7). At the other end of the Christian canon, the book of Revelation is designated as "the prophecy," and John of Patmos pronounces a blessing on those "who keep what is written in it" (1:3). Most of the books that lie between those two extremities make direct or indirect reference to prophetic persons, words, and acts; such reference is especially pronounced in the long corpus of Moses-centered narratives (Exodus through Deuteronomy), the even longer corpus of prophetically oriented accounts of leadership known as Former Prophets (Joshua through Kings), and of course the fifteen books of the Major and Minor Prophets (Isaiah through Malachi). In less concentrated fashion, the New Testament writers frequently allude or make direct reference to the prophetic word, old and new, or the person (or community) who displays prophetic gifts. In sum, the notion of the prophetic is pervasive in the Bible and seems to be indispensable for giving a full account of the experience of God's people in the past and for entering into their (our) ongoing story in the present.

Considered against that background, the relative lack of theological reflection on the notion of prophecy as an aspect of religious experience within the so-called (though now misnamed) mainstream church is puzzling, at the least. In the North American Protestant stream of Christianity that is most formative for my own Christian life, prophecy gets little attention, apart from certain passages that appear in the lectionary, especially during Advent and Lent. While some contemporary figure or movement might be described as "prophetic," within the church and also in our wider culture, the notion is imprecise. Anything edgy is likely to be termed "prophetic," in a positive sense, as long as it makes no particular reference to religious motivation or theological content. However, anyone who uses prophetic language with avowed religious motivation, anyone who could be seen as claiming any degree of prophetic inspiration, anyone who reads biblical prophecy in ways that create direct pressure in contemporary situations— such a person is suspect to many or most, including the majority of Christians. (Although Martin Luther King Jr. might seem to be an exception now, he was not during his lifetime.) In sum, we like to keep the frame of reference for prophecy within the "safe" confines of the Bible, by reading prophecy solely as illuminating what has already happened—the birth, life, and death of Jesus Christ—and not allowing it to meddle much in the current lives of Christians. However, the writers of both Testaments would surely say that in thus limiting our use of one of the fundamental and pervasive elements of biblical thought, we are hampering and even seriously disabling ourselves as responsible interpreters of Scripture.

The present volume is a study of the "prophetic" in the Bible, as it is manifested in persons, words, and actions; more widely, it is a study of a certain "prophetic perspective," a coherent though not homogeneous way of viewing this world and our own lives in the presence of God. The method of study is exegetical; each essay highlights a theme that receives sustained attention within the prophetic traditions and treats it through the close reading of texts— often multiple texts in conversation with one another. At the same time, this is a study undertaken with the life of the church in mind. I try to open up those texts, both Old Testament and New, in ways that may directly inform Christian thought and offer guidance for prayer, discipleship, and ministry.

The volume is designed as a set of closely related essays. Apart from the first essay, which sets forth the "prophetic perspective" and is foundational for each of the others, they may be read alone or in any combination. They treat matters both perennial and timely in the life of the church: intercessory prayer as an aspect of friendship with God (chap. 2); economics, both those that are divinely endorsed or sustained and those that are condemned as idolatrous (chaps. 3 and 5); the integrity of the created order and human assaults upon it (chap. 4); ministry that points to realistic hope out of the midst of disaster (chap. 6); the difficulties inevitably associated with prophetic revelation as the biblical writers understand it (chap. 7); and discipleship in a prophetically informed church tradition (chap. 8).

xii

The brief final chapter reflects how my reading of some prophetic traditions of the Bible has been shaped by my experience of teaching a course with my Muslim colleague, Imam Abdullah Antepli, on "listening together" to our different scriptures. One of the recurrent themes of this study is how central prophetic traditions in the Bible offer possibilities for positive relations between worshipers of Israel's God and the "religiously other." In this generation, it seems apt and even necessary to conclude a study of biblical prophecy by pointing to Islam, which is of all the world religions the one most fully focused on prophets and the prophetically mediated word as guides for serving God faithfully in this world. I hope that the present volume will provide Christians with some resources for thinking about this and thus perhaps prompt theological conversation between Muslims and Christians about our two prophetically informed faiths.

CHAPTER 1

The Prophetic Interpreter

Prophecy is not for the unbelieving but for those who believe.
—1 Cor. 14:22

Whose voice or action might be termed prophetic? What does "the prophetic" look or sound like in our culture? Forty or fifty years ago, many North American Christians who might have self-identified as political liberals would have had a ready answer to those questions: the prophetic role in this and every time is speaking truth to power. Such a definition of the role is supported by numerous biblical examples, chief among them Moses' first recorded words to Pharaoh: "Thus says YHWH God of Israel, Release my people!" (Exod. 5:1). Moses is the foremost exemplar of "the prophetic imagination" as it confronts "the royal consciousness," to use terms from Walter Brueggemann's classic study, *The Prophetic Imagination* (1978). However, in an essay written nearly a quarter-century later, Brueggemann reconsiders that "primal case" of Moses and Pharaoh. Now he judges that in our social, intellectual, and spiritual climate, *"There are deeply problematic things about the model of truth-speaking-to-power"* (*Inscribing the Text*, 10; italics original). Indeed, the basic terms are problematic, for "in a postmodern world, both *truth* and *power* are complex and evasive" (11).

If that is the problem with the model, then it is not confined to the postmodern world; the biblical writers were themselves well

1

aware of the complexities attending truth and power. A number of biblical prophets had complex relations to the royals of their time. Some, such as Jeremiah, one of the disenfranchised priests from the rural village of Anathoth, may have spoken as rank outsiders, but others—Elisha, Isaiah, Huldah—evidently were consulted by kings and those at the center of government. The complexity of truth itself is one of the major themes of the Bible. Pilate's question to Jesus—"What is truth?" (John 18:38)—might epitomize that theme, but in his mouth the query could be heard as merely cynical or despairing. However, prophets, sages, psalmists, and evangelists all struggle at length and in faith with the mystery of truth, which is both revealed and hidden, given as a reliable guide and still to be searched out, known through God's word or in Jesus Christ and yet to be discerned.

Even if speaking truth to power was never a simpler matter to conceive nor an easier thing to do than it is now, Brueggemann is nonetheless right to observe the complexity of power relations in our society and in the church. Lay or ordained, many of us who serve the church are responsible to and for institutions, their personnel, programs, and budgets, and thus to some degree we are arbiters of power. Certainly all those who get a salary (including pastors and religious educators), all who pay tax on anything and submit forms and reports to governmental, denominational, or educational bodies—we all participate in large social systems that further complicate and likely compromise our own relationship to power. Those whose primary responsibility is pastoral may exercise enormous power, and it is a sign of health that this is increasingly acknowledged in the contemporary church; it is no longer assumed that power is a fixed quantity that should remain wholly on the pastor's side of the relationship. Rather, pastors are charged to empower others, instilling in them "the readiness to accept and affirm what power there is, or could be, had we courage to embrace a different notion of power, a different perspective of ourselves in the world" (Brueggemann, *Inscribing the Text*, 11).

Moreover, we stand in complex relationship to the truth as it is relevant to our public roles as pastors, teachers, preachers. Probably no one who bothers to read a book such as this presumes to have a monopoly on the truth, but many of us might lack confidence that we can speak knowledgeably, responsibly, and helpfully on some of the immense problems and questions that the church must address:

global warming, migrant farmworkers and food production, sexual identity and relations. Virtually none of us is off the grid of the global economy, and that inevitably compromises our perception and proclamation of the truth. Thus Brueggemann concludes his analysis of the problematic model of speaking truth to power: "We cannot automatically cast ourselves as Moses or Nathan or Elijah or Daniel, no matter how endlessly we are tempted. Besides, if we are casting to type, it may be that we fit the part of the royally and sinfully acquisitive, rather than the truth-teller" (*Inscribing the Text*, 11).

In this study, I begin with a different scriptural model of the prophetic role, one that was suggested to me a few years ago when I was asked to speak at a conference titled "The Prophetic Interpreter." That phrase was new to me at the time, but I have come to see it as useful for designating a kind of work that crosses borders (as did the conference itself) between the theological academy, the church, and the wider culture. The notion of the prophetic interpreter may help us think about the significance of a variety of leadership roles and modes of service performed in and for the church, including teaching, preaching, writing, and artistic work, as well as public speaking and multiple forms of community service and political work that is done in the service of the church and the wider community. People whom the Bible designates as prophets or as possessing the gift of prophecy engaged in all these forms of work. In word and deed, they interpreted the faith for their time, and equally, they interpreted the times for the faithful. Moreover, the Bible itself represents some of those engaged in prophetic work as learned and innovative interpreters of Israel's scriptural (or protoscriptural) traditions. So I propose that we lift up the prophetic interpreter as an important model for service in and to the church. To illustrate that model, I turn to the first (in canonical order) clear exemplar of the prophetic interpreter within the Bible itself, Huldah of Jerusalem.

Interpreting Current History: Huldah and Josiah

Huldah was a professional prophet, known within the royal circle in Jerusalem during the reign of Josiah of Judah (640–609 BCE). As the story is told (2 Kgs. 22:8–20), "the Torah scroll" is found during Josiah's major renovation of the temple precinct, and it is brought

3

to the king. When he hears the contents of the sacred book—possibly some version of what now forms the core of Deuteronomy (chaps. 12–26), with the appended curses for violators—Josiah becomes alarmed and charges the high priest and his advisers to secure a divine oracle from a prophet. They go immediately to Huldah at her home in the Mishneh, a fashionable district not far from the palace (her husband, Shallum, served the court as keeper of the wardrobe). The prophet would presumably have the strongest personal reasons for retaining Josiah's favor, yet Huldah sends back to the palace this harsh and markedly impersonal word:

> Thus says YHWH God of Israel, "Say to the man who sent you to me: 'Thus says YHWH: I am about to bring evil to this place and upon its inhabitants—all the words of the book which the king of Judah read. Because they abandoned me and burned incense to other gods in order to outrage me with all the work of their hands, my wrath is kindled against this place and will not be quenched.' And to the king of Judah who sent you to inquire of YHWH, thus you shall speak: '. . . Because your heart softened and you humbled yourself before YHWH when you heard what I spoke about this place and about its inhabitants . . . , I too have heard'—an utterance of YHWH. 'And so I shall gather you to your ancestors, and you shall be gathered to your grave in peace, and your eyes shall not look upon all the evil which I am bringing upon this place.'" (2 Kgs. 22:15–20)

The historical validity of the scroll story is much debated. There are reasons that Josiah's admirers, such as the Deuteronomistic Historian, might have invented such a story: to give the aura of ancient authority to Josiah's newly initiated program of religious reform, to avert criticism that the king did not earlier institute reform, since he had been on the throne for a dozen or more years (see 2 Kgs. 22:1 and 2 Chr. 34:3) before he purged Jerusalem and Judah of shrines and images "made for Baal and Asherah and all the host of heaven" (2 Kgs. 23:4). However, it is likely that the story tells us less about the exact circumstances of Josiah's reform than it does about Huldah's role as a prophet. Several things are important for considering the role of prophetic interpreter:

4   1. Huldah's story is the first clear account of someone who encounters God's word in written form and recognizes how it speaks to current and emerging circumstances. As the recipient

and interpreter of Torah (divine Teaching), she stands in the line of authoritative figures that begins with Moses. Indeed, she is the culminating figure in that line, according to the Deuteronomistic History (Deuteronomy through Kings); she stands knowingly on the cusp of the precipitous slide into the great destruction and the exile to Babylon (2 Kgs. 24–25).

2. Huldah of Jerusalem stands in liminal relation to power: she is connected though not subordinated to the very nerve center of the kingdom. Apparently Huldah did not serve with Shallum within the royal palace; it is probable that the position of Judean court prophet, like that of priest, was not open to a woman. But even if she did not give oracles for a salary—perhaps *because* she did not—Huldah was respected and indeed relied upon by the most powerful people in the kingdom; "the man" in the palace heeded her words. So from her position at the edge of the circle of power, she was able to interpret God's word in such a way as to stimulate major change through official channels; in this sense, Huldah is one of the few "successful" prophets of whom the Bible speaks.

3. Huldah's story comes from the circle of theologians, literary scholars, and editors (the so-called Deuteronomists) who likely also collected and shaped the first edition of the Latter Prophets, and especially the book of Jeremiah (Blenkinsopp, *History*, 191–93). Setting Huldah alongside Jeremiah, her contemporary, we may see both of them as liminal figures in a second sense: they stand at the threshold between the age of the great prophets and the age of scribal interpretation. While Jeremiah is represented as a prophet who dictated the divine word into scroll form (Jer. 36), Huldah is the prophet who receives the written word as from God ("Thus says YHWH God of Israel") and recognizes how it applies to her own moment in history. She has the fortitude to interpret it in a way no one would want to hear, and the clarity to make the divine word intelligible and compelling.

4. Josiah exemplifies the person who hears what God is saying through the written word, seeks responsible interpretation, and as a result changes radically and decisively (2 Kgs. 23:1–25). Although Josiah is the most powerful person in the land of Judah, that is not necessarily crucial for what the story has to say to us about hearing God's word through Scripture. Rather, he models the (tragically) rare ability *to hear God's word spoken against one's own apparent interests*. To hear God's word as spoken "against ourselves"—this,

5

Dietrich Bonhoeffer maintained, is what it means to read the Bible seriously, to prefer its thoughts to our own, and thus to "find ourselves again" (*No Rusty Swords*, 185–86). Bonhoeffer was speaking—prophetically, one might say—at the Berlin Youth Conference in April 1932. At that time, his was a nearly isolated Christian voice speaking publicly and persistently against the rise of National Socialism. Bonhoeffer's permanent legacy as a theologian has been to show that in the modern world, as in Josiah's and Huldah's Jerusalem, fostering the discomfiting yet life-giving practice of *reading the Bible against ourselves* is a major public responsibility of the Christian teacher and theologian. In desperate times, as his was and ours may yet prove to be, many may be called to serve thus as prophetic interpreters.

Elements of the Prophetic Perspective

As a clear-eyed interpreter of both text and history, Huldah of Jerusalem may be one of the most important biblical models for those who preach, teach, and interpret Scripture for others in various settings, and Josiah is a model for how we might study and hear God's word for (or "against"!) ourselves. At a given time any Christian might assume either role: Huldah's, of offering an interpretation, or Josiah's, of listening to one; the apostle Paul suggests that every member of the church should be engaged on both sides of the interpretative process (see 1 Cor. 14:26–31). Assuming full responsibility on either side of that process requires that we speak and listen from a perspective that is broadly informed by the prophetic traditions of Scripture, in shorthand "the prophetic perspective."

Here I set forth five essential elements of that perspective on reality as broadly represented in the prophetic traditions of the Bible. My intention in identifying these five is to be suggestive rather than exhaustive, to point to elements that are central to these traditions and, considered together, may provide fruitful ground for theological reflection and ministry in the twenty-first century. Distinguishing them thus at the outset of this study is artificial, even if it may be somewhat useful, for these five elements are everywhere interrelated and overlapping. In the texts treated in the following essays, all these elements appear, in different combinations and

6

with varying degrees of emphasis, but there is no attempt to identify each as discrete. Nonetheless, listing them here may alert readers to some of the elements that make the prophetic traditions of
the Bible distinctive modes of discourse, with the potential to speak
to the church in our own time and varied situations:

1. The radical concreteness of prophetic expression, which both
   engages hearers in particular contexts and makes vivid God's
   engagement with the world
2. The prophetic demand for moral, economic, and religious
   integrity in human communities (Israel or the church) and the
   recognition that human integrity in these several dimensions is
   fundamentally related to the God-given integrity of creation
3. Prophetic participation in the suffering of the vulnerable within
   the created order and the social order, and prophetic witnessing to the suffering of God
4. The prophet as the trusted friend of God, entrusted with a ministry of protest, prayer, healing, and reconciliation
5. Prophetic witness to the theological significance of those who
   do not worship Israel's God, which is *potentially* a witness of
   reconciliation

The remainder of this chapter is an explication of these five
elements.

*1. The radical concreteness of prophetic expression, which
both engages hearers in particular contexts and makes vivid God's
engagement with the world.* The biblical prophets do not traffic in
general ideas, universal ideals, or dispassionate ruminations. Their
settings are particular with respect to place and time; the political
situations they treat are specific; the characters are vividly drawn—
including and especially the character of God. So, for example, Isaiah's language remains radically concrete even when his vision is
heavenly: "In the year that King Uzziah died, I saw my Lord [Ado-
nai] sitting on a throne high and uplifted" (Isa. 6:1a). He cites a
particular year (733 BCE) and thus evokes the politically vexed circumstances that modern scholars call "the Assyrian crisis." It is as
though I were to say, "In the year of 9/11, I saw God. . . ." Historical
circumstance is not all that Isaiah concretizes, as we see from the
immediate continuation of his vision report:

7

> . . . and the hem of his robe fills the temple.
> And flaming creatures are standing at attendance on him, each with
> six wings.
> With two it covers its face, and with two it covers its lower parts, and
> with two it flies.
> And each calls to the other, saying, "Holy, holy, holy—YHWH of
> Hosts!
> His Presence is the fullness of the whole earth."
>
> (Isa. 6:1b–3)

This is a vision with surround sound. In its vivid detail, down to the burning coal thrust right under Isaiah's nose, his report of heaven imaginatively engages every physical sense.

The speech of the biblical prophets is filled with the things of this world; theirs is "a language that pays homage to the splendid grittiness of the physical as well as to the splendor and consolation of the spiritual." This is how the Catholic poet Paul Mariani (*God and the Imagination*, 234) characterizes a tradition of Christian writing that he traces from Dante to Flannery O'Connor and Richard Wilbur. However, it would be accurate to say that all of them take inspiration—even permission—from the Hebrew prophets to write out of a religious understanding "that is not abstracted, not dissociated and world-renouncing" (Wilbur, quoted by Mariani, ibid.). For the prophets and each of these writers, the radical concreteness of expression is not an aesthetic preference in a casual sense; it is motivated and required by a certain theological understanding. Their aim is to show God's inescapable involvement in the world, what Isaiah epitomizes with a single phrase: *'immanû ēl*, "God [is] with us" (7:14; 8:8, 10).

That theological assertion is convincing only within the context of a compelling literary depiction of the world and human existence. And so, like good poets in every tradition, the prophetic poets of the Bible craft sharp images designed to make something visible to the mind's eye—most often viewed from a particular location in space and time, and yet imagined as part of the whole world, inhabited by the hearer as well as the poet. As poets, they must be committed to fidelity, to faithful representation of the world as it actually is, even as they make it possible for their hearers to imagine that God might be doing something radically new in their own time and place. The form of prophetic poetry thus matches its essential content; the poet's faithful framing of words so that they ring true is itself an echo of God's own fidelity to the world.

8

Prophetic poetry often takes the familiar thing, known or readily imaginable, and connects it to what seems to be distant because it is hard to imagine or hard to admit. In a brilliant short oracle, Isaiah ingeniously epitomizes Jerusalem's infidelity to God by contrasting the little local water channel, Shiloah (Silwan), with the massive irrigation system of the mighty Euphrates, the source of agricultural wealth and power for the king of Assyria:

> Because this people has despised
> the waters of Shiloah, which flow gently, . . .
> therefore my Lord is about to raise up against them
> the waters of the River, great and mighty—
> the king of Assyria and all his weighty force.
> And it shall rise up over its channels
> and go over all its banks,
> and sweep through Judah, an uncontainable flood,
> that reaches up to the neck.
> And the spread of [its? his?] wings—
> that will be the fullness of your broad land, Immanuel!
> (Isa. 8:6–8)

For those familiar with the geographic, political, and religious landscape, the immediate situation is bitterly ironic: Judah and Jerusalem, her people and her king, have turned from the God who would be with them (Immanuel) as a life-giving Presence if they trusted YHWH enough to allow it. Isaiah draws on a metaphorical tradition, common among biblical poets, that associates YHWH's Presence with water in a dry land (e.g., Pss. 36:9 [10 Heb.]; 42:1 [2 Heb.]; 63:1 [2 Heb.]). Having spurned that gentle stream, they now face the flood tide of the Assyrian king's invasion. The last lines include a double echo of Isaiah's great temple vision, where God is shown to be the Holy One whose Glory/Presence (*kābôd*) constitutes "the fullness [*mĕlō'*] of the whole earth/land ['*ereṣ*]" (Isa. 6:3). Now there will be a new fullness (*mĕlō'*) in the land ('*ereṣ*, 8:8) of Judah, but whose "wings" are intended is uncertain and probably deliberately ambiguous—are they the alien wings of Assyria's destroying host (sometimes represented as an eagle, cf. Ezek. 17:1–14) or the sheltering wings of YHWH/Immanuel (e.g., Ps. 63:7 [8 Heb.]) or both? The ambiguity leaves us with the question: Is "Immanuel" an assurance only, or also a threat? Certainly the fact that YHWH is "in the midst" of Israel (cf. Isa. 12:6) means that the nations' designs

9

against Judah and Jerusalem will ultimately fail (7:14–16; 10:10), but does this not also create an imminent danger for the people precisely because of their weakness?

This is a considerable poetic achievement. In just a few lines, starting with the concrete image of the small water channel upon which the life of ancient Jerusalem depends, Isaiah offers an analysis not only of international politics of the eighth century but also of religious apostasy in every age—and at the same time of YHWH's constant (and inescapable) Presence. This highly condensed exposition of Judah's situation is a key instance of the prophetic poet's remarkable ability to transform "an experienced reality into a new, coherent, poetic universe" (Alonso Schökel, "Isaiah," 172).

2. *The prophetic demand for moral, economic, and religious integrity in human communities (Israel or the church) and the recognition that human integrity in these several dimensions is fundamentally related to the God-given integrity of creation.* In the coherent universe evoked by the prophetic traditions, connections are assumed or specifically drawn among phenomena that modernity has generally treated as discrete and unrelated. Especially perplexing to moderns is the way these traditions perceive interactions between the moral sphere and what we call the "natural" sphere of physical operations in the nonhuman world.

One notable example is chapter 4 of Amos, an extended oracle that outlines the several dimensions of Israel's transgression and also the several stages of God's punishing response, which is now about to come to a deadly climax. The oracle begins with harsh invective against the

> cows of Bashan who are on Mount Samaria,
> who oppress the poor, crush the vulnerable,
> who say to their lords:
> "Bring and let's drink!"
>
> (v. 1)

This is a vivid picture of the tiny economic elite in Israel's capital city, carousing on the royal acropolis—possibly both women and men, since the Hebrew mixes masculine and feminine grammatical forms. (If "cows" is a mixed-gender reference, then "their lords" refers not to husbands but to pagan gods, as Jerome supposed; see Mays, *Amos,* 71.) The "cows of Bashan" are absentee landowners,

10

who extract their wealth from distant pasturelands east of the Jordan—lands appropriated by the crown from formerly free peasants, and granted to those who render valuable political and military services to the monarch.

Having begun with the iniquitous economic system, the oracle moves on to an indictment of insincere worship at two major state-supported shrines:

> Come to Bethel and transgress,
> to Gilgal and transgress more.
> . . . .
> Burn a thank-offering of leaven,
> and proclaim freewill offerings; make it loud!
> For you love it like that, you Israelites—an utterance of my Lord
>   YHWH.
>
> (vv. 4–5)

YHWH then acidly takes credit for the recent widespread famine:

> And I, yes, I gave you
> cleanness of teeth in all your cities.
>
> (v. 6)

and likewise for the failure of the harvest due to drought:

> And I, yes, I deprived you of the rain
> when there were still three months till harvest.
>
> (v. 7)

On top of that, there was military disaster:

> I killed your young men with the sword—
> along with the capture of your horses.
>
> (v. 10)

As he recounts this series of mounting disasters *brought about by God*, Amos denies Israel and us the freedom to imagine that our "spirituality" can be separated from our economic lives, and that these in turn can be separated from what we experience in the natural order or the social sphere. They are necessarily connected, because everything on heaven and earth is ultimately to be referred to the One

11

who forms the mountains and creates the wind,
who declares to humankind his thinking,
who makes dawn darkness,
and strides on the heights of earth—
YHWH God of Hosts is his name!

(v. 13)

The prophetic perspective, which perceives these various
spheres of our experience as interlocking and interacting, is probably more challenging for interpreters in the modern (or postmodern) period than at any earlier time in history. This is because
accepting the prophetic witness as relevant for ourselves means
that we must consciously reintegrate aspects of our lives that are
habitually separated by the cultural and economic system in which
virtually all of us are immersed, which most of us have come to
think of as "reality." That way of thinking and living, which might
be labeled "consumerism," entails effecting a full separation
between our spiritual life and our material practices, our moral
sense and our economic sense. It requires such separations, for
the perpetuation of consumerism depends upon widespread igno-
rance and denial of the countless ways that we as *consumers* are
currently hurting ourselves and others as *creatures*—that is, as
members of God's creation. Oddly, little attention has been given
to the challenge that prophetic poetry presents to our destructive
habit of self-fragmentation, although the prophets in both Testaments frequently attest to the essential unity of every aspect of
human experience in the world.

3. *Prophetic participation in the suffering of the vulnerable
within the created order and the social order, and prophetic witnessing to the suffering of God.* The prophetic habit of understanding human experience as a unified whole is related to the fact that
the prophets participate fully in the suffering of those whom they
address. When there is "cleanness of teeth" in all the cities of Israel,
Amos himself is hungry. When there is drought in Israel (1 Kgs.
17) or Judah (Jer. 14), Elijah and Jeremiah are thirsty. One of the
great achievements of the Bible's prophetic texts is giving voice to
all those who suffer, whether it is the vulnerable poor, the suffering land itself, the guilty oppressor, or the anguished and angered
Deity. When "Daughter [or "Beloved"] Zion" (*bat-ṣîyôn*) cries out,
it is impossible to distinguish the innocent sufferer from the guilty:

12

For I hear a sound like a woman in labor, in anguish like one bearing
   her first child—
the sound of Daughter-Zion panting; she stretches out her hands:
"O woe is me! My life is fading away before killers!"

(Jer. 4:31)

Thus the prophet uses kinship language to mark his identification
with the whole people, innocent and unrepentant and remorse-
ful (see Jer. 3:22–25) alike, when they fall as one under divine
judgment.

Everyone in Israel, innocent or guilty, suffers alike—and the
Creator along with Israel—but the difference between the prophets and many other Israelites is that the prophets know their suffering is due to human sin. To put it more precisely, they suffer
because the covenantal structure of reality has been violated (see
chap. 4 below). Therefore, when the deep structure of reality has
been violated, the prophet suffers triply:

first, as a creature of God, one who consciously participates in
   the integrated order of creation
second, as one of the people Israel, specially bound to God
   through the covenant with Abraham
third, as the servant who has been chosen to articulate God's
   profound involvement in the life of humanity at a given
   moment in history, and the consequences—negative and
   positive—of that divine involvement for Israel and potentially all peoples

The willingness to suffer in God's service and under divine
judgment is one aspect of the prophets' commitment to the truth.
Preaching on the apostle Paul, Benedict XVI made an observation
that is fitting also for Paul's prophetic predecessors: "In a world in
which falsehood is powerful, the truth is paid for with suffering.
The one who desires to avoid suffering, to keep it at bay, keeps life
itself and its greatness at bay; he cannot be a servant of truth and
thus a servant of faith" (Homily, Rome, June 28, 2008).

Yet even if the prophet accepts suffering as the necessary cost of
bearing true witness for God, that does not mean that the prophet
is a doormat for God. Jeremiah protests to God even as he suffers
knowingly for the sake of God:

13

> Why should my pain be lasting, my wound incurable, refusing to be
> healed?
> Surely you are to me like a delusive stream, waters that cannot be
> counted on.
>
> (Jer. 15:18)

Among those who protest openly in God's service I think of my Haitian student Regine Jean-Baptiste offering this public prayer in the aftermath of the devastating earthquake in her country in January 2010 and in the midst of ongoing violence in East Africa:

> Well, God, here we are, with tears streaming down our faces.
> Well, God, here we are, saying Yes to you, because we can say
> nothing else.
> Well, God, here we are, bearing before you Haiti and Sudan.

There is a kinship between her prayer and Jeremiah's cries of protest (12:1–4; 15:10, 15–18; 20:7–18). All these cries are informed by both anguished love and stubborn loyalty to God; thus they are expressions of a relationship between God and the prophet that is best understood as a kind of friendship, which is the fourth element in the prophetic perspective.

4. *The prophet as the trusted friend of God, entrusted with a ministry of protest, prayer, healing, and reconciliation.* The prophet is God's most trusted human agent, as is expressed already through Amos, the earliest of the so-called writing prophets:

> For YHWH God does nothing
> unless he has divulged his privileged communication [*sôdô*] to his
> agents [*'ăbādāw*] the prophets.
>
> (Amos 3:7)

The word *'ebed,* "agent" (conventionally, "servant" or "slave") may connote a relationship in which the emphasis falls on respect and mutual trust rather than on servile status (e.g., Gen. 18:3; 1 Sam. 20:7–8; Job 1:8). God honors the prophets' moral judgment by admitting them to the sphere of divine decision making (*sôd,* Amos 3:7); as a result, it sometimes happens that they protest to God, not because of their own personal suffering, but on behalf of the doomed people. When God shows Amos the locust swarm that is about to devour the sprouting crops, he cries out: "My Lord YHWH, forgive! How can Jacob stand, since he is small?" (7:2).

14

God does indeed relent, twice, until finally patience is exhausted: "I will not pass by [them] again" (v. 8). This instance of the prophet standing up to God as the loyal opposition is far from isolated; indeed as we shall see (chap. 2), this is one of the core functions of prophetic speech. The role of the prophetic intercessor for the guilty has an obvious connection with Jesus' plea from the cross in Luke's Gospel: "Father, forgive them; for they do not know what they are doing" (Luke 23:34).

A second mode of intercession that appears in the Old Testament and also has great import for understanding the gospel of Jesus is protest on behalf of the innocent. A clear instance is when Elijah confronts God over the death of the young son of the widow of Zarephath, who has taken him, a starving stranger, into her home during a prolonged drought and famine (see chap. 3). There is no more direct confrontation of the Deity in the whole Bible than Elijah's incriminating question: "YHWH my God, would you bring disaster even upon this widow with whom I have found a home, by killing her son?!" (1 Kgs. 17:20). Elijah refuses to accept this death as final, and in response to his challenge, God restores life to the child. For Christians, Elijah's protest is the beginning of a canonical trajectory that climaxes in Jesus' death and resurrection, the ultimate prophetic rejection of death's finality (on this trajectory see Levenson, *Resurrection*).

Intercessory prayer by the prophet, for both the guilty and the innocent, is more than an expression of personal compassion; it also serves to keep intact the covenant relationship between God and Israel and even between God and those outside Israel's covenant with God (such as the non-Israelite widow of Zarephath). Prophets who intercede for the guilty, as Amos and Jesus did, perform the strategic function of preventing God from giving up on humanity. Those who intercede on behalf of the innocent, as Elijah does, may prevent those who suffer and those who grieve with them from giving up on God.

Of course, the biblical writers knew as well as we do that God does not always or usually respond to prayers such as Elijah's by restoring life to a breathless body. More often, God answers our prayers by suffering with us. For that reason, the third element I noted here—the prophetic witness to the shared suffering between God and the created order—is equally essential to the continuance of the covenant relationship. The knowledge that God suffers

15

when we do, whether our suffering is in guilt or in innocence, keeps us from giving up on God. God's "justice"—a shorthand term for intense involvement with the world and with humankind—is not coolly administered. On the contrary, the divine modus operandi is impassioned and demanding on both sides. As the combined witness of the two Testaments shows, for God it is costly beyond calculation.

5. *Prophetic witness to the theological significance of those who do not worship Israel's God, which is potentially a witness of reconciliation.* This is the least obvious of the five elements of the prophetic perspective as identified here. If the possibility of reconciliation with the "religiously other" does not stand out as a pronounced theme in the prophetic traditions, that is likely because the danger of religious apostasy is often highlighted. Further, much attention has been given in scholarly literature (although not in the church's liturgical readings) to the fierce oracles against the nations, which appear prominently in Isaiah (13–23), Jeremiah (46–51), Ezekiel (25–32), Amos (1–2), and Nahum (the latter being entirely an oracle against Nineveh). These oracles should be recognized as more than merely xenophobic. They are present in the corpus of Latter Prophets as strong, repeated statements of divine judgment on the oppressive exercise of imperial power, both military and economic (see chap. 5). Equally, they are statements of YHWH's unbroken (and probably unbreakable) covenantal bond with Israel, even as Israel's and Judah's own acts of oppression are condemned in the prophetic literature.

Yet despite the abiding (and related) concerns of apostasy and oppression, there does appear in the prophetic traditions, and especially in some of the narrative strands, a positive view of how Israelites may relate to members of foreign nations, including those who are not overtly presented as converts to Yahwistic religion. Moses' instruction from Sinai may be the urtext for this aspect of the prophetic perspective: "You shall not subject the sojourner to pressure; you yourselves know the sojourner's very life, for you were sojourners in the land of Egypt" (Exod. 23:9). Embedded in the core of the Sinai revelation (and probably in the oldest layer of that tradition), coming to Israel through the archetypal prophet, this teaching has high standing within biblical tradition. It sets forth a strong point of identification between Israelite and non-Israelite. In this context, that identification implicitly

16

argues for inclusion of the sojourner in the Israelite community's most regular and important religious observance, Sabbath rest (cf. v. 12)—notably, without specifying that in order to qualify, the outsider must worship Israel's God. A variety of prophetic narratives—including those of Elijah and the woman of Zarephath (chap. 3 below), Elisha and the Aramean captives (chap. 7), and even the unwilling Jonah (chap. 2)—suggest that a prophet may sometimes serve as a bridge-builder and peacemaker with those who are not (initially at least, and in some cases ever) worshipers of Israel's God. It seems important to give particular attention to stories such as these in a time when religious extremism in various forms constitutes one of the major sources of violence, within nations and between them, around the globe.

It must be acknowledged, however, that the prophetic traditions of the Bible offer an inconsistent witness on how the foreigner (in most cases a religious outsider) should be viewed and treated. So if we take seriously this fifth element of the prophetic perspective, then we are drawn immediately into ambiguities and contradictions. Two examples will suffice to introduce the difficulty; notably, both illustrate something of the inherent uncertainty associated with the prophetic interpretation of Scripture.

The book of Jonah stands within the canon as an imaginatively wrought countertestimony to the whole genre of the oracles against the nations, and especially to Nahum. Against his own will, Jonah moves the Ninevites to repentance—in the world of the story, although not in the historical record, which does not indicate such a change of heart. So the book of Jonah might be seen as a thought experiment within the corpus of the Latter Prophets, a model of how a whole pagan people *might* be turned "away from their evil way and the violence that was in their hands" (3:8). Further, the humorous story of Nineveh's repentance provides some comic relief and at the same time an ironic contrast to the agonized prophetic account of the suicidal recalcitrance of Israel and Judah, which, though assiduously warned by better prophets than Jonah, nonetheless failed to turn back to God.

Jonah himself is represented as a prophetic interpreter of Torah; in this respect, he might be seen as a negative counterpart to Huldah. He angrily throws back into YHWH's face the divine self-revelation from Sinai: "I knew you were 'a merciful and gracious God, long in patience and abounding in covenant-love' [Exod.

17

34:6], who relents about evil. And now, YHWH, just take my life!" (Jonah 4:2–3). Jonah presumes to control the text with which he indicts God for being merciful, but instead the alert hearer recognizes that Jonah in his hard-heartedness effectively indicts himself. The words of Torah are "active and sharper than any two-edged sword, . . . able to judge the thoughts and intentions of the heart" (Heb. 4:12); they turn against the interpreter who is so foolish as to invoke Scripture against the freedom of God.

The book of Jonah is at odds with other prophetic books, especially Nahum, but even within the single book of Jeremiah we see a contradiction in the prophetic perspective on how Israelites may relate to Gentiles. Jeremiah 29, the letter to the exiles in Babylon, includes the strongest prophetic statement that directly envisions reconciliation between Israelites and their enemies. Jeremiah sends this divine word to those who were carried off in the first tidal wave (597 BCE) of Nebuchadnezzar's onslaught:

> Thus says the Lord of Hosts, God of Israel, to the whole exiled community that I exiled from Jerusalem to Babylon: Build houses and settle down, and plant gardens, and eat their fruit. Take wives and have sons and daughters, and take wives for your sons and give your daughters in marriage, so they may bear sons and daughters. Multiply there; do not decrease. And seek the well-being [*shalom*] of the city to which I have exiled you, and pray for it to the Lord, for with its *shalom* lies your own *shalom*. . . . For thus says the Lord: When seventy years have passed in Babylon, I will take note of you and fulfill for you my promise to bring you back to this place. For I myself know the thoughts that I am thinking concerning you—an utterance of YHWH— thoughts of *shalom* and not of evil, to give you a future of hope. (Jer. 29:4–7, 10–11)

If this were the last word on Babylon in the book of Jeremiah, we might rest content that one major prophetic tradition asserts unambiguously the divine mandate for reconciliation between Israelites and their religious and political enemies. But it is not so simple, for as already noted, the book of Jeremiah ends with six chapters of oracles against the nations, of which the final two are an unrelenting and poetically spectacular diatribe against Babylon. The elaborated message in these chapters runs directly counter to the vision of *shalom* that Jeremiah drew in his letter to the exiles:

Here I am coming at you, O Mountain of the destroyer—an
  utterance of YHWH—
the one who destroys the whole earth.
I will stretch out my hand over you
and roll you down from the cliff-heights
and make you into a burnt-up mountain.
No one will take from you cornerstone
or foundation stone,
for you will be an utter devastation forever—an utterance of YHWH.
(51:25–26)

So what is the prophetic interpreter to do with these contradictory messages within the book of Jeremiah? On what grounds might we accept one and ignore the other? The larger Christian canon offers guidance in this dilemma, a kind of guidance that was not available even to Jeremiah. In calling the exiles to seek God's peace for Babylon, Jeremiah articulated something completely unprecedented, as far as we know. Maybe Jeremiah himself received messages he took to be contradictory. Obviously some who edited the whole tradition of Jeremianic prophecy were doubtful; the final word in the book is that Babylon must perish. But six centuries later, the last and greatest of the prophets said the very same thing that Jeremiah had written the exiles: "Love your enemies and pray for those who persecute you" (Matt. 5:44). With that reiteration, something changed—though certainly not that Christians are now personally disposed to love our enemies; with few exceptions, we feel just the same about them as sixth-century Judeans felt about the Babylonians. What has changed is the set of theological options available to Christians as interpreters of Scripture. We can no longer say that seeking their *shalom* is absurd, as most of Jeremiah's contemporaries would have reckoned it—a figment of an overheated prophetic imagination, perhaps, or a sellout to the oppressor. Jesus speaks, in a sense, directly into the contradiction in the book of Jeremiah and makes explicit that actively seeking *shalom* for our enemies is just what God expects of us. That is what a "future of hope" (Jer. 29:11) looks like in God's own white-hot imagination: people praying without ceasing for their enemies, appealing to God for the godless, putting all their hope in God's ability to craft *shalom*—well-being, peace, true prosperity—out of misery, suffering, and even profound spiritual poverty.

19

Further, even if the historical record does not confirm the repentance of the Ninevites as imagined by the book of Jonah, we dare not say that God cannot turn enmity and present misery to *shalom*. Often enough God has done it, including for the Judean (= Jewish) community in Babylon. In time Babylonian Jews came to live in relative peace alongside their former captors; the Jewish community survived and even thrived in Babylon for more than 2,500 years, until the last century. A thousand years after Jeremiah, it produced the Talmud, to this day the greatest work of Jewish faith and culture apart from the Bible itself. The prophet's vision for the exiles, "a future of hope," was fulfilled, perhaps far beyond his own imagining.

This chapter began with a question: "Whose voice or action might be termed prophetic" in our contemporary culture? The question is not inconsequential, yet in the end I have made no attempt at an answer. The lines of thought I have developed here suggest that there may be better questions for Christians to be asking, questions that aim less at a specific answer than at a certain kind of guided exploration of Scripture:

> What are essential elements of a prophetic perspective on God and the world—a perspective that is firmly grounded in multiple strands of biblical thought in both Testaments?
>
> How might that perspective inform the work of prophetic interpreters—of those who "read" the current historical moment, a certain social situation or problem, and some strands of Christian tradition, all in light of their reading of Scripture itself—as they seek to be responsible guides for the thinking and action of others?

The chapters that follow are probes into the work of prophetic interpretation, examples of the kind of guided exploration of Scripture that may enable Christians in this generation to listen and respond more fully to the diverse prophetic traditions of the Bible.

Works Cited in Chapter 1

Alonso Schökel, Luis. "Isaiah." In *The Literary Guide to the Bible,* edited by Robert Alter and Frank Kermode. Cambridge, MA: Belknap/Harvard University Press, 1987.

Benedict XVI. Homily at the First Vespers of the Feast of Saints Peter and Paul, Rome, June 28, 2008. http://www.vatican .va/holy_father/benedict_xvi/homilies/2008/documents/ hf_ben-xvi_hom_20080628_vespri_en.html.

Blenkinsopp, Joseph. *A History of Prophecy in Israel: From the Settlement in the Land to the Hellenistic Period*. Philadelphia: Westminster Press, 1983.

Bonhoeffer, Dietrich. *No Rusty Swords: Letters, Lectures and Notes, 1928–1936*. New York: Harper & Row, 1965.

Brueggemann, Walter. *Inscribing the Text: Sermons and Prayers of Walter Brueggemann*. Edited by Anna Carter Florence. Minneapolis: Fortress, 2004.

———. *The Prophetic Imagination*. Minneapolis: Fortress, 2001.

Levenson, Jon D. *Resurrection and the Restoration of Israel: The Ultimate Victory of the God of Life*. New Haven, CT: Yale University Press, 2006.

Mariani, Paul. *God and the Imagination: On Poets, Poetry, and the Ineffable*. Athens: University of Georgia Press, 2002.

Mays, James Luther. *Amos*. Old Testament Library. Philadelphia: Westminster Press, 1969.

CHAPTER 2

Friendship with God

The Cost and the Reward

*I no longer call you "slaves," because the slave does not know what [the] master
does. You I have called "friends," because everything that I have heard from my
Father I have made known to you. You did not choose me; rather I chose you,
and I appointed you so that you might go on and bear fruit, and your fruit may
last, so that whatever you ask the Father in my name he may give to you.*
—John 15:15–16

*In every generation [wisdom] passes into holy souls and makes them friends of
God, and prophets.*
—Wisdom of Solomon 7:27 NRSV

Torah is the first long act of the prophetically oriented drama of God,
Israel, Jesus, and the emerging church that constitutes the Christian
Bible. Within this large context, it is significant that in Torah three
Israelites—Abraham, Miriam, and Moses—are named as prophets.
None of them is a prophet in the technical sense that will come to
dominate the fifteen books of the Prophets; they do not proclaim
oracles that denounce injustices against God and neighbor, call hearers to repentance, or offer words of consolation. Rather, their designation as prophets seems to mark these three as belonging to the
close circle of God's chosen agents, a location distinguished not only
by heavy responsibility but also by proximity to divine judgment. It
is a place of privilege and also of testing and suffering. In the overall
judgment of the biblical writers, Abraham and Moses are among the
few who have known God most intimately, served longest and best.

23

Here I focus on aspects of their detailed stories that show the cost as well as the reward of sustained friendship with God. This chapter will consider also the shorter stories of Miriam and (going beyond Torah) of Jonah. They do what short stories—within and outside the Bible—often do best: capture one moment of a life, or illumine one aspect of a complex phenomenon. The stories of Jonah and Miriam function effectively as foils, highlighting the temptations and failures that are necessarily part of every prophet's life in service.

Abraham and the Origin of Intercessory Prayer

So much happens for the first time with Abraham. He inaugurates a completely new stage in the relationship between humankind and God, and not just in terms of his "election," the special blessing that is promised to Abraham's seed. Other aspects of the great *novum* that happens with Abraham bear more closely on the prophetic vocation and begin to shape our understanding of it. Moreover, focusing on Abraham as a prophet yields insight into the critical series of events that center on the moment when God designates him as such (Gen. 20:7). Those events, beginning with Abraham's first recorded act of prayer on behalf of others (Gen. 18) and continuing through the harrowing near sacrifice of Isaac (Gen. 22), arguably constitute the centerpiece of his story.

It is with respect to his capacity for efficacious prayer that God calls Abraham a prophet. God had just stricken barren the whole household of Abimelech, king of Gerar, on account of Sarah, whom Abimelech had taken into his harem. Then God says to the hapless king: "Give back the man's wife, for he is a prophet, and he will intercede for you—and live!" (Gen. 20:7). Accordingly, Abraham prays, and the Gerarites are healed and spared; this would seem at a glance to be a clear instance of the fulfillment of God's initial promise to Abraham: "through you all the families of the arable-land shall experience blessing" (12:3). At least it would be clear, were Abraham not the source of Abimelech's trouble in the first place. Had he told Abimelech the full truth, that Sarah was not just his sister but also his wife, then no healing would have been required.

24   Abraham misled the king and compromised Sarah for the simple but ignoble reason that he feared for his own life, as he admits in response to Abimelech's indignant and bewildered question:

"What did you *see* [or *imagine*], that you did this thing?" And Abraham said, "For I said [to myself], 'It's just that there is no fear of God in this place, and they will kill me on account of my wife.' And in fact she is my sister, the daughter of my father—only not the daughter of my mother—and she became my wife. And so, when God set me to wandering from my father's house, I said to her, 'This is the act-of-loyalty [*ḥesed*] that you should do for me: wherever we go, say of me, 'He is my brother.'" (Gen. 20:10–13)

In excusing himself, Abraham subtly blames the God who set him off on this wandering—a God whom he evidently does not trust to see them through. So the same occasion that shows Abraham to be a genuine prophet also reveals him as deceitful, callous, and lacking the very kind of covenant loyalty he requires of Sarah. As a result, he is guilty before God, wife, and even his Gentile neighbor.

The verb used of Abraham's act of interceding (*p-l-l, hitpaʿel,* 20:7, 17)—and later of Moses' (Num. 21:7; Deut. 9:20) and Jonah's prayers (Jonah 2:2)—has pronounced judicial implications, as John Goldingay observes: "Intercession involves speaking on behalf of someone who has been wronged and asking that the court take action on their behalf, or speaking on behalf of a person guilty of wrongdoing and asking that the court show mercy on them" (*Gospel,* 220). As we have seen (chap. 1, pp. 12–15), Israel's prophets will henceforth engage in both kinds of intercessory prayer, for the innocent and for the guilty. But strikingly here, the originator of intercessory prayer secures mitigation of punishment even though he is himself the first cause of the offense. It is important for the later development of the prophetic role that Abraham the proto-prophet is not innocent; he prays from a position of full involvement in the ways of the world and its failings, even as he continues to "wander" on the way that God has set him (Gen. 20:13).

God's affirmation of Abraham's efficacious prayer comes out of recent experience, since the last scene in which Abraham appeared (18:17–33) showed him to be an audacious intercessor. He is the first person in the biblical history of the world not only to appeal to God's justice but, further, to raise questions about it. That earlier scene began with God's self-questioning about how to proceed: "Shall I conceal from Abraham what I am doing—though Abraham will certainly become a nation great and formidable, through which all the nations of the earth shall experience blessing?" (18:17–18). This question marks the newness that is unfolding through

25

Abraham; for the first time the Deity has fixed upon an interactive modus operandi. Once before God had given a warning—to Noah—of a disaster that would engulf nearly everyone else (6:13), but that was followed by a series of commands, not a conversation. It seems never to have occurred to Noah to question God's stated intention to destroy the world. (The rabbinic tradition criticizes him for not challenging God on behalf of those condemned to die under divine judgment.) It is notable, therefore, that now God deliberately initiates a new way of dealing with human evil, one that entails negotiation with a human moral agent: "For I have known him [yĕda'tîw], so that he may command his children and his house after him and they will keep the way of YHWH, by doing righteousness and justice, in order that YHWH might bring upon Abraham all that he has spoken concerning him" (18:19).

"I have known him"—the connotation of intimacy that often attends the verb y-d-' is well developed by this point in the Genesis narrative: "And the man knew Eve his wife" (4:1a), etc. In the unfolding story of Sodom, the verb y-d-' will appear next to denote the predatory sexual behavior that epitomizes its wickedness (19:5, cf. v. 7). Although sexual intimacy is clearly not at issue between God and Abraham, the biblical tradition does not shy away from acknowledging a deep bond between them. Thus the exilic poet known as Second Isaiah cites God's "pet name" for Abraham: 'ohăbî, "my love," or alternatively, "the one who loves me" (Isa. 41:8); a less literal but better rendering might be "my devoted friend." Friendship is the closest analogy to this bond to be found in the wholly human sphere. There exists between these two the same intimate mutual knowledge and trust that Jesus acknowledges between himself and the disciples: "You I have called 'friends'" (John 15:15). The nature of Abraham's love for God is revealed especially in two momentous encounters: this one over the fate of Sodom, and the equally riveting scene on Mount Moriah a few chapters later (Gen. 22). Considered together, they show that Abraham's devotion to God is unconditional yet not uncritical.

At God's charge, Abraham's two angelic guests (19:1) depart for Sodom, while he remains "standing before God" (18:22). This is the characteristic posture of the prophet (cf. 1 Kgs. 17:1); it normally denotes the servant's readiness to respond to YHWH's command. However, on this occasion Abraham "advances" and poses his own question: "Would you *really* ['ap] sweep away the innocent with

26

the guilty?" (Gen. 18:23). The grammatical particle lends a tone of incredulity and challenge; compare the snake's comment to the woman in Eden: "So God *really* [*'ap*] said you should not eat from any tree in the garden!?" (Gen. 3:1). The ancient rabbis did not miss the fact that Abraham's challenge to God is robust, to say the least. *Genesis Rabbah* ("amplified Genesis"), the classical collection of rabbinic commentary on Genesis, makes this point through a rehearsal of variant interpretations of the phrase "and Abraham drew near" (Gen. 18:23). Each interpretation is supported by another verse that uses the Hebrew verb *n-g-š* to denote a different manner of approach:

> Rabbi Judah said, "This was a drawing near as for battle, as it says, 'So Joab and the people who were with him drew near to battle' (2 Sam. 10:13). [Abraham drew near to fight with God.]"
>
> Rabbi Nehemiah said, "It was a drawing near for conciliation, in line with the usage in this verse: 'Then the children of Judah drew near to Joshua' (Josh. 14:6). The purpose was to conciliate him."
>
> [Anonymous] rabbis say, "It was a drawing near for prayer, in line with the usage in this verse: 'And it came to pass at the time of the offering of the evening offering, that Elijah the prophet came near and said, "O Lord, God of Abraham, Isaac, and Israel, this day let it be known that you are God in Israel"' (1 Kgs. 18:36)."
>
> Said Rabbi Eleazar, "Interpret the verse to bear this encompassing meaning: 'If it is for war, I am coming. If it is for conciliation, I am coming. If it is for prayer, I am coming.'" (Neusner, *Genesis Rabbah*, xlix:viii, 2:202, adjusted)

Once launched into his verbal offensive, Abraham stops for neither breath nor an answer until he has said it all: "Maybe there are fifty innocent people in the city. Would you really sweep them away and not spare the place for the sake of the fifty innocent people who are in it? It is profanation [or, 'alien'] to you to do something like this, to kill the innocent with the guilty. So the innocent should be just like the guilty—that is profanation to you! Should not the Judge of all the earth do justice?" (Gen. 18:24–25). When YHWH concedes that point, Abraham begins to work God down, in a manner that is familiar to anyone who has haggled in a market where no price is fixed: What if there are only forty-five innocent people—or forty? Thirty? Twenty? Just ten? Throughout the whole scene, Abraham vacillates between uncomfortable awareness of

27

his own presumption—"and I am just dust and ashes" (v. 27)—and determination to influence God to do the right thing. Jon Levenson observes that Abraham's apologetic presumption perfectly expresses "both the *necessity* and the *absurdity* of a person's telling God what to do." Thus he acknowledges "both the justice of a human protest against the dubious counsels of God and the inherent limitation upon the right of human beings to lodge such a protest" (*Creation*, 151).

It is a formative moment in the history of covenant. God has just confirmed an "everlasting covenant" (Gen. 17:13) with Abraham and his descendants, and this verbal sparring shows how far Abraham is willing to push in the relationship, how fully he understands that covenant is a relationship of mutuality and trust, even how seriously he takes God, in relation not to himself alone but to the whole world. Thus, in contrast to Noah, Abraham dares to call into question the nature of God's justice and goodness. He becomes the first to intercede for others, and what is more, to plead for those who are not of his household, nor worshipers of his God. And God encourages this human daring, readily acceding to each request to spare Sodom for the sake of a diminishing number of righteous people; Abraham works down to as few as ten (v. 32).

Jon Levenson suggests that in allowing Abraham to bargain over Sodom, God is "testing Abraham's resolve: will the patriarch give up too easily?" (*Creation*, 150). Nathan MacDonald suggests that this is exactly what happens; the scene is "a learning incident," in which Abraham is being instructed in "the forgiving mercy of YHWH," but "drawing the line at ten indicates not only the depth of Sodom's sin but also that Abraham has not plumbed the depths of YHWH's grace" ("Listening to Abraham," 40). Had Abraham been just a little more presumptuous, one might imagine, Sodom would still be standing. However, if we take seriously God's claim to know Abraham intimately (Gen. 18:19), with the implication of trust such a statement implies, then a different possibility presents itself. God has "known" Abraham precisely in order that he might be capable of generating "righteousness and justice" in others. So it seems likely that here God is not testing Abraham (contrast Gen. 22:1) but rather genuinely listening to him, and on the basis of what he says weighing out what constitutes righteousness and justice in this context. These stories of the two covenant partners reveal that God's just dealing is not a quantity fixed once and for all. Rather it

28

is a way forward for God and the world, an opening into the future that must be discovered, each time anew, by God and those God trusts—including and especially the prophets.

In accordance with Abraham's bold and innovative prayer, the midrashic tradition in Judaism represents Abraham as the paradigm of *ḥesed*, the core covenant virtue. Not wholly translatable (though conventionally rendered "steadfast love," "mercy," "loving-kindness"), the term denotes the unstinting commitment that one covenant partner may be called upon to enact toward another. Viewing Abraham as the world's first active proponent of *ḥesed*, the rabbis (with a keen sense of irony) develop Abraham's famous question—"Should not the Judge of all the earth do justice?"—into a *prohibition* on "justice," if that be construed as a strict legal standard. "Said Rabbi Levi, . . . 'If you want to have a world, there can be no justice, and if justice is what you want, there can be no world. You are holding the rope at both ends, you want a world and you want justice. If you don't give in a bit, the world can never stand'" (Neusner, *Genesis Rabbah*, xlix:viii, 2:202, adjusted). Avivah Zornberg comments insightfully: "In order to build the world, *ḥesed*, the generous perception of alternative possibilities, is necessary. . . . *Ḥesed* is the only modality in which a world can survive" (*Genesis*, 110). Abraham dickering with God over Sodom is the first human instantiation of *ḥesed*, of active engagement with God's own generosity. Thus he foreshadows the vital prophetic task of forecasting alternative futures for the relationship between God and Israel, and beyond that, for God and those outside the covenant relationship. Faithful fulfillment of that task would seem to be necessary for the relationship between God and the world to endure.

What God says to the distraught Abimelech implies that it is this exchange over Sodom that wins Abraham the accolade of prophet (20:7). Now, by the strange logic of covenant, it gains him also a second opportunity to stand before God and plead for the non-Israelite—this time, with complete success: "And Abraham interceded with God and God healed Abimelech and his wife and his concubines, and they gave birth" (20:17). The ancient rabbis comment cryptically: "But when our father, Abraham, prayed in this way, that very knot was untied" (Neusner, *Genesis Rabbah*, lii:xiii, 2:241, adjusted)—presumably, the "knot" that had impeded pregnancy. Moreover, it was likewise untied for Abraham's wife; just two verses later, we learn that "YHWH visited Sarah" (Gen. 21:1), and she gave birth. It would seem that all of this is partial fulfillment of God's covenant promise to Abraham: "You will become father of countless nations" (17:4)—the biological father of Isaac, and the "godfather" of Abimelech's issue.

A further link between the scenes in Sodom and Gerar is that both begin with a question about God's justice. When God appears to Abimelech in the night and tells him he is a dead man on Sarah's account, the king unwittingly poses a variant of Abraham's question: "My Lord, even an innocent nation you would slay?" (20:4). Abimelech is evidently a very different kind of Gentile than those we saw in Sodom. Chapter 20 is in several respects the necessary counterbalance for chapter 18; on at least three counts it discredits dangerous generalizations we might reach on the basis of the earlier story alone. First, it prevents us from thinking that all non-Israelites are morally reprobate; specifically, they are not all sexual predators, as we might conclude from the threat of sexual violation when the "men" come to Lot's house (Gen. 19:4–10). Of Abimelech, the narrator says explicitly that he "had not come near" Sarah (20:4); when he swears that he acted "in the innocence of my heart" (v. 5), God believes him, and so do we. Indeed, the king's own prayer provides a striking depiction of non-Israelites; this one morally sensitive king represents the whole "innocent nation" (v. 4) of Gerar.

Second, chapter 20 keeps us from misreading the destruction of Sodom and Gomorrah as proving that Gentiles, or those who do not worship Israel's God exclusively, are wholly beyond the reach of divine mercy. By contrast, this story shows mercy actively extended toward Gentiles *when the conditions for receiving it with understanding are present,* as they were not in Sodom.

Third, chapter 20 corrects any misunderstanding of what qualifies Abraham to be heard by God when he prays. He does not "stand before God" in a state of perfect or permanent innocence; in this case he is more guilty than those for whom he prays. So this story implies a question about God's justice, beyond the question that Abimelech poses directly: Will God heed the prayer *even of the guilty,* if that prayer is offered on behalf of the innocent? The answer is yes. When in Gerar God dubs Abraham a prophet, that means he is qualified to pray for non-Israelites, to intercede for others so they may "experience blessing through him" (18:18; cf. 12:3); it does not mean he is qualified to judge them.

30

One more story is essential for understanding what it means to say that Abraham is God's "devoted friend," namely, the near-fatal binding of Isaac (Gen. 22:1–19). Read in sequence with the portraits of Abraham the feisty intercessor for Sodom (Gen. 18) and the successful intercessor for Abimelech (Gen. 20), the depiction of submissive Abraham, utterly silent before God's command— "Take your son, your one-and-only whom you love, Isaac, . . . and offer him up as a burnt offering"—seems completely out of place. Reconciling these several pictures of Abraham is likely the most difficult exegetical problem in Genesis. I shall offer three distinct lines of approach to the problem, each evidencing a slightly different way of tracing the narrative logic. However, all three lines of approach converge to show the necessity for Genesis 22, when read in sequence with these other stories.

First, just as Genesis 20 corrects certain misconceptions we might infer from Genesis 18, so Genesis 22 corrects certain misunderstandings of the story in Genesis 20. After the encounter with Abimelech, Abraham appears to be riding high, with God's sanction. Indeed, he makes out like a bandit:

> And Abimelech took flock and herd animals and slaves, male and female, and gave them to Abraham, and he returned to him Sarah, his wife. And Abimelech said, "Here is my land before you; wherever looks good to you, settle there." And to Sarah he said, "Here, I have given a thousand pieces of silver to your 'brother,' and here, it will be for you a protection against the [critical] gaze of anyone who is with you; with everyone, you will be cleared." (20:14–15)

From this one encounter, one might suppose that being God's prophet is a rather good deal, requiring relatively little of Abraham. That impression cannot be allowed to stand—hence, the need for the story that shows how Abraham responds when God issues a demand that would cost him "not less than everything."

A second line of approach: The larger story of Abraham must demonstrate his covenantal commitment along two different axes, the vertical and the horizontal. Accordingly, the midrashic tradition follows the Bible in representing Abraham as a man equally driven by total devotion to God and total compassion for the human world; this might well be the essential tension in which the prophet is called to stand. *Psychologically* speaking, it may be nearly

31

impossible to hold those two total commitments in perfect balance. Yet *theologically* speaking, Torah demands both: love for God that withholds nothing of the self (Deut. 6:5) combined with love for the neighbor that is equally unstinting (Lev. 19:18). So the balance that no individual member of the covenant community can achieve *personally* must be upheld *narratively,* in Israel's story and especially in the story of Abraham, for he is the human anchor for the covenant between Israel and God. This need for theological balance within the narrative may explain the fact that Genesis includes portraits of Abraham that otherwise seem to represent two entirely different people. (It should be noted that the difference between the "Abrahams" of chapters 18 and 22 cannot be resolved in purely historical-critical terms, as the so-called Yahwistic source seems to have had a hand in both accounts.)

Abraham's aggressive and partially successful challenges to God (Gen. 18 and 20) established his commitment along the horizontal axis, his concern that God enact justice for all. After that, what remains to be demonstrated is Abraham's commitment on the vertical axis. As we have seen, there is reason to doubt his total trust in God, and perhaps his commitment to God, when he has twice passed off Sarah as his sister (cf. also 12:10–20) to protect himself. One might infer that in Abraham's judgment, *ḥesed* begins at home, with self-care, whatever it may cost others. These troubling stories are part of the background that bears upon God's devastating command, as the narrator implies with the opening phrase: *"After these things,* God tested Abraham" (22:1; emphasis added). The test is a real one, and it is only after Abraham has submitted wholly to God's will that the Deity's doubts about this covenant partner are allayed: "And he said, 'Do not stretch out your hand against the boy and do not do a thing to him, *for now I know that you are a God-fearer*; you did not hold back your son, your one-and-only, from me" (v. 12; emphasis added).

A third line of approach: The stories of Abraham at Moriah and Abraham arguing on behalf of Sodom exemplify the twin moments of the spiritual life that are eventually recognized, however reluctantly, by every person who stays with God through a lifetime: the moment to argue with God, and the moment to trust God, no matter what. The grueling story of the binding of Isaac is most often treated as promoting "absolute and unconditional obedience" as an essential religious virtue (e.g., Levenson, *Creation,* 152; cf.

Moberly, *Bible, Theology,* 83–97). However, it seems to me that when on Moriah God does indeed test Abraham (22:1), the test is designed to gauge his capacity, not for obedience, but for trust. That point is made most effectively by the twentieth-century Orthodox Jewish theologian Eliezer Berkovits, who turned repeatedly to the figure of Abraham, and especially Abraham on Mount Moriah, as he struggled with the question of what it means for Jews to have faith following the Holocaust. Berkovits's answer is that genuine faith is neither the intellectual affirmation of God's existence, nor an irrational leap into the complete unknown. Rather faith is a matter of lived trust, of standing firm in the covenanted life, even in the face of God's incomprehensible demands, or "in the midst of God's exasperating silences" (*With God in Hell,* 125).

The biblical Abraham does not speak a word on Mount Moriah, but Berkovits supplies words to interpret his silence:

> "Almighty God! What you are asking of me is terrible. I do not understand You. You contradict Yourself. But I have known You, my God. You have loved me and I love You. My God, You are breaking Your word to me. What is one to think of You! Yet I trust You; I trust you." Such was the trust of Abraham in God and such was the trust of the authentic Jew in the ghettos and the [concentration] camps. . . . Trust is the bond of love between two who have found each other, who belong to each other. It is not reason that it rejects; it is the hurt that it overcomes. Trust affirms the reality of the relationship. It is the truth of the covenant in action. (*With God in Hell,* 124–25)

Thus Berkovits shows what it means for God to "know" Abraham: it means that they are intimates. Through the covenanted life, Abraham and his descendants are formed so that they can trust God, beyond all knowing and understanding, and reciprocally, so that they may prove to be worthy of God's trust, God's own stake in the relationship. Trust is "the truth of the covenant in action."

If Genesis 22 provides the crucial affirmation of the vertical dimension of covenant relationship, which was still lacking after his intercessory prayers for Sodom (Gen. 18) and for Abimelech (Gen. 20), then we can see how this narrative sequence at the heart of Abraham's story fits together. Further, the whole sequence is foundational for our understanding of what it is to be a prophet. The reference to Abraham as prophet (20:7) points both forward and

33

backward, to two unforgettable confrontations between Abraham and God; it brings their seemingly opposite theological statements together into a "larger, dialectical theology" (Levenson, *Creation*, 153). That larger theology of covenant allows for both presumption toward God for the sake of the world, and submission to God, for God's own sake. (That the submission is for God's own sake is underscored by the form of God's oath of recommitment: "By my own self I swear—an utterance of YHWH—because you have done this thing and have not held back your son, your one-and-only, from me," 22:16.)

Indeed, both presumption and submission toward God are required, for one without the other would make a mockery of biblical religion, as Jon Levenson has argued:

> By itself the theology of Genesis 18 would soon lead to a religion in which God's will had ceased to be a reality: the human conscience, having filtered out all divine directives that offended it, would produce a God that was only itself writ large. . . . Left to its own, Genesis 22, on the other hand, would lead to a religion of fanaticism, in which God would be so incomprehensible that even the praise of him as wise or just would be meaningless, . . . and faithfulness to him would be indistinguishable from mindless, slavish obedience. (*Creation*, 153)

Thus with Abraham the Bible begins to show what it is to serve prophetically in covenantal context: negotiating dual commitments to humanity and to God, from moment to moment discerning when to challenge God on behalf of humanity or Israel, when to submit in trust to the sometimes inscrutable divine will. This kind of dialectical theology operates practically in circumstances more common than those faced by Abraham or by the Jews in Nazi-controlled Europe. A hospital chaplain pointed out to me that when a patient receives a terminal diagnosis, the Genesis pattern of human interaction with God is frequently replicated by both patient and loved ones: first bargaining (Gen. 18), then pleading (Gen. 20), and finally acceptance (Gen. 22).

The rest of the Bible explores those multidimensional covenantal dynamics through many prophetic figures and voices. However, the dynamic of prophetic trust and prophetic challenge becomes explicit most of all through the long story of Moses, the special friend of God.

Moses, Servant of God

Moses towers over all the other larger-than-life figures of the Old Testament—as worker of signs and wonders in Egypt and at the Red Sea, as community leader for forty years in the wilderness, as mediator and teacher of Torah (Instruction) at Sinai. But in biblical memory, he is eminent above all as the servant of God par excellence (Exod. 14:31; Num. 12:7, 8; Deut. 34:5; Josh. 1:1; 18:7; 22:2, 4, 5, etc.), "trusted in all [YHWH's] household" (Num. 12:7). Moses is the only one with whom YHWH would speak "plainly and not in riddles" (Num. 12:8), "face to face, as someone speaks to his neighbor" (Exod. 33:11). And further, Moses is remembered as the one who stood confrontationally "before [YHWH] in the breach, to keep his wrath from destroying" (Ps. 106:23).

The full story of Moses is composite; it embraces multiple strands of tradition and several genres: narrative, legal material, poetry, liturgical recitations, songs, and prayers (i.e., psalms). And all of this contributes to our understanding of what the final book of the Pentateuch may mean when it identifies Moses as the prophet who sets the paradigm for all who are to follow in Israel: "And YHWH said . . . , 'A prophet I shall raise up for them from among their kin, like you, and I shall put my words in his mouth'" (Deut. 18:18). Although Moses sets the gold standard for prophecy, he has no full counterparts, at least within the scope of history known to the Deuteronomist: "There has not arisen another prophet in Israel like Moses, whom YHWH knew face to face" (Deut. 34:10). That notice of Moses' historical incomparability moved Israel to project into the future the vision of another such figure, a projection that is expressed in the New Testament representations of Jesus as Moses' equal and more.

The claim that Jesus stands with Moses is explicit in the several accounts of the Transfiguration (Matt. 17:1–8; Mark 9:2–8; Luke 9:28–36). As Matthew describes Jesus on the "high mountain" (17:1–3), flanked by Moses and Elijah, "his face shone like the sun"—as had Moses' face when he descended from Sinai after speaking with God (Exod. 34:29). Moreover, God identifies him as "my son, the beloved one" (Matt. 17:5)—to alert ears, a probable echo of God's words to another prophet who was faithful *ad extremum:* Abraham on Mount Moriah (cf. Gen. 22:2). Luke, using language that clearly signals a connection with Moses' story, recounts

35

that the two great prophets of antiquity were discussing with Jesus his "exodus" (Greek *exodos*), the departure "he intended to fulfill [*plēroō*]"—the terminology of prophetic fulfillment—"in Jerusalem" (Luke 9:31).

The significance of Moses as the paradigmatic prophet may be traced through three aspects of his story:

1. *The character of Moses*, and particularly his capacity to identify with those who are suffering, as exemplified in his early story and finally in the Deuteronomic account of his death
2. *The mission of Moses*, specifically as a messenger who is sent to speak God's work to Israel and to Pharaoh
3. *The mature relationship between Moses and God*, which calls forth Moses' own work of intercessory prayer, especially following the incident of the golden calf

1. The Character of Moses

The account of the burning bush provides a key indicator of Moses' character; this is, one might say, the moment of attraction, the first encounter in a relationship that will endure through hardship, anger, and disappointment for some four decades. Notably, the relationship does not begin with Moses seeking God. He is out "on the far side of the wilderness" (Exod. 3:1), a likely place to encounter God, from a prophetic perspective (see 1 Kgs. 19; Isa. 40:3; Jer. 2:2; Hos. 2:14–15; Ezek. 20:35–36; Mark 1:9–13, etc.). Yet Moses is just doing his regular work of tending the sheep of his father-in-law Jethro when "an angel of YHWH"—here not a heavenly being fully distinct from God but rather a visible "small-scale manifestation of God" within the realm of ordinary reality (Sommer, *Bodies*, 43)—"appeared to him in a fiery flame from within a certain bush" (Exod. 3:2). Up to this point the narrative has moved quickly through Moses' birth and early history, but now it markedly slows to record Moses' response and its immediate consequence: "And Moses said, 'I've got to turn aside and see this great sight; why does the bush not burn up?' And when YHWH saw that he had turned aside to see, God called to him from within the bush and said, 'Moses, Moses!' And he said, 'At your service'" (3:3–4).

The repeated emphasis on Moses' turning aside caught the ancient rabbinic imagination. One teacher, Rabbi Jonathan, said he took three steps toward the bush, a distance that for the rabbis constitutes entry into a different symbolic space. Another, Rabbi Simeon ben Levi, said, "Moses craned his neck to see"—thereby demonstrating that he is not stiff-necked—and this is what moves God to speak: "'You went to the trouble to see—as you live, you are worthy that I should reveal Myself to you.' Immediately, *God called to him from the burning bush*" (Midrash Tanhuma Shemot 9, quoted in Zornberg, *Particulars,* 79). Possibly the rabbis are inspired to comment because this is not the first time that Moses has set aside business as usual to look hard at something. The only initiative Moses is reported to have taken in his early life is the occasion when he left Pharaoh's palace to go out "to his kinfolk, and he *witnessed* their burdens" (Exod. 2:11; emphasis added). The same distinctive verbal phrase, r-'-h b-, appears elsewhere to denote Hagar's witnessing of her son's (imagined) death (Gen. 21:16), Judah's witnessing of his father's suffering (44:34), and God's compassionate witnessing of Leah's and Hannah's "affliction" (29:32; 1 Sam. 1:11) of both childlessness and contempt.

The clear implication is that Moses shares God's own empathy with those who suffer acutely, and this is confirmed as YHWH continues to speak from the bush: "I have certainly *seen* [r-'-h] the degradation of my people, which is in Egypt. . . . And now, here, the cry of the Israelites has come to me, and also I have *seen* the oppression with which Egypt is oppressing them. And now, go, and I shall send you to Pharaoh; and bring my people, the Israelites, out of Egypt!" (Exod. 3:7, 9–10; emphasis added). John Goldingay comments, in a narrative mode the rabbis themselves would appreciate, "The cry causes God to look. God is like a king sitting in his palace courtyard at one of the higher points of the city and hearing a cry in the street outside. His job is not to ignore that but to find out what is going on" (*Gospel,* 301).

There is one more early and enormously consequential reference to Moses' seeing, when "he saw an Egyptian man striking a Hebrew man, one of his kin. And he turned this way and that and *saw that no one was there*, and he struck down the Egyptian" (Exod. 2:11–12; emphasis added). Again, the same phrase is used elsewhere of God:

37

And YHWH saw, and it was evil in his eyes, for there was no justice.
And he saw that no one was there and was stunned that no one
    intervened
and so his own arm worked deliverance.

(Isa. 59:15–16)

On the basis of that intertextual echo, Goldingay argues persuasively that Moses is not looking around to make sure no one will
see him; evidently Hebrews are around to see him strike down the
Egyptian (see Exod. 2:14). Rather, like God in Isaiah's poem, "he
is looking to see if anyone is coming to take action in the face of
injustice" (*Gospel*, 309), and specifically injustice as experienced by
Israelites. Moses' willingness to act while others stand by costs him
his lifestyle, at least: "And when Pharaoh heard this thing he sought
to kill Moses, and Moses fled" (2:15). That was the end of his life as
prince of Egypt.

From now on, Moses' costly identification with the sufferings of
his people is one of the constants of his character as represented in
every biblical tradition. The Deuteronomic tradition gives ultimate
expression to that identification and shows its cost. To his great distress, Moses is barred from entering the promised land, not for any
failing of his own, but because of the people's sin: "For YHWH was
indignant with me, too, on your account, saying: 'Neither shall you
go there'" (Deut. 1:37; cf. 3:23–28; 4:21–22). Patrick Miller comments: "We do not have here a full-blown notion of the salvation
and forgiveness of the many brought by the punishment of the one,
but we are on the way to that" ("Moses," 253).

2. The Mission of Moses

The most obvious way that Moses functions as the prototype for
subsequent prophets is that he is the first biblical character to have
a mission in the true prophetic sense. That is, he is the first one who
is explicitly *sent to speak God's word in a situation where authority
is disputed, and especially the authority to shape the life and des-
tiny of the people Israel.*

We begin with the fact that Moses is "sent" (Exod. 3:10); as the
narrative presents it, this is the immediate consequence of God's
portentous seeing that Israel suffers. The word š-l-ḥ ("send") occurs
repeatedly in the scene at the burning bush (e.g., 3:12, 13, 15, cf.

20), where Moses is commissioned to serve as YHWH's messenger to Pharaoh. Within the narrative world, it would not be lost on any of these characters that the erstwhile prince now is charged with a role that is the direct analogue to the royal messenger that Pharaoh or any other ancient Near Eastern monarch would commission (Ross, "Prophet"). Moses is famously reluctant to assume the role: "Who am I that I should go to Pharaoh?" (3:11). Moses' prolonged attempt to get out of it serves as a model for other prophetic objections that God overrides, especially Jeremiah's (Jer. 1:6–10). However, this is by far the most detailed and heated argument between the Deity and the designated emissary about God's choice, and its dramatic conclusion is fraught with unresolved tension.

To Moses' insistence that he is "heavy of mouth and heavy of tongue" (Exod. 4:10), YHWH finally responds,

> "Who put the mouth in the human being? . . . Is it not I, YHWH?! And now go, and I myself will be with your mouth, and I will teach you what you should say."
>
> But [Moses] said, "I pray, my Lord, send by whatever hand you may send!"
>
> And the anger of YHWH flared against Moses, and he said, "What about Aaron your brother, the Levite? I know that *he* will certainly speak. . . . And you shall speak to him and put the words in his mouth; and I myself will be with your mouth and with his mouth, and I will teach you both what you should do. And he will speak for you to the people, and it will happen that he will become a mouth to you, and you will become a god to him! And this staff— take it in your hand so you can perform the signs with it."
>
> And Moses went. (4:11–18)

Citing the great thirteenth-century Jewish commentator Rabbi Moses ben Nachman (= "RaMBaN," aka Nachmanides) on this passage, Avivah Zornberg observes that "God's anger is directed against a prophet who refuses to grow into prophecy, who does not even, as Ramban points out, *ask to be cured* of his speech problem: 'so great was his desire not to go on the mission, that he did not pray to God to remove the heaviness of his mouth. . . . And, since he did not pray, God did not want to heal him'" (Zornberg, *Particulars*, 119).

But perhaps there is another reason that God did not want to heal him. The fact that Moses was chosen at all suggests that

39

in speaking for God, glibness is no advantage, since God will provide the words; Jesus gives his disciples the same assurance (Matt. 10:19–20; Luke 12:11–12). Indeed there is a sense in which Moses *must* lack natural adeptness in speech, so there can be no doubt about whose is the authoritative word he speaks, to both Pharaoh and the Israelites. In this connection, it is notable that as soon as they are out of Egypt, the people begin complaining against Moses (Exod. 15:24), and he is constrained to distinguish between Aaron and himself as agents and YHWH as Author of the exodus and the One who provides for the people: "When YHWH gives you in the evening meat to eat and your fill of bread in the morning, when YHWH hears the complaints that you are making against him— and what are we? Your complaints are not against us but against YHWH" (16:8).

So likely Moses' ineptness as a speaker is a meaningful lack; it registers a suspicion, in the words of Emmanuel Lévinas, "of any rhetoric which never stammers." As a characteristic of the prototypical prophet, it points to the Source of revelation and also says something about the kind of revelation it is: "one which does not forget the weight of the world, the inertia of men, the dullness of their understanding" (*Levinas Reader,* 197). In a sense, Moses "prophesies" or models those who will hear this word; what he struggles to articulate, we struggle to interpret.

This extended confrontation between God and Moses marks a turning point in biblical history: it is the first time in the Bible that God is explicitly reported as getting angry. Moses' culpable failure at this point is his unwillingness to trust God to equip him for the task he has been given, and that is one of the most serious and consequential of spiritual failings. The midrashic tradition dramatizes this moment and traces the logic of God's anger in a teaching that exposes Moses' mistrust as a lapse of the essential prophetic virtue of compassion:

> R. Yehuda said: God said to Moses, "I am master of the universe, I am full of compassion, I am reliable in paying reward, My children are enslaved by human beings—and you say to Me, Send by whose hand You will send!"
>
> R. Nechemia said: "God said to Moses, 'The anguish of My children in Egypt is revealed and known to Me, as it is said, "God saw the children of Israel, and God knew." [Exod. 2:25] My children dwell in anguish and you dwell at ease; and I seek to set

40

them free from Egypt—and you say to Me, Send by whose hand You will send!" (Zornberg, *Particulars*, 90–91, citing *Midrash haGadol* [= *Midrash Rabbah*] 6:2)

In the end, according to this midrash, Moses' lack of trust in God proves fatal to his mission; for this failing (and not the sin of the Israelites, as Deuteronomy maintains) Moses is barred from the promised land. The midrash concludes:

R. Akiva said: God said to Moses, "By speech, and by decree, and by oath, it is decided by Me that you shall not enter the Holy Land." So God says, "Therefore you shall not bring this community into the Land . . ." (Num. 20:12). (Ibid., 91–92)

Despite his unpromising initial resistance to being sent by God, Moses becomes the greatest of divine messengers in the Old Testament. Not only does he deliver God's word to Pharaoh—a simple and straightforward message, however unwelcome it might be—he also performs the infinitely more complex and demanding task of delivering to the people Israel the great Teaching at Sinai. It is chiefly because he is a perfectly clear channel for divine communication that Deuteronomy hails Moses as the greatest of prophets and the exemplar for every divine spokesman to follow: "A prophet I shall raise up for them from among their kin, like you, and I shall put my words in his mouth, and he will speak to them all that I command him" (Deut. 18:18).

However, Moses is much more than a mouthpiece for God; even in Deuteronomy and the tradition that proceeds from it, he is remembered also as the greatest of all those who challenge God to show mercy—that is, those who make intercession for Israel (see Deut. 9:18–29; cf. Jer. 15:1). At the burning bush, Moses' resistance to God is unproductive; it only moves God to anger and delays, however slightly, Israel's deliverance. But there are other occasions when Moses' resistance to God's stated intention actually produces a change, one that is fruitful for the Israelites. Those two consistent features of his prophetic work stand in some tension throughout the story of Moses in the wilderness: on the one hand, speaking for God to Israel, and on the other, pleading, cajoling, arguing with God on Israel's behalf. As we shall see in the next section, his intercession is no less a part of the great covenantal drama at Sinai than is his role as messenger.

41

3. The Mature Relationship between Moses and God

Already in Egypt, Moses showed his ability to issue a productive challenge to God. His first mission to the royal court, to present the divine demand to release Israel, had ended in apparent failure; Pharaoh's only response was to take away the straw for making bricks. "And Moses returned to YHWH and said, 'My Lord, why have you made things worse for this people? Why did you send me here? Ever since I went to Pharaoh to speak in your name, he has made things worse for this people—and you certainly have not delivered your people!'" (Exod. 5:22–23). There is nothing heroic or selfless in this protest; Moses is trying to weasel out of going to Pharaoh again (see 6:12). Yet even so, he is beginning to see things from the perspective of the Israelites and bring their urgent needs before God: Take responsibility for *your* people!

It is the debacle of the golden calf that forces Moses to mature in his role as intercessor. The full account appears in Exodus 32–34 (recapitulated in Deut. 9:11–10:2), in a series of somewhat loosely connected vignettes that show two titanic powers struggling together and between themselves with the question of how to deal with Israel's unfaithfulness. YHWH's first impulse is to exterminate: "And now let me be, and my anger will flare up at them and I will finish them off—but I shall make you into a great nation!" (Exod. 32:10). But Moses resists that impulse, first with an appeal to God's international reputation—"Why should Egypt say, 'He brought them out with evil intent, to kill them in the mountains'?" (v. 12)— and then by invoking God's personal promise to the ancestors: "I shall multiply your seed like the stars of the heavens" (v. 13). And remarkably, God backs off, at least some distance, "and YHWH relented concerning the evil which he had said he would do to his people" (v. 14).

In a second act of intercession, Moses is more daring, and for the first time he puts himself directly at risk. His prayer begins with a word of forceful entreaty: 'ānnā', which appears elsewhere in Torah only when Joseph's brothers plead with him, ostensibly on behalf of their dead father, to forgive their ghastly sin against him (Gen. 50:17). Now Moses makes a similar appeal to God: "'ānnā', this people has sinned a great sin and made for themselves gods of gold. And now, if you will bear their sin . . . But if not, then wipe me out of your scroll that you have written!" (Exod. 32:31–32).

Goldingay's comment points to Moses' audacity and also suggests how he has grown in God's service:

> In his previous prayer [32:11–13], he identified with God and pleaded with God on the basis of God's purpose and God's reputation. Here he identifies with Israel and argues with God on that basis. His proposal actually reverses YHWH's earlier one that YHWH should abandon the people and start again. . . . Now he declares he will have nothing to do with it. If YHWH will not have Israel, YHWH cannot have Moses. (Goldingay, *Gospel*, 421)

The question must be asked: What do these bold acts of intercession imply about the nature of Moses' servanthood? Is Moses overstepping his bounds, or is this a role that God intended him to take up and wishes him to continue for Israel's sake? The answer offered by the rabbinic tradition is a resounding yes, as expressed by this ingenious midrash, commenting on Exodus 32:10:

> Is Moses holding back God's hand, so that God must say, "Let go of me"? What is this like? A king became angry at his son, placed him in a small room, and was about to hit him. At the same time the king cried out from the room for someone to stop him. The prince's teacher was standing outside, and said to himself, "The king and his son are in the room. Why does the king say 'stop me'? It must be that the king wants me to go into the room and effect a reconciliation between him and his son. That's why the king is crying, 'Stop me.'" In a similar way, God said to Moses, "Let Me at them." Moses said, "Because God wants me to defend Israel, He says, 'Let Me at them.'" And Moses immediately interceded for them. (Muffs, *Love and Joy*, 34, quoting *Shemot Rabbah* 42:9)

In styling Moses as teacher to a prince, the midrash plays on his role as the preeminent teacher of the people who at Sinai are designated God's *sĕgullâ* (see also Exod. 19:5; Deut. 7:6; 14:2; 26:18), conventionally rendered "treasured possession" (NRSV, also phrased this way in the New Jewish Publication Society Bible). In biblical Hebrew and cognate languages of the ancient Near East, the term is used to denote valued property—or by metaphorical extension, persons—to which a god or a monarch lays exclusive claim or has at his disposal (see Eccl. 2:8 and 1 Chr. 29:3; Sarna, *Exodus*, 104); the most closely analogous English term might be "royal peculiar."

43

Like the biblical writers themselves, the rabbinic theologians understand that the dynamics of human relationships afford the best insight into the character of God's relationships, indeed, of God's emotions. In drawing inferences that go beyond what the Bible says, they are guided by what it does say: in this case, that God's anger flares and then God relents, that Moses is trusted above all others in YHWH's household (Num. 12:7), and especially here, that "Moses, his chosen one, stood in the breach before him" (Ps. 106:23). Therefore Moses must have been chosen just because he had the chutzpah, the sheer nerve, to face off with God. Another midrash makes that point even more explicitly, interpreting the assertion that God spoke to Moses face to face thus: "God said to Moses, 'Did I not make a condition with you, that when you are angry with them, I will soothe *your* anger, and when I am angry with them, you will soothe *My* anger?" (Muffs, *Love and Joy*, 34, citing *Shemot Rabbah* 35:2). Much further along in the biblical story, God speaks through Ezekiel about what happens when no one in the house of Israel assumes that prophetic responsibility: "And I sought among them someone who would repair the [defense] wall, who would stand in the breach before me on behalf of the land, so I would not destroy it, but I found no one. And I poured out upon them my indignation; with the fire of my rage I finish them off; I requite their conduct on their head, an utterance of the Lord YHWH" (Ezek. 22:30–31).

The golden calf incident is not the only time that Moses stands in the breach to fend off God's annihilating wrath. Later in the journey, when the scouts return from the promised land with a terrifying report of its gigantic inhabitants, the people stage a revolt: "Let's head on back to Egypt!" (Num. 14:4). God is ready to send an annihilating plague, topped off with disinheritance (v. 12), until Moses intercedes with an appeal to God's own covenantal commitment and the history of the relationship: "'I pray, pardon the iniquity of this people according to your great *ḥesed* and as you have borne with this people from Egypt to here.' And YHWH said, 'I pardon according to your word'" (vv. 19–20). God listens to Moses and makes a major concession, yet there are limits to how far YHWH will relent: "Nonetheless, as I live and the glory of YHWH fills all the earth, all the people who see my glory and my signs that I did in Egypt and in the wilderness, and have tested me these ten times and have not heeded my voice—they will not see the land

44

that I swore to their ancestors. All who are contemptuous of me, they will not see it!" (vv. 22–23). God is "long-suffering, abounding in *ḥesed*, and regularly bears with iniquity and transgression" (v. 18), and yet justice and divine judgment remain part of the structure of reality. In the end, according to the Priestly tradition in Numbers, the sword of God's judgment turns even against Moses, and he too is forbidden entry into Canaan. This point is taken up in the next section, as we look at Moses' ultimate and most costly failure, and also at the failings of two other prophets whose weaknesses become evident precisely because they are brought so close to God.

Even Real Prophets Go Wrong: The Failures of Moses, Miriam, and Jonah

Antiheroism is a striking feature of the biblical representation of YHWH's prophets. To the extent that their characters are known to us, it is evident that none of them is flawless. In several cases—two of them in Torah, that is, in the foundational accounts of prophecy—the temptations and distorted (self-)understandings to which YHWH's prophets are prone are exposed with remarkable honesty. These stories serve as a warning to all who participate in a tradition that takes prophecy with utmost seriousness, including those whose own work may have prophetic dimensions.

1. Moses

The outstanding failure is Moses' own, and its consequences are ultimately the most serious. As we have seen, the book of Deuteronomy reports that it was wholly on Israel's account that Moses was barred from the land, but the Priestly source in Numbers tells a different story. It begins, as usual, with the people gathering against Moses and Aaron, desperate and enraged by the lack of water:

> "Why did you make us go up from Egypt to bring us to this awful place?" . . . And Moses and Aaron went away from the congregation to the entrance of the tent of meeting, and they fell on their faces, and the glory of YHWH appeared to them. And YHWH spoke to Moses: "Take the staff and gather the community, you and Aaron your brother, and address the rock in their sight, and

45

it will yield its water. So you shall bring out for them water from the rock and you shall give drink to the community and their beasts." And Moses took the staff from before YHWH, just as he had commanded him. And Moses and Aaron gathered the congregation before the rock, and he said to them, "Listen now, you rebels! From this rock shall we bring forth water for you?" And Moses raised his hand and struck the rock with his staff, twice, and much water came out, and the community drank, and their beasts. And YHWH spoke to Moses and Aaron: "Because you did not place trust in me so as to sanctify me in the eyes of the Israelites, therefore you shall not bring this congregation to the land that I have given them." Those are the waters of Meribah. (Num. 20:5–13)

The conclusion of this incident implies a stark contrast to repeated comments from this same Priestly source on this (v. 9) and other occasions, namely that Moses and those working under him had done "just as God had commanded" (e.g., Exod. 39:1, 5, 7, 21, 26, 29, 31, 32; 40:16, 19, 21, 23, 25, 27, 29, 32, etc.). At the same time, the language here draws an implicit connection with the scene cited just above. Moses "did not place trust in [God]," just as the people Israel had failed to do, when they lost courage at the report of the scouts: "And YHWH said to Moses, 'How long will this people show contempt for me? How long will they not place trust in me, despite all the signs that I performed in their midst?'" (Num. 14:11). In both cases the divine decree is the same; the disposition of mistrust will not be authorized and carried into the land of Canaan.

Yet exactly how Moses failed to affirm YHWH's sanctity is ambiguous enough to have occasioned centuries of debate; some modern commentators suggest the sin has been deliberately obscured to protect Moses' reputation (Milgrom, *Numbers*, 448). Did Moses err in striking the rock rather than speaking to it (Friedman, *Commentary*, 495; Olson, *Numbers*, 127–28)? If so, why was he told to take the staff, which God had previously had him use to bring forth water (see Exod. 17:6; see Milgrom, *Numbers*, 449–50)? Did he overdramatize by striking it twice, thus attracting attention to himself? Or is it because he turned on the people ("you rebels!") rather than responding to their real need (Olson, *Numbers*, 129)? There may be more than one good answer, but the psalmist's interpretation is the earliest, and it remains convincing:

And they aroused fury over the waters of Meribah,
and it went badly for Moses on their account.
For they embittered [or "rebelled against"] His [or "his"—i.e.,
   Moses'] spirit,
and he blurted out with his lips.

(Ps. 106:32–33)

The third line here is ambiguous and may refer to an act against either God or Moses; I take it as a reference to grieving the spirit of God (cf. Eph. 4:30). The following line certainly refers to Moses; according to this interpretation, his sin lay in ill-considered words—or perhaps in just one letter of one Hebrew word. The twelfth-century Jewish exegete Joseph ben Isaac of Orléans epitomizes the problem as a tiny but telling grammatical slip: "The sin resulted from saying *notsi'*, 'shall we draw forth,' and they (Moses and Aaron) should have said *yotsi'*, 'shall He draw forth'" (quoted in Milgrom, *Numbers*, 451).

At that moment, Moses for the first time failed to be transparent to God's power. It is noteworthy that the text does not suggest that God's response of barring Moses from the land is an expression of anger—although that is the divine response to the people's breach of faith (Num. 14:11). It seems more likely that here God is less vindictive toward Moses than protective toward the people. Moses' lack of transparency to the One he serves—possibly his delusion of indispensability—is dangerous to the people, not just in the present but in generations to come. "The severity of the punishment demonstrates the seriousness of the offense" (Friedman, *Commentary*, 495).

Moses' rash speech shows the heavy spiritual cost of leadership, including and especially leadership in God's name. This is a paradigmatic story treating the greatest leader in the Old Testament, the most godly leader of a large community in the Bible. It points to a failing that few if any spiritual leaders are spared, and maybe especially the most conscientious and influential of them. Moses exemplifies the tragic flaw of those who have so long carried the heavy burden of responsibility for God's sake, lived so single-mindedly for God's cause that sometimes they forget that the power is not their own. When Moses fails to place his trust wholly in God, then even he must be eliminated. This story takes place at Kadesh, which means "holy." This story of Moses' ultimate failure to hallow

47

YHWH thus finds subtle yet powerful resonance in the prayer that Jesus would later teach his disciples: "Our Father in heaven, hallowed be your name" (Matt. 6:9; Luke 11:2). That declaration and petition is the basis of the kind of prophetically informed leadership that the New Testament sets forth for the church.

2. Miriam

Miriam is explicitly identified as a prophet—a title that, interestingly, is never attached to Moses within the book of Exodus, and is assigned to Aaron only metaphorically: he plays the articulate "prophet" to Moses' silent "god" when they approach Pharaoh (Exod. 7:1). Miriam, however, has a more clearly defined prophetic role. She was a musician, and music was associated with prophecy in the ancient Near East, including Israel (1 Sam. 10:5), and further associated with prophetic performance in the context of worship (1 Chr. 25:5–6). Wilda Gafney cites Exodus 15:20–21 as an instance of "interpretive prophecy," part of "the first religious musical performance in post-Exodus Israel" (Gafney, *Daughters*, 80–81): "And Miriam the prophet, sister of Aaron, took the timbrel in her hand, and all the women went out after her with timbrels and with dancing. And she chanted back to them:

> Sing to YHWH, for he has greatly triumphed;
> horse and its rider he has cast into the sea."

The sketchy account of Miriam's (temporary) fall from grace as a prophet appears in the complex series of events that unfolds through Numbers 11 and 12; its unifying theme is the widening of prophetic responsibility beyond the person of Moses. The segment that concerns Miriam begins in medias res: "And Miriam spoke, and Aaron, against Moses regarding the Cushite woman whom he had married: 'He has married a Cushite woman!' And they said, 'Is it only through Moses that YHWH has spoken? Has he not also spoken through us?' And YHWH heard. Now the man Moses was very humble, more than any other human on the face of the earth" (12:1–3). YHWH descends in a pillar of cloud and summons the three siblings out to the tent of meeting, where Aaron and Miriam are then called forward like misbehaving schoolchildren and instructed about the difference between Moses and every

48

other prophet: to the others, God appears in a vision and speaks in a dream, whereas to Moses, YHWH speaks "mouth to mouth"—and what is more, "he beholds the manifestation [*tĕmûnâ*] of YHWH. Now why," God asks pointedly, "did you not fear to speak against my servant Moses?!" With that the angered Deity departs, "and whoa! Miriam is stricken with scale disease, like snow!" (vv. 8–10). Aaron, in shock, appeals to Moses: "My lord, do not hold against us the sin that we have so foolishly committed!" Moses immediately prays for healing, and the prayer is granted, but only after Miriam "bear[s] her shame for seven days," shut out of the camp. However, "the people did not journey on until Miriam was readmitted" (vv. 14–15).

The story tells much less than we would like to know about the incident; therefore any interpretation must consist largely of questions that admit of no final answer. What is Miriam's objection regarding the Cushite woman, and why is it raised now, long after Moses' marriage to Zipporah (see Exod. 2:21)? Is it ethnic contempt (as most think), because Moses' wife is an outsider? If so, then Miriam's punishment of being set *outside the camp* is an application of the core biblical principle of "measure for measure" ("an eye for an eye," Exod. 21:23–25; Lev. 24:20; Deut. 19:21), a principle that is generally applied metaphorically, as here. Or is she objecting that Moses has taken another wife after Zipporah, whom Moses once sent away (Exod. 18:2)? Or perhaps the Cushite is the same person as Zipporah the Midianite, since Habakkuk seems to identify Cushan with Midian (Hab. 3:7). If this is so, then the point may be that her ethnic difference is only now apparent to everyone, since Zipporah has just recently joined the Israelite camp (Exod. 18:5). In any case, this objection appears to be a pretext for the real issue of prophetic authority: Does it belong exclusively to Moses? There may indeed be a connection between the two issues of marriage and authority, since Zipporah is the daughter of a priest, and so it is likely that Moses elevated his religious status by that marriage. Perhaps Miriam is now trying to bring him down a peg (see Bellis, *Helpmates*, 91).

Again, why does Miriam take the force of God's rage on her own body, while Aaron gets off scot-free—at least on this occasion? (As discussed below, Aaron is treated even more harshly than Miriam for his later act of rebellion at Meribah.) Perhaps Miriam was simply hit first, since she had spoken for them both, and Aaron confessed the sin just a moment before the scale disease struck his own body. More likely, it is because Aaron, as the high priest, cannot suffer a punishment that would disqualify him for his office; those with scale disease were regarded as ritually dead (cf. Num. 12:12), and according to Leviticus 22:4, any man from Aaron's line who gets such a disease must be cleansed before eating from what has been sacrificed. But even if either or both of these is the case, it is also true—and this realistic narrative detail should not be lost on hearers of the story—that in many modern cultures as in the ancient world, women have very often been publicly humiliated for offenses, real or perceived, that equally involve men. Further, women are frequently discouraged from claiming religious status and punished when they do. It is therefore especially important to underscore the fact that out of respect for the prophet Miriam, the Israelites did not continue their journey until she was reintegrated into the community.

Further, it is crucial to recognize that this memorable and disturbing story appears in the context of several accounts of complaints, appeals to God, and power sharing among prophets. As Jacob Milgrom has shown (see *Numbers*, 376–80), there is a strong thematic and structural connection between this story and the one in Numbers 11:4–34, where Moses hits bottom under the burden of leadership and whines mightily to God: "I cannot bear this people all by myself; it is too heavy for me. If this is how you are going to do me, then go ahead and kill me—if you really care about me—so I don't have to witness [*r-'-h b-*] my own misery!" (vv. 14–15). Accordingly, God takes some of the prophetic spirit laid upon Moses and distributes it among seventy elders. Whether or not this represents a diminution of Moses' powers—as Joshua clearly thinks it does (v. 28)—Moses welcomes the relief: "If only all YHWH's people were prophets!" (v. 29). Moses' genuine humility and God's willingness to distribute the prophetic spirit have thus anticipated Miriam and Aaron's objection about power sharing and rendered it unnecessary.

Taken together, the stories of the three siblings yield several insights into the power dynamics of prophecy, and also of the burden and the cost to those who bear it:

1. Prophecy is not a solo enterprise for anyone, including Moses, nor is it an open competition. The prophetic spirit is a manifestation of God's grace, granted in community and for the sake of the community. Within the Bible this notion is developed most

fully by the apostle Paul (1 Cor. 14), as we shall consider in chapter 7 (pp. 197–205 below).

2. The exercise of prophecy is not a career opportunity governed by rules of "fairness." God's gift of grace is apportioned freely, and differently to each. The spirit of prophecy can be temporarily withdrawn by God, and ultimately God takes it from every good servant, including Moses.

3. Most importantly, there is no such thing as a prophet without flaws—indeed flaws that may profoundly impair one's service, at least for a time. What is more, the prophet's burden reveals and exacerbates those flaws; it is a punishing job that comes close to destroying those who do it. God's judgment ultimately falls on each of the three siblings, with the same result: none of them enters the land of Canaan. When Aaron is punished for the "rebellion" at Meribah (Num. 20:24), his humiliation would seem to be even greater than Miriam's: stripped of his priestly robes, he is sent off to die on Mount Hor. "And the whole community saw that Aaron had perished [*g-w-ʿ*]" (v. 29)—tellingly, the Priestly source uses the same verb elsewhere with reference to death that results from sin: in the flood (Gen. 6:17; 7:21), in the Korahite rebellion (Num. 20:3), of Achan (Josh. 22:20). Goldingay observes perceptively: "Being drawn into the fulfillment of YHWH's purpose brings extraordinary privileges, but it is also a dangerous business, and the reasons for the cost it brings cannot necessarily be explained. Blessing and danger cannot be dissociated" (*Gospel*, 313).

3. Jonah

Jonah epitomizes the genuine prophet who goes far wrong, literally. Sent eastward to Nineveh on the Tigris, he immediately fled to the Mediterranean port of Jaffa and found a boat heading due west, to Tarshish. What makes his story apt here is that Jonah is so clearly styled as the antitype to the progenitors of the prophets, Abraham and (especially) Moses. If Abraham is the great exemplar in the Bible of the prophet interceding for the Gentile nations (see Lipton, *Longing*, 108–40), in the case of Sodom even taking the initiative against God's expressed intention, then Jonah is the one who did all he could to get out of that commission when he was specifically called to give Gentiles a chance to be reconciled to God.

51

Equally, Jonah is shown to be the antitype to Moses at Sinai, when Jonah *"interceded [p-l-l, hitpa'el]* to YHWH and said, *"ānnâ* YHWH'!" Jonah utters the same strong particle of entreaty, used only in addressing the Deity, with which Moses began his prayer (Exod. 32:31) over the sin of the golden calf, when he laid his own life on the line for the Israelites. Indeed, Jonah's "intercession" is a distorted inversion of that prayer: "Isn't this what I said when I was still on my own soil? That's why I went ahead and bolted for Tarshish—because I know that you are 'a gracious and merciful God, long in patience and abounding in *ḥesed*, who relents about evil.' And now, YHWH, just take my life, since my dying is better than my life!" (Jonah 4:2–3). Jonah cites *against* God the signature revelation to Moses, who had pleaded to God, "Just show me your glory!" (Exod. 33:18). When Moses saw who God really is, "he quickly bowed low to the ground and worshiped" (Exod. 34:8); Jonah fumed and then went off to grab a ringside seat (Jonah 4:5), still hoping against hope that something bad might happen to Nineveh. Jonah's anxiety is the polar opposite of the consistent concern of Abraham and Moses, that God should not overlook anyone in the community who might be innocent or who might yet turn back to God. The last thing Jonah wants is a whole city of Ninevite penitents.

The book of Jonah is a parody on prophecy, as many have said, but what makes it apt for consideration here is that it is essentially a parody on YHWH's friendship with the prophet. The importance of this story and also its poignancy lie in the fact that the Deity does not give up on Jonah, even as he sits in a hot sulk under his withered vine, hoping to God that he will die. Instead God addresses him in a tone any one of us might use with a disgruntled and estranged friend:

> "You're good and angry over that plant, aren't you?"
> And he said, "Yes, I'm good and angry, enough to die."
> And YHWH said, "You felt protective toward that plant, though you did not labor over it nor grow it, which appeared and vanished between one night and the next. And I, I should not feel protective toward Nineveh, the great city that has in it more than 120,000 people who don't know their right from their left—plus a lot of livestock?" (Jonah 4:9–11)

52   In this story God speaks directly only to Jonah—not to the great king of Assyria, nor to any other Ninevite. This appeal for Jonah's empathetic understanding is the climax of the pursuit of Jonah,

God's chosen friend, that constitutes the plotline of the book. From the moment he runs to Joppa until now, after the prophetic charge has been successfully if grudgingly fulfilled, God is after Jonah. We are not told whether God needed him in particular to reach the Ninevites. But what is clear from this speech is that God desires not only to reclaim the Gentiles but also to have Jonah as an understanding friend. God wishes him to know and appreciate how it feels to be the One who made all these dumb creatures, Ninevites included.

In the context of the canon, the book of Jonah functions as an extended proto-midrash, a story that amplifies Scripture, likely taking its inspiration from the Deuteronomic Historian's reference to "the word of YHWH God of Israel that he spoke by the hand of *his servant Jonah*, son of Amittai, the prophet" (2 Kgs. 14:25; emphasis added). Particularly this parodic story amplifies the notion of what it would mean to be a prophet in the line of God's servant Moses, who was "faithful in all God's household" (cf. Num. 12:7). It should mean sharing God's compassionate concern for every creature, human and beast.

Curiously, the storyteller does not record how Jonah responds to God's appeal, which stands as the final word in the book. Thus, narratively speaking, God goes unanswered—unless some reader hears the appeal and offers God the understanding that betokens genuine friendship. Jonah's silence puts on us the burden of prophetic response.

Works Cited in Chapter 2

Bellis, Alice Ogden. *Helpmates, Harlots, and Heroes: Women's Stories in the Hebrew Bible.* Louisville, KY: Westminster John Knox Press, 2007.

Berkovits, Eliezer. *With God in Hell: Judaism in the Ghettos and Deathcamps.* New York: Sanhedrin Press, 1979.

Friedman, Richard Elliott. *Commentary on the Torah.* New York: HarperCollins, 2001.

Gafney, Wilda C. *Daughters of Miriam: Women Prophets in Ancient Israel.* Minneapolis: Fortress Press, 2008.

Goldingay, John. *Israel's Gospel.* Old Testament Theology 1. Downers Grove, IL: InterVarsity Press, 2003.

53

Levenson, Jon D. *Creation and the Persistence of Evil: The Jewish Drama of Divine Omnipotence.* New York: HarperCollins, 1988.

Lévinas, Emmanuel. *The Levinas Reader.* Edited by Seán Hand. Oxford: Blackwell, 1989.

Lipton, Diana. *Longing for Egypt and Other Unexpected Biblical Tales.* Sheffield: Sheffield Phoenix Press, 2008.

MacDonald, Nathan. "Listening to Abraham, Listening to YHWH: Divine Justice and Mercy in Genesis 18.16–33." *Catholic Biblical Quarterly* 66 (2004): 25–43.

Milgrom, Jacob. *Numbers.* JPS Torah Commentary. Philadelphia: Jewish Publication Society, 1990.

Miller, Patrick D., Jr. "'Moses My Servant': The Deuteronomic Portrait of Moses." *Interpretation* 41:1 (January 1987): 245–55.

Moberly, R. W. L. *The Bible, Theology, and Faith: A Study of Abraham and Jesus.* Cambridge: Cambridge University Press, 2000.

Muffs, Yochanan. *Love and Joy: Law, Language and Religion in Ancient Israel.* New York: Jewish Theological Seminary of America, 1992.

Neusner, Jacob. *Genesis Rabbah: The Judaic Commentary to the Book of Genesis: A New American Translation.* Atlanta: Scholars Press, 1985.

Olson, Dennis T. *Numbers.* Interpretation series. Louisville, KY: John Knox Press, 1996.

Ross, J. F. "The Prophet as Yahweh's Messenger." In *Israel's Prophetic Heritage,* edited by Bernhard W. Anderson and Walter Harrelson. New York: Harper, 1962.

Sarna, Nahum. *Exodus.* JPS Torah Commentary. Philadelphia: Jewish Publication Society, 1991.

Sommer, Benjamin D. *The Bodies of God and the World of Ancient Israel.* New York: Cambridge University Press, 2009.

Zornberg, Avivah Gottlieb. *Genesis: The Beginning of Desire.* Philadelphia: Jewish Publication Society, 1995.

———. *The Particulars of Rapture: Reflections on Exodus.* New York: Doubleday, 2001.

Hosting God's Power of Life

Elijah and His Gospel Legacy

Then take, O God, thy power and reign.
—"Ride On! Ride On in Majesty!"
Henry Hart Milman, 1791–1868

The hands that know how to give never stay empty.
—Latvian proverb

Entering the Prophetic Era

As the Bible tells it, the prophetic era in Israel begins in earnest with Elijah. He is the first prophetic protagonist in the land of Israel, that is, the first prophet after Moses whose career is narrated as a full-scale drama in several acts. At the core of the drama is the confrontation between the outlier prophet Elijah and Ahab, certainly one of the most powerful kings in Israel's history. Earlier kings of Israel and Judah were of course attended by prophets, such as Nathan and Gad in David's court. This reflects the standard practice of ancient Near Eastern monarchs, who kept prophets, sometimes by the hundreds (1 Kgs. 18:19; 22:6), to give counsel in matters of domestic and foreign policy, and perhaps especially to guide and encourage their military exploits (e.g., 1 Kgs. 20). But the biblical account emphasizes another prophetic role, one that in historical context was probably exceptional: prophets operating inside

55

and outside court circles challenge the power of the king and others in positions of influence, and sometimes they succeed in influencing action at the highest level. Of all the prophets closely associated with Israelite monarchs, Elijah stands as primus inter pares, first among equals—or better, as primus ante (before) pares. Because his story is found within the so-called Former Prophets (the books of Joshua through Kings), Elijah is positioned canonically near the head of the line of those who stand before God and speak God's truth to kings.

Moreover, Elijah is the first after Moses to exercise public influence on a large scale, on the people and not just on the king. After his grand prophetic performance on Mount Carmel, "all the people saw, and they fell on their faces and said, 'YHWH, *he* is the [real] God; YHWH, *he* is the God'" (1 Kgs. 18:39). Elijah is also the first prophet to anoint a disciple and successor (19:16–21). Both the public contest on Carmel and the anointing of Elisha might be viewed as signaling the beginning of something like a prophetic movement. Scholars speak of a "YHWH-alone party" or "movement" that seems to have begun in the ninth century; its proponents insisted strongly—perhaps violently (18:40)—on the exclusive worship of Israel's national God. His very name might be emblematic of the movement; *Eliahu* means "Yah is my God." The religious position that we call monotheism may have persisted for some centuries as a minority opinion in Israel before it became, after the exile, the dominant view of early Judaism and in the Bible (see Smith, *Palestinian Parties*; Lang, *Monotheism*, 26–50).

All the events in this detailed saga stem more or less directly from Elijah's intense and prolonged confrontation with Ahab. Here we see how much their interaction runs against the grain of the ancient Near Eastern custom of prophets in the service of kings. Even when Nathan exposed David's sin, he remained his trusted adviser, but Ahab names Elijah plainly as "troubler of Israel" (1 Kgs. 18:17) and "my enemy" (21:20). No less than Elijah, Ahab is an emblematic figure. Measured in terms of military achievement, he was spectacularly successful, a mover and shaker, with the result that he is the earliest Israelite king to enter into the extrabiblical historical record.

56   As we shall see, the contest between Elijah and Ahab focuses attention on this question: Who holds the power of life? Is it YHWH or is it "the king"—that is, powerful individuals and social

institutions, along with the idols they worship and stand for? Further, the Elijah story and the whole prophetic trajectory that unfolds from it draw attention to these questions: How do humans serve as channels through which God's power of life flows? Conversely, how might they obstruct that power, bringing doom upon themselves and death to others? The story of Elijah sets the crucial terms by which those questions will be addressed and answered throughout the rest of the Bible. As we shall see, it does so in a way that illumines a matter of great urgency for our own time, namely, the human responsibility to tend and share the physical means of life, those few essentials without which we cannot long survive: water, food, and arable land. These are the concrete terms of the struggle between Elijah and Ahab.

Scholars debate whether the Elijah narrative may have been an early source from which the Deuteronomistic History developed (see Halpern and Lemaire, "Composition," 145–48) or alternatively, one of the latest parts, the tower on the edifice that gives coherence and memorable form to the whole (see Brodie, *Crucial Bridge,* 76–77). What is certain is that it is developed and positioned as an indispensable hermeneutical key to the stories and books of the prophets that follow, from Elijah's immediate successor, Elisha, all the way through to the evangelists' representations of Jesus. As I shall show, continuity and difference with the Elijah saga is especially important in Luke's portrait of Jesus and those who recognize and hail him as the Lord of life.

Because he was taken up live into heaven, biblical tradition consistently reads Elijah as the prophet who is still active in God's service. Therefore his is the name that concludes the canonical division of the Prophets:

> I am about to send to you the prophet Elijah,
> before the coming of the great and fearsome Day of YHWH.
> (Mal. 3:23 [4:5E])

Positioned thus in the penultimate verse of the Christian Old Testament, Elijah points forward into the New Testament, where his name appears twenty-nine times (with twenty-seven instances in the Gospels). In the first verse of chapter 3, Malachi says:

57

> I am about to send my messenger,
> and he will prepare the way for me.

The earliest of the Gospels begins with an implicit citation of that divine promise (with variation):

> I am about to send my messenger before *you*,
> who will prepare *your* way.
> (Mark 1:2; emphasis added)

The messenger, John the Baptist, then erupts onto the scene as suddenly as did Elijah (1 Kgs. 17:1), with a message of doom for those who persist in opposition to God, and later Jesus will affirm that "Elijah has come" (Mark 9:13; cf. Matt. 17:12). Above all, what makes Elijah crucial for the New Testament writers is his status as the first person in the Bible to challenge the finality of death and prevail. His revival of the son of the widow of Zarephath prefigures Jesus' identifiably "prophetic" act of raising the son of the widow of Nain (see Luke 7:16), just as Elijah's bodily ascent into heaven prefigures Jesus' own death and resurrection.

The Life-Giving Word

Elijah comes out of nowhere, both narratively and geographically. Without introduction, Elijah of Tishbe (an otherwise unknown place) strides onto the biblical stage and addresses Ahab with an air of complete command: "As YHWH lives, the God of Israel before whom I stand, there shall not be dew or rain in these years, *except by my word*" (1 Kgs. 17:1; emphasis added). The prominence and power of the prophetic word is the clearest marker of the new era that begins with Elijah. Earlier prophets may have spoken to the king in oracles and parables, but here the prophetic word emerges as a dominant entity—almost a character in the biblical story—as it will continue to be until the end of the monarchy and on into exile (see Jer. 36 and Isa. 55). Prophets and prophetically oriented historians inscribe a history in which the word of God directs every faithful action and every truthful word spoken. Moreover, the divine word spoken to and through the prophet provides a standard for judging whatever may proceed from bad faith, including some of Elijah's own actions and words. Although in the end no one can prevail against it, "the primary goal of the [divine] word is not to dazzle or destroy, it is to give life and, when life is endangered, to

58

heal and nourish" (Brodie, *Crucial Bridge*, 71). Elijah swears by YHWH as the *living* God, the Source of life for every creature. The threat of dew and rain withheld focuses attention directly on the point of greatest vulnerability in the semi-arid land of Canaan, where drought is an ever-present threat, too often realized.

In the ninth-century reign of Ahab (871–850 BCE) and his queen Jezebel, Elijah's theological assertion was highly contentious. In the few preceding verses the narrator has set the stage, so we can appreciate just how contentious it is:

> And Ahab the son of Omri did what was evil in the eyes of YHWH, more than all who were before him. And as though it were too little for him to walk in the sins of Jeroboam son of Nebat, he took as wife Jezebel the daughter of Ethbaal, king of the Sidonians, and he went and served Baal and bowed down to him. And he raised an altar to Baal in the house of Baal that is in Samaria. And Ahab made the Asherah and did more to provoke YHWH the God of Israel than all the kings of Israel who were before him. In his days Hi'el the Bethelite built Jericho; at the cost of Abiram his firstborn he founded it, and at the cost of Segub his younger child he set up its doors [of the gates], in accordance with the word of YHWH that he had spoken by Joshua bin Nun. (1 Kgs. 16:30–34; cf. Josh. 6:26)

The brief concluding notice about Hi'el of Bethel is much more than a throwaway line. This is usually taken as a reference to human sacrifices made at the foundation or (re)dedication of a city and assumed to be a sign of evil influence from (supposed) Canaanite religious practice. However, there is no evidence, either archaeological or textual, that Canaanites or Israelites engaged in such a practice. The biblical narrator presents this as the fulfillment of Joshua's curse upon anyone who would rebuild Jericho (Josh. 6:26). In the present context, the notice of death in Jericho also foreshadows Elisha's miracle of "healing" the poisonous waters of that place, which were causing early death (2 Kgs. 2:19–22). It is likely that the narrator gives this brief account of a family's tragedy in order to draw attention to the polarity between curse and blessing in the land of Israel. The ancient curse upon the city that constituted the gateway into the land reached its fulfillment, ironically, "in [Ahab's] days"—to all appearances, a time of prosperity for Israel. The implication is that this is an emblematic tragedy; it is no

59

coincidence that Hi'el hails from Bethel, a royal sanctuary (Amos 7:13), which was for the Deuteronomists the chief site and source of apostasy for the kings and the whole nation (1 Kgs. 12:29–13:32). Nevertheless, rereading this notice in light of Elisha's healing miracle, we may see a sign of hope for Israel, or at least for that part of Israel that attends to the word and work of YHWH as mediated by prophets such as Elijah and Elisha. The irruption of divine blessing evidenced in the healing of Jericho's waters is likewise emblematic; it makes the city—and by extension the land—wholesome for habitation "until this day" (2 Kgs. 2:22).

The rest of the overview of Ahab's reign makes clear what it was to be king in a world in which religion and politics were inseparable. By marrying the daughter of Ethbaal (reigned ca. 887–ca. 856 BCE; Sweeney, *I and II Kings*, 206) and making her his chief wife, Ahab gained an advantageous alliance with a powerful royal house. The king of Sidon had unified the major Phoenician city-states and aggressively expanded the opportunities for its maritime trade. The partnership created new trade opportunities for Ahab as well, and especially outlets for his most valuable commodities, olive oil and wine (Master, "Institutions of Trade"). No less importantly, it provided crucial regional support in western Asia against the growing threat of the Assyrian Empire to the east. Royal protocol would require that Ahab offer religious hospitality to his new wife by making room for or giving greater prominence to the god to whom she was fervently devoted, the Canaanite rain-and-vegetation god Baal. For Elijah and the Deuteronomistic Historian, this is the crux of the matter.

Ahab, along with most of Israel as the Deuteronomist represents it, subscribed to "the flexible logic of polytheism" (Lang, *Monotheism*, 28), so Baal and the goddess Asherah were worshiped alongside YHWH in the capital city of Samaria. In this matter, Jezebel and Elijah were exceptional; both were religiously intolerant, although they took opposite sides in the battle. Both would (and did) slaughter prophets in large numbers to assert the rights of their deity as the national god of Israel. Elijah confronts Israel with the same choice that Moses posed to them in his farewell address, the classic Deuteronomic choice between "life and what is good, and death and what is evil" (Deut. 30:15). The point of Elijah's rich story is to demonstrate that Baal is not just less powerful than YHWH; he is dead. The various scenes show from different angles how the

60

forces of death threaten profoundly and perennially, yet ultimately they cannot stand against YHWH's power of life and power for life (see Hauser and Gregory, *From Carmel,* 11–89).

The account of Moses and Israel in the wilderness is one of two important backstories that establish the depth dimension of the Elijah saga. The other, less evident backstory is the Canaanite epic of a battle between two gods, Baal ("Master") and his fierce opponent Mot ("Death"). According to this mythological tradition, Baal battles against Death, and in the hot, dry land of Canaan the god associated with rainstorms and annual vegetation inevitably succumbs, as reflected in these lines of the epic poem:

> We came to the pleasant land of the outback,
> To the beautiful field of Death's Realm.
> We came upon Baal fallen to earth;
> Dead is Mightiest Baal,
> Perished the Prince, Lord of the earth.
> (Parker, *Ugaritic Narrative,* 149)

But that is not the end of the story; Baal symbolizes not only the green growth that dries up but also the rain that revives it. He is the Cloudrider, who stretches out over the earth and saturates it, inseminating it with life-giving moisture. In the cycle of mythical events and the agricultural year, Baal rises from the dead. In the epic, the high god El has a vision of rain, and he announces with relief,

> My spirit within can rest.
> For Mightiest Baal lives,
> The Prince, Lord of the Earth, is alive.
> . . . .
> May Baal restore the furrows of the ploughed land.
> (*Ugaritic Narrative,* 158)

Against this background it is evident that when Elijah boldly asserts that dew and rain will fall only by *his* word, as the servant of the living God, he is issuing a direct challenge to Baal. Although the narrator does not explicitly say that the prolonged drought is punishment for Israel's sin of apostasy, that inference is readily drawn by anyone who knows the Deuteronomic curse that falls upon Israel when it refuses to listen to YHWH and "to keep and do all his commandments and ordinances": "The sky that is over your head will be bronze, and the land that is beneath you, iron. YHWH will

61

make the rain of your land powder and dust; from the sky it will fall upon you until you are exterminated" (Deut. 28:23–24).

Although Elijah begins by speaking of "my word," the narrative immediately makes it clear that it is YHWH's word that is determinative. In the next verses the divine word sends him into "hiding" in a wadi, a torrent canyon that empties into the Jordan Valley, with the promise: "I have commanded the ravens to sustain you there" (1 Kgs. 17:4). While drought-afflicted Israel descends into famine, Elijah eats as only royalty did in ancient Israel, with meat twice a day. The mention of bread and meat, morning and evening (v. 6), alludes specifically to Israel's eating to satiety in the wilderness (Exod. 16:8, 12). The point of that ample feeding of the ancestors was not merely survival; rather it was, as YHWH instructed Moses, "that you [plural] may know that I am YHWH your God" (16:12). It is noteworthy that the earlier story of miraculous feeding in the wilderness is the first fully developed account of the experience of the people Israel once they have been delivered from slavery in Egypt. We might infer that the foundational cultural act for this people, or any people who might be judged godly, is to recognize the divine Source of their food. That recognition is the base on which all other religious knowledge is built (see Davis, *Scripture, Culture*, 66–79).

Hospitality in the Face of Death

After a time Elijah too is affected by the drought; the seasonal stream in the wadi dries up, and YHWH's word puts him back on the road, to the small city of Zarephath, just a few miles from Jezebel's hometown of Sidon, where her father Ethbaal is king. Sending Elijah there is a kind of divine counteroffensive, an instance of what traditional rabbinic interpreters call "measure for measure": just as Israel crossed the border, figuratively speaking, to worship the national god of the Phoenicians, so now YHWH calls for a prophetic advance into Baal's own territory. As he sets off for Sidon, Elijah receives an assurance parallel to the one with which he went into the wilderness of the Jordan: "Look, I have commanded a widow woman there to sustain you" (1 Kgs. 17:9). YHWH's word operates with equal power both inside and outside the land of Israel, both in the world of nonhuman creatures and in the land of the Sidonians.

What happens in Zarephath is crucial; it establishes key themes of the Elijah story and of prophecy throughout the Bible; in Luke's Gospel, this story is emblematic for Jesus' ministry (Luke 4:25–26). The feeding of Elijah by the widow is no less miraculous than his feeding by the ravens. She and her child are exactly one meal away from starvation when he shows up asking for food—and what is more, asking her to feed him *first* (v. 13). She does so, although at this point she appears to have no real faith in the God, foreign to her, in whose name Elijah offers this assurance: "Do not be afraid. . . . For thus says YHWH God of Israel: The jar of meal shall not be exhausted nor the vat of oil run out, until the day when YHWH gives rain upon the face of the fertile earth" (17:13, 14).

The widow of Zarephath is perhaps the most outrageous and courageous biblical exemplar of hospitality—the social virtue that, today as in biblical times, is valued above all others within traditional communities in the Mediterranean world—although she is not widely recognized as such (Abraham and Sarah feeding the angels in Gen. 18 are the traditional Old Testament icon of hospitality). Those of us who live in thoroughly modern cultures may regard hospitality as mere "entertaining," a social nicety that is optional and increasingly neglected in our busy lives. Because we do not find time to open our homes to guests, hospitality has become an "industry," a commodity to be purchased. But in the ancient world there were no restaurants; inns were far between and not always safe. Roads were for the most part sparsely traveled and dangerous, and there were no consulates to protect the interests of their citizens abroad. Very few ancients traveled for pleasure; most people on the open road were displaced persons, which is what the term "sojourner" (Hebrew *gēr*) implies. In a kinship-based society such as ancient Israel, the outsider had no social standing, no natural claim to any form of social protection or to the basic means of subsistence: work, land, shelter, food, even water from the community well.

In such a situation, hospitality is literally a matter of life and death, a sacred duty that every household is bound to fulfill. Accordingly, within the Bible there are dozens of references, direct and indirect, to the cultural mandate to offer food, shelter, protection to the sojourner (Exod. 23:9; Lev. 19:34; Luke 11:5–8; contrast the story of Sodom and Gomorrah in Gen. 19). Lord Jonathan Sacks, former chief rabbi of the United Hebrew Congregations of the (British) Commonwealth, reflected on the ramifications of this

63

biblical mandate in his Jewish New Year message of September 2001, just one week after the tragic events of 9/11:

> I used to think that the greatest command in the Bible was "You shall love your neighbour as yourself." I was wrong. Only in one place does the Bible ask us to love our neighbour. In more than thirty places it asks us to love the stranger. Don't oppress the stranger because you know what it feels like to be a stranger— you were once strangers in the land of Egypt. It isn't hard to love our neighbours because by and large our neighbours are people like us. What's tough is to love the stranger, the person who isn't like us, who has a different skin colour, or a different faith, or a different background. That's the real challenge. It was in ancient times. It still is today. (quoted in Russell, *Just Hospitality,* 101–2)

The widow of Zarephath fulfills the challenge to be hospitable in the most radical way possible within the cultural world of the Bible. As an unmarried woman with no grown son to support her, she herself has little if any social standing; no one is obligated to keep her and her son alive. She is herself as vulnerable as this stranger to whom she gives the meager protection of the one meal she assumes will be her last.

Yet Elijah tells her, "Do not be afraid." The empty meal jar is reason enough to be afraid, but to those whose ears are attuned to biblical idiom, Elijah's charge might suggest another, less obvious situation of threat, and thus another dimension to the unfolding story. In most of its occurrences in the Deuteronomistic History and elsewhere, the admonition "Do not be afraid" is spoken by a prophet to a king, combatants, or others "caught up in terrors and ravages of war" (Conrad, *Fear Not,* 34; see, e.g., Exod. 14:13; 2 Kgs. 6:16; Isa. 7:4). In these contexts, it functions as a call to trust in YHWH to fight on behalf of the people. It would seem that there is a war in progress between YHWH and Baal, or YHWH and Ahab, and the prophet calls upon the widow of Zarephath to contribute to the war effort. In her compliance she is a traitor, from a Baalite perspective—the perspective of Jezebel and her royal father—for giving material aid to the enemy. But from the perspective of the Deuteronomistic Historian, she is another heroic noncombatant like Rahab of Jericho (Josh. 2). Both these non-Israelite women live on the margin, in terms of both social status and physical location. Rahab the prostitute lives in a house built into the city wall (a good place to attract customers just in from the road); likewise the nameless widow of Zarephath likely lives near the entrance to the city, since she is the first person Elijah encounters there. Lacking social and economic support, even respect in their own communities, these "foreign women"— sometimes a dubious classification in the Bible (explicitly in Prov. 7:5; Ezra 10:2, etc.)—nonetheless prove their valor and good faith in combat situations that are nothing other than struggles for Israel's faithfulness to its God.

The widow who gives Elijah the gift of life receives it in return, through two successive miracles. First the promise of food is fulfilled: the meal jar and the vat of oil are continuously replenished, and the household eats in the midst of famine, "for a long time" (1 Kgs. 17:15). But that deadly threat is no sooner relieved (from the reader's perspective) than another replaces it. Immediately the narrator reports, "After these things, the son of the woman, the mistress of the household, became ill, . . . to the point that there was no breath left in him" (v. 17). The desperate woman turns fiercely on Elijah: "What have you got against me, man of God? Have you come to me to bring my sin to remembrance, and to kill my child?" (v. 18). Elijah's response merits careful examination, for it discloses the extent to which accepting the widow's costly hospitality has been transformative, so that his own life has become inseparable before God from the lives of the woman and her son. "And he said to her, 'Give me your son,' and he took him from her lap and took him up to the upper room where he was living and laid him on his [own] bed" (v. 19).

Laying the child on his own bed, the prophet exposes himself to whatever power of death (apparently unknown) has overcome the boy. It is an act of complete solidarity, in which Elijah imitates and reciprocates the woman's action of giving all that she has to answer the needs of the other. Standing over the inert body, he utters the words the mother does not yet know how to pray. Taking into himself the full force of her desperate need, he redirects it straight at the God of life: "YHWH my God, would you even do evil to this widow with whom I have taken shelter, by killing her son?!" (v. 20). Then, in a final act of willing vulnerability and solidarity, Elijah stretches his own body out full-length upon the still child and prays, "YHWH my God, let the life of this child return to his body!" (v. 21). It happens just as he prays in this, the first

65

resurrection account in the Bible. Thus this second miracle of life restored is the sign that attends Elijah's own demonstration of risky hospitality, just as the first miracle—the bottomless jars of meal and oil—attended the widow's prior demonstration of foolhardy generosity to a stranger.

The scene reveals not only the total solidarity between the prophet and the Canaanite widow and child; it also reveals just how intimate is the relationship between the prophet and God. This moment of bold prayer on behalf of a foreigner is a distant parallel to Abraham's prophetic intercession for Sodom and Gomorrah (Gen. 18:16–33). There is, however, an ironic contrast between the two scenes, specifically with respect to the key social value of hospitality to the stranger. Abraham pleads in vain for the Sodomites, who would in the very next scene determine to abuse the (angelic) strangers in their midst (Gen. 19:1–11); by contrast, Elijah is heard when he prays for a woman who has shown selfless generosity to the stranger. Although the God to whom Elijah prays may not yet be known to her, she matches perfectly the psalmist's depiction of the one who fears YHWH:

> . . . gracious and compassionate and just;
> good is the person who enacts grace and lends.
> (Ps. 112:4b–5a)

Somehow these acts of courageous hospitality open the way for God's power of life to enter into history, breaking the power of death. Justo González's astute comment about the nature of miracles illumines the connection between the character of the widow and her completely unlooked-for response to Elijah and God's miraculous actions through the prophet: "A miracle is not an interruption of an order, but rather the irruption of the true order—the order of the creator God—into the demonic order of the present world. . . . It is an announcement that the new order is at hand, that ultimately power belongs to the God of creation, of true order, freedom, and justice" (González, *Luke*, 83–84). The prolonged drought signals clearly (for those who can read signs and wonders) the temporary triumph of the demonic order within Israel's royal house and populace at large. Across the border, the twin miracles of food in the midst of famine and life restored to a breathless body come to a household where a woman who does not yet know YHWH nonetheless practices the righteousness of a true God-fearer. These are

66

signs pointing to the inevitable victory of the God who built into the very structure of the world the divine attributes of righteousness, generosity, and compassion (see, for example, Pss. 33 and 111). Meanwhile, as we shall see, the king of Israel is profoundly confused about wherein resides the power of life.

Ahab: Failing to Recognize the Power of Life (1 Kings 18, 20)

The Sidonian peasant woman rises above every man in the story, including even Elijah himself (cf. 1 Kgs. 19), as a model of unflagging courage in the midst of (spiritual) warfare. Likely ancient hearers of the story would have been struck especially by the contrast between the gutsy Canaanite peasant and the Israelite king, for Ahab was a renowned warrior, whose reputation extended well beyond his own borders. He merits mention in the massive Kurkh monolith, erected by the Assyrian ruler Shalmaneser III in celebration of his purported victory in the battle at Qarqar on the Orontes (today in Turkey) in 853 BCE. (The fact that the Assyrians did not push farther west at that time suggests that the outcome of the battle was in actuality a standoff.) Shalmaneser lists eleven kings in the western states who formed an alliance against him, and the largest force among them belonged to "Ahab the Israelite," who reportedly brought to the field 2,000 chariots and 10,000 foot soldiers (Pritchard, *Ancient Near Eastern Texts*, 278–79). The number is astonishing for the time; even if (as some suppose) Shalmaneser exaggerated for effect, Ahab was surely a force to be reckoned with.

The biblical narrator gives Ahab's military exploits more attention than those of any king since David, and the portrayal is distinctly antiheroic. His famous chariot force should haunt our memory when we read of Ahab's strategic response to the drought:

> Ahab summoned Obadiah, the palace administrator.... And Ahab said to Obadiah, "Go through the countryside, to all the springs of water and all the wadis. Maybe grass can be found, and we can keep the horses and mules alive, so we will not be cut off, with no animals." And they divided between themselves the countryside, to go through it; Ahab went in one direction by himself, and Obadiah went in another direction by himself. (1 Kgs. 18:3a, 5–6)

67

People are dying in the king's own city, but the horses and mules must live. So the king and his chief aide leave the starving population and go to find sustenance for those precious beasts without which he cannot field his chariots and keep the army supplied. Obadiah is a loyal servant of the king, managing all the most important affairs of the palace establishment, and none is more important than maintaining supplies for the army. Yet as the narrator shows us, Obadiah leads a double existence, a fact that gives a sharp irony to this little scene. He serves YHWH as well as Ahab, as his name ("the one who serves Yah[wh]") suggests. Even as Jezebel is hunting down the prophets of YHWH, bent on exterminating them, Obadiah keeps a hundred of them hidden in caves virtually under the royal noses, maintaining them (presumably) from the dwindling palace supplies of food and water (18:4). Obadiah fears YHWH; but he fears Ahab too, and he is terrified of being exposed as a supporter of Elijah and his kind (18:7–14). Unlike Elijah, Obadiah does not confront the royals openly; yet he sustains the prophets of YHWH, just as the widow of Zarephath did, and with no less risk to himself. Thus he keeps the truth alive in Samaria, the center of Israelite power that is directly opposed to the power of YHWH.

The consequences of his action are very great, as we may judge from the activity of some of those anonymous prophets of YHWH in 1 Kings 20, an account of Ahab's battles with Ben-hadad of Aram (Syria). Although its historical background is debated by scholars (see Sweeney, *I and II Kings*, 238–40), the theological intent of the account is clear: it shows how the king's failure to rely on YHWH plays out in the sphere of international politics. When Ben-hadad brings a coalition of thirty-two (!) kings to lay siege to Samaria, Ahab is terrified, immediately ready to capitulate and pay the heavy tribute—silver and gold, wives and sons—required: "According to your word, my lord king; I am yours and all that I have" (v. 4). But Ben-hadad pushes the humiliation one step too far with his demand to search the palace and the homes of the courtiers; at this the king and his elders and even "all the people" (v. 8) balk. So the battle is on, and Ahab rises to the occasion, answering Ben-hadad's dire threats with this cool riposte: "Let not the one who girds on [weapons, armor] boast like the one who ungirds" (v. 11).

68   Yet tellingly, the king of Israel never thinks to consult YHWH about the situation. So the Deity takes the initiative, sending "a

certain prophet" to Ahab with this message: "Thus says YHWH: Have you seen this whole great crowd? Look, I am giving them into your hand today—and you will know that I am YHWH" (v. 13). That last phrase is the common "recognition formula" (cf. v. 28), which appears always in situations where God's power is not clearly perceived by Israel (e.g., Exod. 16:12; Ezek. 20:38) or is contested between Israel and the nations (2 Kgs. 19:19). The promised victory for Israel will be only incidentally a military and political event. Essentially, it is an educational strategy; its aim is wholly theological.

Accordingly, the tide turns in Ahab's favor, in two successive seasons of battle, and Ben-hadad's coalition army is badly trounced. Nonetheless, it is evident that Ahab learns nothing from this precipitous change in circumstances; he is "theologically pathetic" (Hens-Piazza, *1–2 Kings*, 201), never recognizing that his well-being depends entirely on YHWH. He simply makes a minor shift in his political and economic calculations, concluding an advantageous treaty or "covenant" (*brît*) with the king he is now content to call his "brother" (1 Kgs. 20:32–33). In response to that casual alliance, Ahab receives a devastating message from another of YHWH's prophets: "Because you have let go free the man I had doomed, it shall be your life instead of his, and your people instead of his people" (v. 42). From here to the end of Ahab's story, there will be no more instances of God's grace extended to him, no more theological education opportunities.

This might be seen as an instance of what so many Christians expect to find in the Old Testament: a God who rejoices over dead pagans and stands in the way of peace. It is true that the Old Testament writers are not pacifists, with a few possible exceptions (Isaiah being the most likely). But neither do they idealize war. To many of his contemporaries, Ahab may well have seemed like a great military hero; he managed to stave off the Assyrian advance in his generation, and the northern kingdom endured for another 130 years. Yet from the prophetic perspective of the Deuteronomistic Historian, he was an egregious failure. Despite his experiences of YHWH's power and mercy, he never enacts in his kingship a properly theological recognition of the disposition of power among the nations.

The psalmist articulates the kind of insight that Ahab could and should have gained from these events:

> Now I know that YHWH delivers his anointed!
> . . . .
> Some [count] on chariots, and some on horses,
> but *we*, we count on the name of YHWH our God.
> *They*, they crumple and fall;
> but *we*, we rise up and endure.
> O YHWH, save the king!
> Answer us on the day we cry out!
> (Ps. 20:7–10 [6–9E]; v. 10 emended)

Because he never learns truly to recognize, to "count on," YHWH, Ahab will in the end crumple and fall dead—perhaps inevitably, in one of his world-famous chariots (1 Kgs. 22:34–35).

The unforgettable concluding moment of Elijah's story points to the true power of life for Israel and thus ironizes Ahab's status as commander of a powerful chariotry. As the young prophet Elisha sees his master one last time, in a chariot of fire with horses of fire, ascending to heaven in a whirlwind, he cries out, "My father, my father, the chariotry of Israel and its horsemen!" (2 Kgs. 2:12; similarly of Elisha himself, 13:14). The pride and strength of God's battle force are faithful prophets, not the iron chariots and horses on which Ahab so foolishly relies.

Inherit the Earth (1 Kings 21)

After the battle that ends with an anonymous prophet foretelling the king's death, there remains for Ahab one more momentous encounter with Elijah, who foretells the downfall of the royal house altogether, the end of the powerful Omride dynasty founded by Ahab's father. The occasion for the fateful encounter is the judicial murder of the farmer Naboth, a crime precipitated by Ahab's land greed and masterminded by his Canaanite queen, Jezebel.

Read in historical context, this beautifully crafted narrative points to a major social and economic shift that occurred in Israel, likely beginning with the Omride period. Archaeological and textual evidence from both the northern and the southern kingdoms suggests that, starting about the ninth century and advancing rapidly through the eighth and seventh centuries, there was widespread appropriation of family-held landholdings and their produce by the crown and the aristocracy. Thus the traditional

70

system of ancestral land inheritance was undermined by those whom Isaiah denounced as

> the ones who, annexing homestead after homestead, join field to
> field,
> until there is no more room, and you dwell all by yourselves in the
> midst of the land.
>
> (Isa. 5:8)

The system of independent small family farms was part of what defined Israel over against the Canaanite city-states. It was not simply an economic system; it was the cornerstone of social and religious identity. "The household, with its landed property, stood as the basic unit at the center of several spheres of Israel's life." It was the "fundamental cell of the kinship structure of the nation" and also "had a crucial role in maintaining the covenant relationship between the nations and God and in preserving its traditions through succeeding generations" (Wright, *God's People*, 1–2). It is noteworthy that we have no record, biblical or archaeological, of an Israelite selling farmland on the open market. Arable land was not a commodity but an intergenerational trust, granted on the condition of covenant faithfulness to God and neighbor.

This distinctly theological, even sacramental, understanding of the institution of land tenure, which signals the life-giving bond between God and the people Israel, is a tenet of biblical thought; especially, it is a recurrent theme in both Former and Latter Prophets. Witness Micah's vivid, precisely targeted denunciations of those wealthy people who plot on their beds to deprive others of their ancestral inheritance, and then

> in the morning's light they accomplish it, for their hand is godlike.
> They covet fields and seize them, and homesteads, and appropriate
> them.
> . . . .
> You drive the women among My people away from their delightful
> homesteads;
> from their infants you take away My splendor, forever.
>
> (Mic. 2:1b–2a, 9)

From a Deuteronomic perspective, it is precisely the role of Israel's king to protect the sacred land rights of his people. So Naboth the Jezreelite is rightly scandalized when "Ahab the king

71

of Samaria" (1 Kgs. 21:1)—a telling title, which identifies him with the dynastic capital built by his father, Omri—proposes to buy his vineyard, which lies adjacent to the king's winter palace in the lushest agricultural region of the country. Naboth's answer is the clearest possible articulation of the religious principle for which he will shortly die: "It is a desecration for me before YHWH to give my ancestral inheritance to you!" (v. 3).

When Ahab tries to buy the land, he claims he wants to convert the vineyard to a palace vegetable garden. However, when we examine that claim under a historical lens, it looks like a scam, and not only because Israelites, and especially their royals, seem not to have prized vegetarian cuisine (MacDonald, *What Did the Ancient Israelites Eat?* 77–79). Much more likely, Ahab wants the vineyard's valuable yield for himself. The Omride dynasty greatly expanded Israel's international commerce, and especially of fine wine and olive oil. Commodity agriculture was not confined to the northern kingdom; industrial-scale wine production is attested at Ashkelon and Gibeon in Judah in the eighth and seventh centuries BCE, the period and place in which the Elijah narrative likely assumed its present form (see Halpern and Lemaire, "Composition"). Ahab's marriage alliance with the Phoenician royal house gave him crucial access to maritime trade, and the bazaar in Damascus secured through his "covenant" with Ben-hadad gave him a lucrative market at that nexus of land routes. The monarch who knew how to exploit opportunities such as these would be a major international player— and at the same time a tyrant who succeeded by depriving his own people of life and land. Ahab "does kingship over Israel"—to echo the wording of Jezebel's bold challenge to her husband to take what he wants (v. 7)—in a way that runs directly contrary to God's *torah* (instruction) for the king, which is meant to ensure "that his heart may not be exalted over his kinfolk" (Deut. 17:20). Thus he betrays YHWH and the people Israel, and even himself and his royal house. In effect, he forfeits his own inheritance, as Elijah's oracle of doom implies: "*Because you have sold yourself* to do what is evil in the eyes of YHWH, I am about to bring evil upon you, and I shall consume everything after you" (1 Kgs. 21:20b–21a; emphasis added).

Perhaps no prophetic narrative speaks more strongly and urgently to our contemporary social and economic practices than does this one. Instead of royal appropriations of arable land, we have land-grabbing by governments (and sometimes their militias)

72

and the handful of multinational corporations that now dominate agriculture around the globe. Millions of small farmers have been reduced to poverty and rural communities to desperation, including rampant suicides, violence, and sex trafficking. Cities have been overwhelmed by the influx of the now-landless encamped more or less permanently around their perimeters. Further, the earth itself is impoverished and poisoned from some seventy years of industrial agriculture. About 40 percent of its soils are degraded and eroded; rivers, lakes, and underground aquifers are drained to the danger point, if not drained dry; and there are hundreds of dead zones at points where chemical-laden water empties into the oceans. Local and regional ecosystems are collapsing as a result of drastic reductions in genetic diversity among both animals and plants, including all our major food crops. And for all that, hunger is again on the rise around the world, even as the natural resources needed to combat it shrink in ways that are not recoverable in historical time. Moreover, "part of the 'externalized' cost of this [industrialized food system] is war after war" (Berry, "Agrarian Standard," 26).

In short, appropriation and commodification of arable land for the further enrichment of the powerful is revealed in our own time to be more than bad economics. It is murderous in the present and destructive of generations yet to be born, because the land is the proximate and indispensable source of life.

> If you have no land, you have nothing: no food, no shelter, no warmth, no freedom, no life. If we remember this, we know that all economies begin to lie as soon as they assign a fixed value to land. . . . Whatever the market may say, the worth of the land is what it always was: It is worth what food, clothing, shelter, and freedom are worth; it is worth what life is worth. (Ibid., 28)

Wendell Berry's insight reiterates in our context the perennial prophetic message delivered by Elijah to Ahab in the ninth century: for "the royals" to appropriate land for their own aggrandizement runs directly counter to the life-giving intention of the living God.

Elijah and Luke's Jesus

73

A major reason the Elijah saga is important for Christians is because echoes of his story figure so prominently in the two-volume work

Luke–Acts. From the beginning, Luke gives particular attention to prophets—Zechariah (Luke 1:67), the infant John (1:16), and Anna (2:36)—with the paradigmatic prophet Elijah clearly perceptible in the background. Even before John is born, the angel who promises a son to Zechariah announces that he will "be filled with the Holy Spirit . . . and turn many Israelites back to the Lord their God, and he will go before him in the spirit and power of Elijah" (1:15–17). Furthermore, a strong thematic echo with Elijah's story is Luke's emphasis on the word of God as active and consequential; small communities of the faithful gather in response to it. More than other evangelists, Luke names the peculiar blessedness of "those who hear the word of God and keep it" (8:21; 11:28; cf. 8:11, 15; see Johnson, *Prophetic Jesus*, 72–95).

Jesus himself is hailed by the people as "a great prophet" (7:16). Yet as we shall see, Luke shows that understanding of Jesus' person and ministry is finally insufficient. The thrust of Luke's repeated emphasis on prophecy is to show that prophecy as Israel has known it is being simultaneously fulfilled and surpassed. John the Baptist is "a prophet, yes, . . . and more than a prophet," as Jesus declares (7:26); how much more is this true of Jesus himself? In order to understand Jesus' person and work as represented in Luke's Gospel, it is helpful to explore the two key passages is which Elijah's prophetic ministry is evoked, first explicitly and then implicitly: the scene in the synagogue in Nazareth, when Jesus reads from the Isaiah scroll (4:14–30), and his raising of the widow's dead son at Nain (7:11–17).

Having withstood the devil's temptations in the wilderness, Jesus returns to Galilee "in the power of the Spirit" (4:14); entering the synagogue on the Sabbath, he is handed the scroll of Isaiah. The importance of the scene is underscored by the fact that this is Jesus' first public address; further, it is "the most dramatically elaborated story in [Luke's] Gospel" (Evans, *Saint Luke*, 266). Unrolling the scroll, Jesus lets the Scripture speak for him, naming both his identity and his mission:

> The Spirit of the Lord is upon me,
> wherefore he has anointed me to bring good news to the poor [or "afflicted"];
> he has sent me to proclaim to captives release
> and give sight to the blind,

to let the oppressed go free
to proclaim the year of the Lord's favor.

(4:18–19)

The anointing Jesus claims for himself should be understood in part as prophetic; he will shortly comment wryly that "no prophet receives favor in his hometown" (v. 24). But at the same time, it recalls the angelic proclamation to the shepherds in Bethlehem: "To you is born this day a savior, who is *Christos*/Messiah/the Anointed, the Lord" (2:11). A prophet and more than a prophet is here.

Jesus' anticipation of a bad reception in his native place is a self-fulfilling "prophecy"; he incites his hitherto admiring audience to a murderous rage by recalling how Elijah passed over all the widows in Israel and followed God's call to the widow in Zarephath (4:25–26). Ahab called Elijah a "troubler [LXX *diastrephōn*] of Israel" (1 Kgs. 18:17), and this scene in the synagogue offers the first indication of how Jesus himself will come to be seen by the elders, priests, and scribes as one who "troubles [*diastrephonta*] our nation, . . . saying that he is himself *Christos*/Messiah, a king" (Luke 23:2). Jesus' own programmatic statement in the synagogue suggests how he will be troublesome. Like Elijah with Ahab, he will disturb the powerful with his message that it is self-deception for Israel and its leaders to assume God's favor *without* making the commitment, which is always costly, to trust in God alone. By recalling Elijah's life-giving sojourn with a foreign widow, Luke establishes at the outset of Jesus' ministry his message "of salvation-as-reversal, of status transposition, of insiders becoming outsiders, of grace for unexpected people" (Green, *Theology of the Gospel,* 86).

The rest of the Gospel narrates how the mission statement from Nazareth is realized in the life and ministry, and ultimately in the death and resurrection, of Jesus. As C. Kavin Rowe observes, "the reading process moves first from person to manner of fulfillment," so it is important "to pay close attention to the person of Jesus himself to see how and in what way Luke narrates the enactment of the Lord's 'program'" (*Early Narrative,* 82). An important moment in that enactment is the second Lukan passage that evokes the memory of Elijah in Zarephath; Luke 7:11–17 is another story of life restored to a widow's "only begotten" (*monogenēs*) son (v. 12). Christopher Evans observes that the passage is exceptional for its "strongly Semitic" literary style, with eighteen past-tense verbs

75

mostly connected by "and." He suggests that Luke was trying to reproduce the style of ancient oral tradition, but one could say more than that. Likely Luke was using syntax, along with multiple verbal and thematic links, to reinforce the parallel with that particular story. To anyone familiar with the Elijah tradition, the echoes are unmistakable. Both stories begin, "When he came to the gate of the town . . . ," and end with an acclamation affirming the holy man's intimacy with God. When the son was revived, Elijah and Jesus both "gave him to his mother" (1 Kgs. 17:23; Luke 7:15).

Each story shows the personal involvement of the one who brings life out of death: Elijah is morally outraged that God should do evil to the woman who had taken him into her home, and Jesus is likewise deeply moved by the mother's grief. Yet the way in which Jesus' involvement is reported points to the profound difference between him and the ancient prophet: "And seeing her, the Lord had compassion [*esplanchnisthē*] upon her, and he said to her, 'Don't cry'" (Luke 7:13). The same verb is used later in the Gospel to describe the pity that moved the Samaritan to tend the wounds of the traveler on the road to Jericho (10:33) and the powerful emotion that overwhelmed the father of the returning prodigal, when he saw him "still far off" and ran to throw his arms around his lost son (15:20). However, in this context we are led to see that something more than even extraordinary human compassion is involved. This is the first time that Luke, using the voice of the "omniscient" (third-person) narrator, unambiguously calls Jesus "the Lord" (*ho kyrios*). The other evangelists reserve that term for Israel's God, following the Septuagint, the ancient Greek version of the Hebrew Bible. As Rowe has argued persuasively, Luke is deliberate in introducing that designation for Jesus here and in the next scene, when John sends his disciples to "the Lord" (7:19) to ask Jesus to reveal his true identity: Is he "a great prophet" (v. 16), as the crowd acclaims him, or is he "the one who is to come," the Messiah? In calling Jesus "the Lord," Luke gives the reader his own answer to that question, "thereby qualifying the category of prophet as christologically insufficient" (*Early Narrative*, 120).

Moreover, in using this designation in combination with the verb denoting compassion, Luke creates an echo within his Gospel that gives insight into both the character of Jesus and the new action of God in him. The first occurrence of the word "compassion" in the Gospel is in Zechariah's prophecy over his infant son, declaring

76

that through the "merciful compassion of our God," dawn is about to break upon those who "sit in darkness and the shadow of death" (Luke 1:78–79). Thus at the beginning of the Gospel, Luke points to the ministries of John and (even more) of Jesus as evidencing God's compassion for his people (v. 77). Now, in the scene at Nain, the evangelist shows that Jesus is himself the embodiment of divine compassion: the pity he feels in his own body (the Greek word literally refers to the guts, the seat of strong emotion), his hand on the bier, his word: "Young man, I say to you, rise!" (7:14). Jesus does not need to pray fervently to God, as Elijah did; his word to the dead man is itself the inbreaking of God's light for those who were sitting in death's dark shadow. "A great prophet has come among us!" the people exclaim. But then they make an even stronger claim, one that is truer than they may know: "God has visited his people!" By creating the echo between Zechariah's prophecy and this scene of release from death, Luke gives "implicit unity to the action of Jesus and the God of Israel at the point of the power of their compassion" (Rowe, *Early Narrative*, 121).

By drawing out so fully the parallel with Elijah's story, Luke enables us to see how unprecedented is this present action of God, even as it is consistent with the character of God as Israel has always known it. In Zarephath, Elijah's prayer and actions on behalf of the widow and her son were a channel through which flowed God's power of life. Now in Nain, Jesus himself is shown to be the Lord of life. In the context of Luke's Gospel, this story of a widow's son restored to life is a powerful fulfillment of the opening statement of Jesus' great teaching to the crowd gathered on the plain (6:20):

> Blessed are you who are poor,
> for yours is the kingdom of God.

In Luke's vocabulary, "poor" (*ptōchoi*) denotes those who are not just economically disadvantaged but also lacking social position, a "voice" before those with status and power. In the ancient world, from Elijah's time to Jesus' and Luke's, widows who lacked the support of an adult male were the most abject of "the poor." As Joel Green notes, Luke's story of the raising of the widow's son "is in reality much less about the dead man and much more about his mother" (*Theology of the Gospel*, 97)—another nameless, socially nonexistent woman, whose piteous condition calls forth the surprising action of God.

From Luke's perspective, then, what Elijah did in Zarephath portends Jesus' early ministry. Like Jesus, Elijah entered into full community with the powerless—being at that time powerless himself, in the wilderness of Sidon, in the middle of a killing drought and famine. He depended on her radical hospitality, became part of her household, and there he became a channel for God's power of life, evidenced first by daily bread, and then by life restored from death. What Robert Karris rightly observes about "the Lukan Jesus' kingly ministry" (*Luke*, 58) is no less true of Elijah's mutual ministry in Zarephath, that "God shares food with all, even those considered 'non-elect,'" and what is more (quoting Joachim Jeremias) "sharing a table means sharing life" (ibid.).

Moreover, Luke–Acts throughout highlights several themes that are especially prominent in the story of the widow of Zarephath: the inclusion of women in the new movement inspired by the word and Spirit of God, the manifestation of God's grace and power to non-Israelites and within communities where the socially powerless live together and share what little they have. All these are aspects of the "prophetic embodiment and enactment" of God's word— that is, how Luke not only states but *shows* "the character of God's vision for humanity" (Johnson, *Prophetic Jesus*, 72–73).

In one other place, Luke explicitly evokes Elijah's story, apparently with a view to showing how far Jesus differs from the ancient prophet in doing the surprising work of God and indeed surpasses him precisely on the point of mercy. Shortly after the Transfiguration, when Peter, James, and John saw Jesus talking with Moses and Elijah (9:28–36), the evangelist notes that "the days drew near for [Jesus] to be taken up" into heaven—as Elijah had been taken up before him—and "he set his face to go to Jerusalem" (9:51 NRSV). Jesus sent ahead messengers, who went to a Samaritan village looking for hospitality for their master, but they were turned away. James and John indignantly appealed to Jesus: "'Lord [*Kyrios*], do you want us to command fire to come down from heaven and wipe them out?' [Jesus] turned and chastised them" (9:54–55). It seems that these disciples, under the influence of what they had seen on the mountain, expected Jesus to answer this Samaritan offense just the way Elijah had, when Ahaziah, "king of Samaria" (2 Kgs. 1:3), sent troops after him. He called down fire to consume two companies of fifty men each and reduced the surviving soldiers to terror (vv. 9–14).

78

But Luke's presentation of Jesus uses Elijah both as type and antitype. In this case, Jesus' refusal to act according to the script provided by the ancient presentation of Elijah signals a serendipitous extension of clemency and mercy that will be matched both by the exemplary behavior of other Samaritans in the journey narrative (10:25–37; 17:11–19) and in Acts, by the proclamation and reception of the message of the kingdom of God in Samaria (Acts 1:8; 8:5–26). (Green, *Gospel of Luke*, 406)

In Jesus' forbearance we see how much "more than a prophet is here." In him "the merciful compassion of our God" (Luke 1:78) irrupts into our world, and its consequences become visible, in Israel and beyond.

A final point of connection between Luke's Gospel and the prophetic saga is the vindication of Elijah and Jesus, those two "troublers of Israel," at the end of their earthly ministries. Elijah's ascent into the heavens in the fiery chariot shows him to be just what Elisha says: "Israel's chariots and horsemen" (2 Kgs. 2:12), a source of power that is not delusory; in his proclamation of and public devotion to the true God, Elijah performs crucial prophetic functions that serve to keep the people alive. Similarly Jesus' mission of bringing good news to the poor and sharing life with the powerless and indeed his own "royal" power (23:2, 38) are vindicated finally and publicly in his ascent to heaven. Jesus was taken up "while he was still bestowing his blessing," in the very act of imparting fullness of life, with the result that all present were full of joy, and henceforth "they spent their time continually in the temple, giving praise to God" (24:51–53). The continuous flow of blessing and praise among Jesus' disciples is testimony to God's power of life at work among them.

Works Cited in Chapter 3

Berry, Wendell. "The Agrarian Standard." In *The Essential Agrarian Reader*, edited by Norman Wirzba. Lexington: University Press of Kentucky, 2003.

Brodie, Thomas L. *The Crucial Bridge: The Elijah-Elisha Narrative as an Interpretive Synthesis of Genesis-Kings and a Literary Model for the Gospels*. Collegeville, MN: Liturgical Press, 2000.

Conrad, Edgar W. *Fear Not Warrior: A Study of 'al tîra' Pericopes in the Hebrew Scriptures*. Brown Judaic Studies 75. Chico, CA: Scholars Press, 1985.

Davis, Ellen F. *Scripture, Culture, and Agriculture: An Agrarian Reading of the Bible*. Cambridge: Cambridge University Press, 2009.

Evans, Christopher F. *Saint Luke*. TPI New Testament Commentaries. Philadelphia: Trinity Press International, 1990.

González, Justo. *Luke*. Louisville, KY: Westminster John Knox Press, 2010.

Green, Joel B. *The Gospel of Luke*. New International Commentary on the New Testament. Grand Rapids: Eerdmans, 1997.

———. *The Theology of the Gospel of Luke*. Cambridge: Cambridge University Press, 1995.

Halpern, Baruch, and André Lemaire. "The Composition of Kings." In *The Books of Kings: Sources, Composition, Historiography and Reception*, edited by André Lemaire and Baruch Halpern. Supplements to Vetus Testamentum 129. Leiden: Brill, 2010.

Hauser, Alan J., and Russell Gregory. *From Carmel to Horeb: Elijah in Crisis*. Sheffield: Almond Press, 1990.

Hens-Piazza, Gina. *1–2 Kings*. Abingdon Old Testament Commentaries. Nashville: Abingdon Press, 2006.

Johnson, Luke Timothy. *Prophetic Jesus, Prophetic Church*. Grand Rapids: Eerdmans, 2011.

Karris, Robert J. *Luke, Artist and Theologian*. Eugene, OR: Wipf & Stock, 2008.

Lang, Bernhard. *Monotheism and the Prophetic Minority*. Sheffield: Almond Press, 1983.

MacDonald, Nathan. "Listening to Abraham, Listening to YHWH: Divine Justice and Mercy in Genesis 18.16–33." *Catholic Biblical Quarterly* 66 (2004): 25–43.

Master, Daniel M. "Institutions of Trade in 1 and 2 Kings." In *The Books of Kings: Sources, Composition, Historiography and Reception*, edited by André Lemaire and Baruch Halpern. Supplements to Vetus Testamentum 129. Leiden: Brill, 2010.

Milman, Henry Hart. "Ride On! Ride On in Majesty." In *Hymnal 1982: according to the use of the Episcopal Church*. New York: Church Hymnal Corporation, 1982.

Nelson, Richard D. *First and Second Kings*. Interpretation series. Atlanta: John Knox Press, 1987.

Parker, Simon B. *Ugaritic Narrative Poetry*. Society of Biblical Literature Writings from the Ancient World. Atlanta: Scholars Press, 1997.

Pritchard, James B. *Ancient Near Eastern Texts Relating to the Old Testament*. Princeton, NJ: Princeton University Press, 1969.

Rowe, C. Kavin. *Early Narrative Christology: The Lord in the Gospel of Luke*. Grand Rapids: Baker Academic, 2006.

Russell, Letty M. *Just Hospitality: God's Welcome in a World of Difference*. Louisville, KY: Westminster John Knox Press, 2009.

Smith, Morton. *Palestinian Parties and Politics That Shaped the Old Testament*. New York: Columbia University Press, 1972.

Sweeney, Marvin A. *I and II Kings: A Commentary*. Louisville, KY: Westminster John Knox Press, 2007.

Wright, Christopher J. H. *God's People in God's Land: Family, Land, and Property in the Old Testament*. Grand Rapids: Eerdmans, 1990.

CHAPTER 4

The Pain of Seeing Clearly

Prophetic Views of the Created Order

*There seems to be a law that when creatures have reached the level of
consciousness, as men have, they must become conscious of the creation; they
must learn how they fit into it and what its needs are and what it requires of
them, or else they pay a terrible penalty: the spirit of the creation will go out of
them, and they will become destructive; the very earth will depart from them
and go where they cannot follow.*

—Wendell Berry, "A Native Hill,"
in *The Long-Legged House*, 193

Perhaps the most urgent, fresh, and indeed surprising message that
the biblical prophets speak to contemporary society concerns the
God-given integrity of the created order and how it is disrupted
through the ungodly, disorderly actions of humans. This theme,
which is so peculiarly and tragically apt for our time, appears frequently in the prophetic corpus from the eighth century BCE to
the exile, and probably beyond. Its freshness derives from the fact
that its centrality to Israel's prophetic vision is only beginning to
command consistent scholarly attention and is still not widely recognized in the church.

My chapter title, "The Pain of Seeing Clearly," is inspired by
Abraham Joshua Heschel's distinction between, on the one hand,
conventional seeing—which is often not seeing at all but rather
overlooking, ignoring the things that should cause us to change our
mind and our ways—and, on the other hand, the often painful and
always surprising experience of insight. "What has been closed is

83

suddenly disclosed. . . . Insight is knowledge at first sight" (*Prophets*, 1:xii). It is apt in this connection that an early term for a prophet in Israel is *rō'eh*, "seer" (1 Sam. 9:9). Amaziah, the priest at the royal sanctuary of Bethel, uses a similar term when he contemptuously calls Amos "you visionary" (*ḥōzeh*, Amos 7:12). Nonetheless the term is appropriate (cf. the editor's use of the corresponding verb in Amos 1:1), for the encounter with Amaziah immediately follows a report of three painful visions that Amos has received from YHWH: a devastating locust plague, then fire, and finally a plumb line. All of them point to divine judgment on deviant Israel, a judgment that will not be revoked. "What do you see, Amos?" (7:8)—God's question underscores the fact that the prophet is literally a clairvoyant, one who sees clearly what others habitually look past.

This chapter explores how the classical Prophets see the created order and the human place within it. Despite the variety of their treatments, there is much consistency in what they see. The aim of this chapter, then, is to provide a framework for considering the many expressions of that theme, although only a few of them can be treated here. I offer a set of closely related theses that govern the prophetic understandings of God, humanity, and the earth—six insights that challenge the ways we customarily think about the world, even as they speak with a terrible directness to our current situation.

Thesis 1: There exists an essential three-way relationship among God, humanity, and creation.

In contrast to the North American church, which currently invests much energy in the debate about evolution and creationism, the biblical writers dwell little on the question of the origins of life. That question receives a rather simple answer from the psalmist, who in this matter speaks for all the others: "With [God] is the source of life" (Ps. 36:10 [9E]). The far more vexed question, and therefore the one to which they return again and again, starting with Genesis and continuing through the Torah, Prophets, and Writings, is this: How are the various creatures bound in relationship to each other and to God?

84

In their essential elements the Prophets' approaches to that question are congruent with the basic view of the Old Testament as a whole. A useful schematic model is Christopher J. H. Wright's influential representation of the triangular interrelationship among YHWH, the people Israel, and the land of Israel/Canaan (*God's People*, 105), which he has subsequently expanded into diagrams that consist of YHWH, humanity, and the earth, in both fallen and redeemed states (*Old Testament Ethics*, 183–87). Hilary Marlow posits an "ecological triangle," connecting God, humanity, and non-human creation (*Biblical Prophets*, 111). This model in its several variations points to the three irreducible elements in the set of obligating relationships that shape human existence, which the Israelite prophets construe as covenantal existence. Because it moves beyond conventional understandings of covenant as a two-party relationship between God and humanity or God and Israel, an even more appropriate name for the model might be "the *covenantal* triangle."

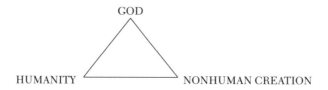

This model corresponds to God's "eternal covenant" with Noah and "every living being among all flesh" following the flood, thereby setting the conditions for continued life on earth (Gen. 9:8–17). Again, it illumines a key covenantal statement, such as the divine vow that appears in Leviticus, as it "forecasts" the exile of Israel from the land: "I will remember my covenant with Jacob, and yes, my covenant with Isaac, and yes, my covenant with Abraham I will remember—and the land I will remember" (Lev. 26:42). The inverted order in which the ancestors are listed—Jacob, Isaac, and Abraham—points to the preeminence of the land, which takes its rightful place in covenantal history, even at the head of the line of ancestors. Before Abraham was, the land is (cf. John 8:58). Both of these examples show the need for thinking of covenant as involving three parties, even while they also imply the importance of the dimension of time, which the flat geometric figure cannot accommodate. So one might supplement this geometric figure with the image of covenant as a dance, both ordered and dynamic, in which each creature interacts with every other creature, and all of them with the Creator.

85

The first inference to be drawn from this covenantal triangulation is that human and nonhuman creatures are in God's eyes, and therefore in reality, inseparably connected in their well-being. Contemporary readers of the Bible may well recognize here the essential agrarian insight that the health of an individual, and certainly the health of any human community, is entirely bound up with the health of the "entire human and nonhuman neighborhood" (Wirzba, *Agrarian Reader,* 4). The way of thinking and living called agrarianism, which in this generation Wendell Berry has articulated most fully (and in the view of many, "prophetically"), is not a sentimental throwback to some imagined Arcadia. Rather it is a complex worldview, grounded in science, philosophy, history, and theology, "that holds together in a synoptic vision the health of land *and* culture. . . . However much we might think of ourselves as post-agricultural beings or disembodied minds, the fact of the matter is that we are inextricably tied to the land through our bodies—we have to eat, drink, and breathe, and so our culture must always be sympathetic to the responsibilities of agriculture" (*Agrarian Reader,* 5).

While concern with the land and the responsibilities of agriculture may seem to modern readers very far from the central concerns of the prophets, they were in fact all members of agrarian communities, whether in the city or in the village. Therefore their perceptions and experiences of God and their own humanity were fundamentally informed by an awareness of the earth and nonhuman creation in ways that most of us can scarcely imagine. Moreover, the prophetic movement gained traction in the eighth century, a nodal point in the history of ancient Israel's agricultural economy, when the traditional system of independent family farms was yielding to a system of state-controlled agriculture. As the crown and the aristocracy were growing rich through trade in the three commodities of the Levant—grain, wine, and oil—the smallholders, virtually everyone else in the population, were (literally) losing ground. In the midst of this massive social and economic upheaval, the early prophets Amos, Hosea, Isaiah, and Micah, as well as many of their successors, spoke out for the floundering farmers and even for the land itself (see Davis, *Scripture, Culture,* 120–38; on Amos, Hosea, and Isaiah, see Marlow, *Biblical Prophets*).

86   A further inference to be drawn from the covenantal triangle is that human and nonhuman creatures are both connected with God in similar ways, in genuine relationship that is intended by God to

be intimate and enduring. Among all the biblical writers, Hosea is the one who speaks most suggestively, even mystically, of a covenant between God and the creatures:

> And it shall happen in that day—an utterance of YHWH—
> that you will call [me], "my husband," and not call me anymore "my
>   Ba'al."
> And I will remove the names of the *ba'alim* from her mouth,
> and they will not call their names to mind anymore.
> And I will cut for them a covenant on that day
> with the animals of the field and with the birds of the skies and the
>   creepers of the soil,
> and bow and sword and war I will break off from the earth,
> and I will have them lie down securely.
> And I will betroth you to myself forever.
> I will betroth you to myself with [the bride wealth of] righteousness
>   and with justice
> and with covenant-loyalty and with compassion.
> I will betroth you to myself with faithfulness, and you shall know
>   YHWH.
> And it shall happen in that day, that I will answer—an utterance of
>   YHWH.
> I will answer the skies, and they will answer the earth.
> And the earth will answer the grain, and the new wine and the oil—
> and they will answer "Jezreel" ["God sows"].
> And I will sow it myself in the earth.
>   (Hos. 2:18–25a [16–23a E])

In this intimate cosmological vision, the restoration of a faithful "monogamous" relationship between Israel and YHWH is set in a larger covenantal context, in a world without war (cf. Isa. 2:1–4//Mic. 4:1–4) or any hint of threat. Gone is the mutual hostility between animals and humans, which the Bible dates back to the primeval era (Gen. 3:15; 9:2; contrast Isa. 11:6–9). Indeed, in this anticipated covenant, which includes the wild animals as primary partners, there is no suggestion that humans have any "special species" status with respect to the birds of the skies, the field animals, or the ground creepers— the same categories among which humans are to exercise "skilled mastery," according to the cosmology of Genesis 1 (vv. 26, 28).

The most striking feature of the passage is the promise of betrothal, spoken by YHWH to an unspecified addressee who is, grammatically speaking, feminine singular. Laurie Braaten proposes that the bride is the personified Land (of Israel) and that the family who witnesses the covenant and receives the bride wealth is the whole "Earth community," humans included ("Earth Community," 195–99). Yet it is equally possible and theologically desirable to see the bride also (and at the same time) as the people Israel, with the land community ratifying the covenant. This vision anticipates a time when God's sowing the seeds of life and prosperity will give new meaning to "Jezreel," the richest agricultural district in Israel, which was famous as the site of royal grabs for land and power (Hos. 1:4–5; cf. 1 Kgs. 21; 2 Kgs. 9). The intertwined metaphors of marriage and agriculture point to the twin aspects of God's "husbandry" of Israel, both its people and its land; they are bound together in their well-being, "for better, for worse."

The intimate tone of the passage pushes the hearer to see justice, righteousness, and faithfulness as more than purely human ethical or religious attributes. They are qualities of interaction that are deeply inscribed throughout the world order that God has established; righteousness can and should abide in fertile farmland (Isa. 32:16) and not just in human society. Intriguing in this regard is the suggestion of Margaret Barker that the notion of righteousness, which is so central to covenantal discourse in the Bible and the literature of early Judaism and Christianity, often has a meaning that is close to our notion of sustainability (*Creation*, 144).

With its steady repetition of the key verb '-n-h, "answer, respond" (cf. Hos. 2:15 [17 Heb.])—a secondary meaning is "sing," which might suggest an antiphonal call and response (Marlow, *Biblical Prophets*, 176, 180)—this passage is a superb example of what Terence Fretheim calls the "interresponsiveness" characteristic of the interaction between God and the earth with its creatures. God has a genuine relationship with the so-called natural world, which moderns generally conceive as inert, an "it" to be acted upon rather than a "thou," capable of interaction. However, "this language of interresponsiveness shows that God's presence to and relationship with the earth and its creatures is more than external"; these have "an inwardness and interiority" that make mutuality possible (*God and World*, 173). "To speak in this way does not necessarily lead to panpsychism or vitalism, but it certainly suggests a greater continuity between the animate and the inanimate than moderns have commonly been willing to claim" (255).

The richness of the biblical concept of interresponsiveness, and its innovative religious character, is evident when the passage from Hosea is compared to a text from the Canaanite tradition of epic poetry from the Late Bronze Age. Here the storm god Baal is speaking to his sister Anat about the structure of the cosmos, and the nature of communication within it:

> For I have a word to tell you,
> A message I will recount to you,
> A word of tree and whisper of stone,
> Converse ["answering"] of Heaven with Earth,
> Of Deeps to the Stars.
> I understand the lightning Heaven does not know,
> And Earth's masses do not understand.
> Come, and I will reveal it,
> In the midst of my mountain, Divine Sapan,
> In the holy place, on the mount of my possession,
> In the pleasant place, on the hill of my victory.
> (Ugaritic tablet, ca. 1200 BCE;
> see Smith, *Early History of God*, 74)

There is a kinship between the two passages, especially signaled by the key notion of "answering" (expressed here in a Ugaritic word cognate with Hebrew '-n-h). Yet Hosea's vision introduces something that is absent from the Baal myths, namely, any indication of genuine relationship between the divine and human realms (Marlow, *Biblical Prophets*, 171). Here the god offers to share knowledge with the goddess, knowledge that is explicitly withheld from "Earth's masses." By contrast, the prophetic vision looks to a time when the bride—both land and people—will "know YHWH," and that knowledge will bring healing on and for the earth.

The other five theses are all closely related to the first. The next two point to the suffering shared among all three partners in the covenantal triangle, in our broken world.

Thesis 2: Human and nonhuman creatures together are "the poor and vulnerable"; they suffer together, and both stand in need of deliverance.

In her provocative study *The Body of God*, Sallie McFague makes the striking proposal that "the distinctive characteristic of Christian embodiment is its focus on oppressed, vulnerable, suffering bodies. . . . In an ecological age, this ought to include oppressed

89

nonhuman animals and the earth itself" (*Body*, 164; italics hers). I depart from the christological presuppositions of McFague's study, which "relativize the incarnation in relation to Jesus of Nazareth" and "maximize it in relation to the cosmos" (162). Nonetheless, her notion that in this century "human beings have caused nature to be the new poor" (166), used and misused, like the "old poor" of Jesus' parables, seems to be fully congruent with numerous representations of the nonhuman world in both Testaments, including Prophets, Psalms, and Paul's Letter to the Romans.

Possibly the most succinct biblical affirmation that God's restorative justice extends to humans and nonhumans alike comes from Psalm 36, whose theme is YHWH's covenant-loyalty as it is experienced by pilgrims in God's "house," the temple:

> Your righteousness is like the (al)mighty mountains; your justice,
>   the great deep;
> humans and beasts you deliver, O YHWH.
>
> (Ps. 36:7 [6E])

It is against the background of that statement that we should read a prophetic indictment such as this one from Hosea:

> Hear the word of YHWH, you Israelites,
> for YHWH has a charge against the inhabitants of the land/earth ['*ereṣ*]:
> There is no truthfulness and no covenant-loyalty
> and no knowledge of God in the land/earth.
> Perjury and cheating and murder and stealing and adultery
> are rampant, and bloodshed follows upon bloodshed.
> Therefore the land/earth mourns and all who dwell upon it languish,
> including the animals of the field and the birds of the skies,
> and even the fish of the sea are perishing.
>
> (Hos. 4:1–3)

The passage represents the tragic countertestimony to the covenant vision in Hosea 2. Instead of a lasting covenant that unites with bonds of affection and loyalty every living creature in the land or on the earth (the Hebrew word '*ereṣ* can mean both), human misconduct is rampant, bringing a blight upon the whole created order. Tellingly, what is missing is precisely the covenant-loyalty (*ḥesed*) and the knowledge of God (*daʿat 'ĕlōhîm*) that should be sources of healing and security for the earth and all its inhabitants. The absence or rejection of such knowledge constitutes Hosea's central complaint against the Israelites and their priests (cf. Hos. 4:6). The root *y-d-ʿ*,

90

"know," occurs no less than sixteen times in the book, in both nominal and verbal forms (2:10 [8E], 22 [20E]; 4:1, 6 [2x]; 5:3, 4; 6:3, 6; 7:9 [2x]; 8:2; 11:3; 13:4, 5; 14:10). In all but one place (7:9), it refers to the mutual knowing that exists (or is lacking) between Israel and YHWH, and the devotion that follows from true knowledge of God. What Israel lacks is not cognitive religious knowledge but rather an active embodiment of God's revealed will, as is clear from the list of crimes (4:2), with its clear echoes of the Decalogue. When YHWH cites Israel's cry, "My God, we know you!" (8:2), it is a statement of commitment to a certain way of living, however insincere it may be. Thus Hosea witnesses to the reality that the whole created order is being undone because the human inhabitants of the land (or earth) lack the one thing required of them: a wholehearted response to YHWH's self-revelation, the ultimate and most intimate gift of the God who has also provided superabundantly for the material needs of the people (cf. Hos. 2:10 [8E]). Richard Bauckham observes, "What can only seem grossly hyperbolic in its original context looks only too realistic in the context of our own situation of worldwide ecological catastrophe" (*Bible and Ecology*, 93).

The most vivid and extended prophetic account of the devastation of human and nonhuman creatures together is Joel's portrayal of a locust infestation as mercilessly destructive as any war. The dominant literary feature of the passage is verbal repetition, with the same language used to describe the activity and experience of the soil, the crops, and the people:

> Wail like a young woman girded with sackcloth, over the husband of her youth!
> Grain offering and libation is cut off from the house of YHWH.
> Mourn, you priests, servants of YHWH!
> The field is laid waste, the soil mourns;
> For the grain is laid waste, the vintage is withered, the oil crop has failed.
> Farmers are withered [or, "put to shame"], vintners howl over the wheat and over the barley;
> for the harvest of the field is lost.
> The vine is withered and the fig has failed;
> pomegranate, even date palm and apricot—all the trees of the field wither.
> Indeed, joy is withered away from human beings.
>
> (Joel 1:8–12)

91

The passage begins with a call to wail; although the identity of the feminine singular addressee is not specified, it must be the grapevine and fig tree (both feminine in gender) whose wasting is described in the preceding verse (v. 7). Likewise the priests are called to mourn, even as the soil is already doing (vv. 8–9). The most frequently repeated root, *y-b-š*, "be dried up, withered," appears here four or five times in several different forms. The occurrence in verse 11 is ambiguous: are the peasant farmers "withered" or "put to shame"? The latter translation would derive the form *hobišu* from the root *b-o-š*, as in Jeremiah 8:9, 12. This perfect and presumably deliberate ambiguity drives home the point that the farmer's emotional and physical well-being cannot be separated from the well-being of the farmland, as any farmer or rancher or gardener will tell us. When one fails to thrive, so does the other. Speaking to and for a culture in which virtually everyone outside the tiny elite class was a farmer, Joel reveals the extent to which human experience inevitably reflects the prosperity or suffering of the places on which our lives depend.

In a recent study, Richard Bauckham proposes that Paul's description of the groaning creation in Romans 8:19–23 is to be read against the background of the prophets' accounts of the mourning earth, with the death of plants and animals. Specifically, he suggests that the vivid picture drawn by Joel "may serve to fill out Paul's rather abstract language" (*Bible and Ecology*, 97) of the creation "subjected to futility" and put in "bondage to decay" (Rom. 8:20–21). His conclusion is worth quoting at length:

> Crucially, what becomes clear is that Paul assumes the same kind of close relationship between human wrongdoing and the well-being of the non-human creation that the prophets do. . . . That is not to say that Paul or the prophets understood the connection between human behaviour and ecological degradation in the way that we are now able to do, but what modern scientific knowledge makes possible is mainly a fuller understanding of how human physical behaviour . . . has extensive and destructive consequences for the ecosystems of the planet. For the ethical and spiritual dimensions that pervade such human behaviour it is we who can learn from the biblical writers. (100)

As Bauckham rightly notes, the most difficult theological problem raised by the common experiences and linked fates of human and nonhuman creation is the suffering of the innocent, and how ecological degradation and destruction may be related to divine judgment and justice. "While there is some justice in human wrongdoers suffering from the lack of the essential resources of the Earth, the non-human creatures themselves are the undeserving victims of the consequences of human behaviour" (101). In speaking of the futility to which the creation has been subjected, Paul may well be recognizing that "this kind of judgment on a large scale is bound to be, the world being as it is, relatively indiscriminate. Those most responsible are by no means always those who suffer most" (ibid.). This difficulty brings us to the next thesis.

Thesis 3: God feels pain and anger when the earth and its creatures suffer.

In his classic and lyrical study of the Prophets, Abraham Joshua Heschel identifies the prophet as the one who feels and articulates "divine pathos" at the injustice and suffering rife in the world: "The pages of the prophetic writings are filled with echoes of divine love and disappointment, mercy and indignation. The God of Israel is never impersonal" (*The Prophets*, 1:24). Therefore the prophet's message is to be "seen in three dimensions. Not only the prophet and the people, but God Himself is involved in what the words convey" (6). "The prophet hears God's voice and feels His heart" (26).

The centrality of divine pathos must be seen in connection with the historical situation that, as Heschel puts it, "drove" him to a study of prophecy that "involves sharing the perspective from which the original understanding is done" (xiv). That involved stance contrasts with the sociological or psychological approaches to prophecy that were standard fare during his years as a philosophy student at the University of Berlin. In time he came to see such uninvolved studies as irrelevant and ultimately irresponsible, as he observes:

> In the academic environment in which I spent my student years philosophy had become an isolated, self-subsisting entity, . . . indifferent to a situation in which good and evil had become irrelevant, in which man became increasingly callous to catastrophe and ready to suspend the principle of truth. I was led slowly to the realization that some of the terms, motivations, and concerns which dominate our thinking may prove destructive of the roots

93

of human responsibility and treasonable to the ultimate ground of human solidarity. (xiv)

Heschel completed his doctoral studies (on biblical prophecy) in 1933; five years later, he was expelled from Germany to Poland. Although he left Warsaw for London six weeks before the German invasion, Heschel's mother and three of his sisters died in the German bombing or in concentration camps. *The Prophets*, published some twenty years after these tragic events, is dedicated "To the martyrs of 1940–45."

Against the background of his immediate historical experience, Heschel reads the prophet's word as "a scream in the night," a "blast from heaven" directed against "a coalition of callousness and established authority" (16). In light of the new, humanly engineered catastrophe that occupies our own generation, it is revealing to use his approach to read Jeremiah, who, as Heschel says, "lived in an age of wrath . . . To Jeremiah his time was an emergency, one instant away from a cataclysmic event" (106). What makes Jeremiah's words especially apt in our contemporary critical situation is that no other prophet gives such full expression to God's anguished attachment to the land, as in this powerful outpouring of intermingled grief and rage:

I have abandoned my household, forsaken my Heritage.
I have given the darling of my life into the hand of her enemies.
My Heritage has become to me like a lion in the forest.
Over me she raises her voice; for this I hate her.
Has my Heritage become to me a bird of prey, a hyena? Let birds of
    prey encircle her!
Go, gather every beast of the field; bring them to devour!
Many shepherds wreck my vineyard; they trample my portion;
they turn my delightful portion into desolate wilderness.
They have desolated, made her into a desolation; she mourns to me,
    desolate.
The whole land/earth is made desolate, yet no one takes it to heart.
On every height in the wilderness, despoilers have come.
For a sword belonging to YHWH devours, from one end of the land/
    earth to the other;
all flesh is deprived of well-being [*shalom*].
They have sown wheat and harvested thorns; they make themselves
    sick and profit nothing.

Be ashamed, then, because of your yields, because of the burning
wrath of YHWH.

(Jer. 12:7–13)

This is an impassioned lament, not an oracle of judgment, and
the distinction is important for our understanding of God's involvement in the devastation of the land. In Terence Fretheim's insightful words, "the 'Godward' side of wrath is always grief" ("Earth
Story," 101). God grieves extravagantly, as does Jeremiah (e.g., Jer.
8:23 [9:1E]; 14:17), and even the land itself (4:19–20; 12:11); they
all model the only sane response—mourning—to the disaster that
no one among the people "takes to heart." Yet the situation is complicated, for God's giving "the darling of [God's] life" into the hand
of her enemies is itself part of the unfolding disaster. So how does
YHWH's admitted abandonment relate to the suffering of the land?
Countering Walter Brueggemann's assertion that "Yahweh has withdrawn fidelity," thus exposing the land to loss of fertility, Fretheim
offers a solution that is more consonant with the logic of the biblical
writers. YHWH's withdrawal is not the first cause of the land's suffering; rather, "the already devastating effects of the people's wickedness are thereby brought to completion in the moral order which
God mediates" ("Earth Story," 106). The relation of human crime
to divine punishment might be compared with that in the primeval
flood story. The earth is "ruined before God" (Gen. 6:11), because
"all flesh had ruined its way on the earth" (v. 12); only when the
fact of ruin is fully established (v. 13a) does God resolve to "effect-
their-ruination" (v. 13b). With four iterations of the verb, the narrator shows a punishment that not only fits the crime but is essentially
identical with it. The ruin God effects is no more than the full manifestation of what "all flesh" has already done to itself and the earth.

Jeremiah's original hearers, most of them farmers, might also
have drawn the close connection between human irresponsibility
and the desolation of the land in a second way, based on common
agricultural experience. "They have sown wheat and harvested
thorns"—this is a succinct and accurate description of what happens to overtilled earth, especially in a thin-soiled, semi-arid environment such as the fragile uplands of Judah (George W. Fisher,
personal communication, March 2012).

The passage altogether makes it clear that YHWH's way of
responding to the actions of the "household" is far from a top-down

95

imposition of the divine will. Although the several references to "my vineyard, my portion" leave no doubt about God's strong and particular connection with or ownership of the land, "God delegates responsibility for the land to others—with all the attendant risks" (Fretheim, "Earth Story," 106). It would seem that the biggest risk of all is borne by God, as suggested here by the several remarkable verbal images of Israel roaring over YHWH, like a ravenous lion over its prey, a vulture or a hyena picking up roadkill. In the whole Bible, there is probably no more striking statement of human rapacity and divine vulnerability. Here we see a clear instance of a theological claim that Christians often wrongly ascribe solely to the New Testament: God is vulnerable to human sin, threatened by it even (to push the boundary of the prophetic metaphors) unto death. The divine lament in Jeremiah is a prophetic witness to the divine vulnerability that is fully revealed only on the cross. Conversely, the next thesis considers how humans may experience the suffering of the earth.

Thesis 4: The suffering of the earth itself is a primary index of the brokenness in the human relationship with God.

Beginning in Eden, as the Bible tells the story of the created order, human alienation from God is directly mirrored in the condition of the land. God tells the man, after the original disobedience, "Cursed is the arable-land ['ădāmâ] on account of you [ba'ăbûrekā]" (Gen. 3:17). That the soil should be disgraced because of human misconduct may seem arbitrary, at least when viewed from the urban perspective shared by many North American readers of the Bible, but such a perception itself reflects our alienation from the immediate sources of our life. I once asked a group of young farmers—all highly educated and ecologically sensitive, and probably none of them a regular churchgoer—what they thought of that strange curse in Genesis. Is this just another instance of the (supposedly) grumpy God of the Old Testament? For a moment they looked puzzled that I would even pose a question whose answer was so self-evident; then one answered for all: "If we are out of sync with God, then the soil is going to be the first to suffer."

96

That elemental connection between the human ('ādām) and the arable-land ('ădāmâ) underlies one of Jeremiah's most fully developed oracles. Like an increasing number of people in our own time, he lived through a deep, extended period of droughts. Moreover, like the prototypical prophet Elijah, Jeremiah saw and proclaimed that disaster as a judgment from God. When the people are unfaithful, rain is withheld (Jer. 3:2–3). This is a core tenet of the Deuteronomists (cf. Deut. 28:22–24), the stream of tradition that preserved and edited the words and stories of both Elijah and Jeremiah, and it informs this message "concerning the droughts":

> Judah mourns and her gates languish; they bow in gloom to the earth,
> and Jerusalem's outcry rises up.
> Their nobles send their servants for water. They come to the water holes;
> they do not find water; they return with their vessels empty.
> They are ashamed and humiliated and cover their heads.
> On account of [ba'ăbûr] the arable-land ['ădāmâ], which is shattered [or "dismayed"]—
> for there has been no rain in the land—
> the plowmen are ashamed; they cover their heads.
> Yes, even the deer in the field gives birth and abandons; for there is no grass.
> And the wild asses stand on the heights; they pant for breath like jackals;
> their eyes pine, for there is no herbage.
> If our iniquities speak against us, YHWH, act for the sake of your name!
> For our backslidings are many; against you have we sinned.
> Hope of Israel, its Savior in time of trouble—
> why would you be like a sojourner in the land, or like a traveler who stays [just] for the night?
> Why would you be like someone stunned, like a strongman who cannot save?
> Yet you are in our midst, YHWH, and your name is proclaimed over us.
> Do not leave us!
>
> (Jer. 14:2–9)

Jeremiah is one of the greatest poets ever to have worked in the Hebrew language, and this oracle shows his subtle and supple use of language. Humans experience shame on account of the "shat- 97 tered" soil. As in Joel 1, that telling word, which is normally applied to people, reveals the interpenetration between the human and nonhuman spheres of experience. Even more telling is that humans experience shame, and not just desperation. The latter might be the natural response to drought—that is, a response uninformed by revelation. But shame is precisely the theologically informed response for which the preceding divine lament calls: "Be ashamed, then, because of your yields, because of the burning wrath of YHWH" (Jer. 12:13). Jeremiah and the peasant farmers in Judah understand this terrible drought as a silent indictment from YHWH.

The multiple references to the experience of shame invite us to explore a concept that was evidently central to Jeremiah's theological understanding but is largely foreign to our own. The experience of shame on account of the arable-land and its (meager) yields would seem to be a deliberate allusion to the story of the first time humans became alienated from God and the fertile soil, their partners in the covenantal triangle. While once the soil was cursed "on account of" the humans, now the Judean farmers are ashamed "on account of" the soil. Shame might well be understood as the subjective, distinctly human response to the enactment of a curse. "The opposite of being blessed, is to be shamed," says Robin Stockitt, in a probing theological study of shame (*Restoring the Shamed*, 66). The servants' and plowmen's shame is a sign that once again humans have overreached themselves, acting as though they—we—were the rulers of creation and not the creatures of God. When we act against our true nature—a deviance within the created order that can originate only with humans—then the whole order of creation is thrown out of kilter; the doe abandons her fawn, just as YHWH seems to be abandoning Israel. Shame is the appropriate human response to a curse, and thus it corresponds to the "mourning" of the earth: "Because of a curse, the land/earth mourns; the pastures of the wilderness dry up" (Jer. 23:10; cf. the land mourning to YHWH in Jer. 12:11).

Stockitt identifies the experience of shame as "the sense that something is essentially damaged, distorted, infected at the core of our being" (*Restoring the Shamed*, 19). Shame fundamentally threatens our sense of belonging, of being in communion with God and "protected by the larger web of relationships in which one's own life can flourish. This sense of belonging is inter-dependent" (30). When the social or (as in the case of Judah's drought) physical conditions of our existence inhibit flourishing, the resulting sense of shame "strikes at the very heart of what it means to be human"

98

(41). Although Stockitt includes only God and other humans in the essential web of relationships, we might adapt his basic insight to include the whole covenantal triangle. Construed thus, it illumines the shame that the Judean plowmen experience when they see the shattered soil and dying animals and sense that God has turned away from this place and its inhabitants.

It was a fundament of Deuteronomic theology that God was immediately present to Judah because of Jerusalem and its temple, viewed as the place God has chosen as a permanent dwelling place for God's "name" (Deut. 12:5–7, 11–12; 14:23; 16:6, etc.). Jeremiah's own theology is closely associated with that tradition ("Your name is proclaimed over us," Jer. 14:9), although he also exposes its potential for idolatry (7:1–4). Now the prophet and those who have eyes to see perceive that God is present only as a casual traveler might be, passing through and leaving Judah and Jerusalem to their suffering. According to Deuteronomic theology, blessing and curse coexist in a volatile polarity, which directly reflects the state of human covenantal obedience and is in turn reflected in the prosperity or suffering of land and animals (Deut. 27 and 28). Now that polarity has shifted dramatically against Judah and Jerusalem. Witnessing the disruption of the sustaining relationships that convey blessing, the servants and plowmen recognize the dissolution of the community of Creator and creatures. Therefore they cover their heads (Jer. 14:4), shrinking in shame.

Shame is not the same as guilt. Jeremiah certainly does not regard the plowmen—small farmers or (likely here) field laborers employed by the "nobles" (v. 3)—as bearing a great weight of personal guilt. Here and throughout his prophecy, he ascribes guilt chiefly to the rulers, prophets, and priests who have led the whole people astray (vv. 14–15, 18). Yet he shows a realism about the corporate dimensions of moral behavior and its consequences that our own highly individualistic culture often lacks. Jeremiah and the other prophets "remind us of the moral state of a people: Few are guilty but all are responsible" (Heschel, *Prophets*, 1:16). Moreover, it may well be the case that the small farmers and field laborers, those at or near the wide bottom of a society in which most are relatively poor, are able to see the truth to which the privileged few are blind, namely, how far the whole people has moved away from God. "The poor and vulnerable" (or "needy") see and therefore feel shame, because they are in the habit of turning to God, seeking

99

protection and blessing. By contrast, the still-confident prophets and opinion leaders are used to relying on their own resources, social and material.

In another subtle phrasing, God is addressed as *miqwēh yiśrā'ēl*, "Hope of Israel" (Jer. 14:8). The word *miqwēh* is unusual, used in the sense of "hope" only five times in the Bible, three of them in Jeremiah (also 17:13; 50:7). But in this oracle concerning the droughts, it is tempting to think that Jeremiah means his Hebrew-speaking hearers to hear the resonance of the homonymous word meaning "a gathering"—generally of waters (Gen. 1:10; Exod. 7:19; Lev. 11:36). Addressing God as *miqwēh* thus recalls the original divine structuring of creation and at the same time suggests that the physical and spiritual spheres of experience are not fully separable. God is the Source of hope; God is also the One who provides water for the creatures, or withholds it.

The earth is allied with God in its suffering and lament (thesis 3), and its shattered condition testifies to the broken relationship between humans, or Israel, and God. The next thesis points to yet another way in which the nonhuman creation partners with God.

Thesis 5: The earth and its nonhuman inhabitants serve as divinely appointed witnesses to and agents of judgment.

Amos, the earliest of the so-called writing prophets, establishes the basic contours for our understanding of how the earth provides both voice and agency for God's acts of judgment. He prophesied around the time of a great earthquake (1:1), one that did serious damage in the vicinity of Jerusalem (Zech. 14:5) and made a strong impression on the prophet's imagination. He testifies to God as

> Lord YHWH of hosts,
> who touches the earth and it melts away, and all who dwell on it mourn,
> and it rises like the Nile, all at once, and sinks, like the Nile of Egypt.
> (Amos 9:5)

What is most interesting is how the book of Amos relates that memorable quake to human iniquity. Another mention of it occurs immediately after the famous denunciation of those who plot "to buy the destitute for silver and the needy in exchange for sandals" (8:6), when YHWH swears:

> I will never forget all their doings.
> Is it not for this that the land/earth shakes and all who dwell on it mourn,
> and it rises like the Nile, all at once, and churns and sinks like the Nile of Egypt?
>
> (8:7–8)

The key theological issue raised by the way Amos draws this connection concerns our understanding of causality with respect to what we normally call "natural disasters"—but insurance companies call them "acts of God," and often enough, so does the general public, many of them churchgoers. And indeed, if we identify God as First Cause of every geophysical event, then it makes sense to us to ask questions such as: Why did God allow Hurricane Katrina or the Indonesian tsunami to happen, or cause appalling earthquakes in Haiti or Japan, and searing fires in the American West (to name just a few)? My own first theological instinct would be to dismiss such a question as totally misguided or simply unanswerable, yet I suspect that Amos and a number of other Israelite prophets might not set it aside so quickly. What is certainly misguided is any answer that costs the so-called prophet nothing by way of either compassion or suffering, such as Pat Robertson's infamous explanation of the 2010 earthquake in Haiti as divine retribution for the people's "pact with the devil."

One difference between Amos and Robertson is that Israelite prophets (in contrast to the media mogul and best-selling author Robertson) characteristically suffered *along with* the people—their own people—even as they announced God's judgment upon them. Amos's younger contemporary Isaiah gives the clearest expression to the true prophet's sense of ineluctable belonging to a doomed people: "I am done, for I am a man of unclean lips, and among a people of unclean lips I am living" (Isa. 6:5). Isaiah and Amos stand in clear contrast to Robertson, who points the finger at people in whose fate he has no share. The Letter of James sets forth precisely such sharing as a mark of those whom God has sent: "Friends, take as an example of suffering evil and forbearance the prophets, who spoke in the name of the Lord" (5:10). Real prophets suffer evil

101

along with the people they address, and therefore they often plead for divine forbearance in the face of human frailty (see Amos 7:1–6).

Certainly we must be cautious and exceedingly circumspect in considering whether Amos's understanding of judgment should have any bearing on our own way of thinking. He ventures a theological explanation for one disaster in his own time and homeland; it should not be viewed as a "one-size-fits-all-disasters" answer. Nonetheless, if we take seriously prophetic understandings of the covenantal triangle, with the multidimensional interresponsiveness that obtains among God and both human and nonhuman creatures, then the situation becomes complicated. We may have to entertain questions about causality that do not come readily to contemporary Westerners.

In a sensitive exegetical study of eighth-century prophets from an ecological perspective, Hilary Marlow says that in Amos, the natural world operates as God's "megaphone" to rouse an unhearing world (*Biblical Prophets*, 146): "Rather than declaring God's glory as in Psalm 19, the non-human creation proclaims his anger— and so is part of the 'dialogue' between YHWH and Israel. Since the people have not listened to warnings mediated through God's *human* agent, the prophet, God chooses to speak through his *cosmic* one" (152, italics original). Moreover, there is evidence that the earth itself listens to God in a way most humans fail to do. In several places God "calls to" (*qārā' l-*) the waters of the sea (Amos 5:8 and 9:6) and fire (7:4). These are rare instances of God "calling to" nonhuman elements of creation; apart from the creation account itself (Gen. 1:5, 10), the phrase "almost always denotes the summoning of the natural world against the human population" (*Biblical Prophets*, 137). The summons to the waters are reported in a passage where their (evidently) immediate response contrasts with the people's fatal slowness or failure to heed God's call (Amos 5:4–6; 9:1–4).

All of this suggests that for Amos, flood and earthquake and fire are indeed instruments of God's judgment, but they are more than mechanical instruments, sticks with which God beats people. Rather, it seems that the earth in its various elements responds to human crimes with some of the same indignation that God feels; it rises up as a genuine ally. It is noteworthy in this regard that the earth (like any other ally who enters into a fray) is not immune to suffering and deleterious change, be it from the effects of God's

102

judgment, the human misconduct that necessitates it, or likely both. The opening lines of Amos's prophecy declare,

> YHWH roars from Zion, and from Jerusalem raises his voice,
> and the shepherds' pastures mourn, and the top of Carmel is dry.
> (1:2)

Uncomfortable though it may be, the biblical view that the nonhuman creation warns of and somehow participates in God's judgment is an idea with clear theological import for our time. If we are to interpret it responsibly, then we must see that the biblical writers consistently represent divine judgment as the fierce yet ultimately loving exposure of injustice, of oppressive practices that diminish or destroy the creation and thus fundamentally distort God's own intentions for it. Deuteronomy, which is in its entirety a prophetically informed statement of God's fierce love for Israel, expresses it thus:

> For YHWH will judge his people and on his servants he shows compassion,
> when he sees their strength is used up and there is no one, enslaved or freed.
> (Deut. 32:36)

Marlow points to the urgent need to reckon with this strangely relevant prophetic perspective: "If Amos and his contemporaries were proclaiming their message today, they would surely be talking about global warming and its impact on the poor and on the rest of creation" ("Justice," 207). She acknowledges an apparent difference in their view of the sequence of events and our own: the biblical prophets consider that disregard for the poor causes the land's desolation, whereas we see that overexploitation and abuse of the earth may itself be the root form of injustice to the poor. She then concludes,

> But perhaps these are just two ways of saying the same thing: that the world is an interconnected whole and we ignore this at our peril. The prophets' call for social justice . . . calls us as Christians to examine carefully the impact our own actions have not merely on other human beings but on the rest of the natural world as well. To do any less than that is to make our worship of God into a hollow and meaningless charade. (208)

103

The prophetic view that the nonhuman creation acts for God, and indeed far outshines Israel (at least) as a prophetic agent and ally for God, reaches its fullest and funniest expression in the book of Jonah. Humor can be an effective yet gracious way of pressing home unconventional perceptions and uncomfortable truths, and making them stick. Here the prophet succeeds in his mission against his own will, and only because every *other* creature under heaven heeds with alacrity YHWH's expressed will. The storm at sea, the pagan sailors, the fish, the Ninevites themselves and their beasts, the scorching east wind—each of them makes a distinctive contribution to getting Jonah to Nineveh instead of his own intended destination of Tarshish. Several creatures are specifically identified as being "appointed" by YHWH: the fish (2:1), the qîqāyôn plant (4:6; the name of this otherwise unknown species sounds strikingly like an abbreviation of the memorable phrase "[it] disgorged Jonah" in 2:11; see Brent Strawn, "On Vomiting"), and also the worm (4:7) that destroys it, as well as the wind that delivers to Jonah's unsheltered head the coup de (divine) grâce (4:8). Megan McMurtry draws from this slapstick account the elegant conclusion "that the interaction between the cosmos and the prophet becomes the prophetic act and thus the vehicle for divine communication . . . The cosmos takes the place of the 'prophet' as the medium for the communication of the divine's message and thus it becomes a perpetual 'prophet' that outlives any human counterpart" ("The Cosmos in Jonah").

The (ahistorical) representation of Nineveh's dramatic repentance and YHWH's pity upon that great city of clueless people and a lot of cattle is one of many indications within the prophetic corpus that God's action does not end with condemnation and destructive judgment. The last thesis points to what is in fact its ultimate horizon, from a prophetic perspective.

Thesis 6: God already intends a restored or "new" creation.

The phrase "new creation" recalls the most extravagant prophetic statement of the final horizon for God's work:

> For I am about to create new heavens and a new earth,
> and the first ones will not be remembered; they will not come
> to mind.

(Isa. 65:17)

Almost every prophetic book includes some vision of restoration of the land of Israel (and many envision the converse, the
destruction of its enemies). However, no other prophet's vision
extends as far as does this one of Third Isaiah. So for the sake of
developing a general thesis, it may be useful here to focus on the
more typical restoration vision of Joel 2, whose terms correspond
closely to the vision of desolation in Joel 1:

> Do not be afraid, O soil! Rejoice and be glad, for YHWH has done
>   something great!
> Do not be afraid, O animals of the field! For the pastures of the
>   wilderness are in grass,
> for the tree bears its fruit; the fig and the vine assert their strength.
> And people of Zion, rejoice and be glad in YHWH your God!
> For he gives you the early rain for right-order [ṣĕdāqâ] and makes the
>   rain fall,
> early and late rain, as it did before.
> The threshing floors will be full of grain, and the vats overflow with
>   new wine and oil.
> I will repay you for the years that the locust consumed,
> the hopping-locust and the destroying-locust and the
>   cutting-locust—
> my great force that I set loose against you.
> And you shall eat, eat your fill, and you shall praise the name of
>   YHWH your God,
> who has dealt so wondrously with you, and my people shall never
>   again be put to shame.
> And you shall know that I am in the midst of Israel—
> and I, YHWH, am your God, and there is no other,
> and my people shall never again be put to shame.
>
> (Joel 2:21–27)

Notice that soil (or maybe it should be "Soil," with a capital
S) and the animals of the field are addressed in the second person, and before the humans. At least two assumptions are operative
here. First, soil and animals are treated as subjects, not objects.
Soil, beasts, trees, grapevine—all are sentient beings. They can
feel fear; they can also hear God's word and thus be released from
fear. The familiar prophetic assurance, "Do not be afraid" (Exod.
14:13; 1 Kgs. 17:13, etc.) may well have originated as a war oracle, a prophetic address to the king or the commander of troops
(Conrad, *Fear Not*), and that background is relevant to Joel's use

of it. In chapter 1, images of agriculture and war interpenetrate in the description of the locust plague, to such an extent that scholars debate whether this is a human army advancing like a locust swarm or (as I prefer) a locust swarm advancing like an army. Probably we are meant to be a little confused; both were life-threatening situations with which Israelites were, to their grief, well acquainted.

The second underlying assumption is closely related to the first: All the nonhuman creatures addressed or mentioned here stand in immediate relationship with God. Joel envisions them delivered from a condition of shame and restored to a condition in which all life can flourish. They can and will fulfill their vocation to productivity: putting forth grass and fruit, and thus asserting their strength. The religious and poetic vision here is akin to that of the nineteenth-century Jesuit poet Gerard Manley Hopkins in his sonnet "As Kingfishers Catch Fire." Attending to the voices of kingfishers and dragonflies, tumbling stones and rung bells, he perceives that

> Each mortal thing does one thing and the same:
> Deals out that being indoors each one dwells;
> Selves—goes itself; *myself* it speaks and spells,
> Crying *What I do is me: for that I came.*

Thus each "mortal" thing has interiority; it is capable of self-expression. One might even say that every creature is *capax Dei*, "possessed of a capacity for God," to use a phrase of medieval Christian theologians. (That we would not normally reckon stones and bells as "mortal" is irrelevant.) The cry that Hopkins hears is a not-so-distant echo of Jesus' words to Pilate: "I was born for this, and for this I came into the world, that I might bear witness to the truth" (John 18:37).

It is regrettable that this passage from Joel 2:21–27 is rarely heard in the church, where it has been much overshadowed by the familiar lines that follow immediately:

> And it shall happen afterward, that
> I will pour out my spirit on all flesh, and your sons and your
>   daughters shall prophesy.
> Your elders shall dream dreams, and your youths shall see visions.
> And even on slaves, male and female, in those days I will pour out
>   my spirit.
>
> (Joel 3:1–2 [2:28–29E]; cf. Acts 2:17–18)

As the opening phrase indicates, the two passages are meant to be heard together; most English Bibles include these two verses in chapter 2, although in the Hebrew text they begin a new chapter. Yet because we normally overlook verses 21–27, we miss the crucial way they prepare the ground for what comes next. It would seem that for Joel, restoration of the nonhuman creation is the precondition for the outpouring of the genuine spirit of prophecy, for true dreams to be dreamed, true visions to be seen. This literally fruitful connection between the restored land and true prophecy contrasts sharply with Jeremiah's denunciation of the false prophets who proclaim "lying visions . . . and deception out of their own imagination [heart]" (Jer. 14:14)—and they do so in the midst of a drought (14:1), which Jeremiah recognized as both evidence and consequence of the nation's faithlessness. Peter's citation of this passage from Joel on Pentecost in Jerusalem (Acts 2:17–18) might underscore the connection between the fruitfulness of the land and the outpouring of the divine Spirit in the form of true prophetic utterance, since Pentecost marked the conclusion of the two grain festivals (for the firstfruits of barley and wheat) observed at the Jerusalem temple. However, one might doubt how conscious of the connection Peter and his audience (or Luke and his audience) might have been; by the first century the agricultural nature of the Pentecost had been greatly overshadowed by its significance as the anniversary of the Sinai revelation and covenant.

Joel's vision is radically inclusive and thus potentially transformative; God's spirit is no respecter of gender, age, or social standing. This vision may be seen as one of the precursors for the apostle Paul's "prophetic" declaration to the Galatians: "There is no [room for] Jew or Greek, nor slave or free, nor male or female; for you are all one in Christ Jesus" (Gal. 3:28). Tellingly, this vision appears to be not just socially but also biologically inclusive; "all flesh" will receive the outpouring of the prophetic spirit. The phrase would seem to be a deliberate echo of God's covenant with Noah and "all flesh" (Gen. 9:15–17), and it implies a crucial theological claim, which James K. Bruckner states succinctly: "Creation is the necessary reality from which redemption emerges" (quoted by Fretheim, *God and World*, 193). Always and everywhere God is involved on both "sides" of the ceaseless work of redemption. The renewal of creation involves the remaking of human society, and human society is entirely dependent upon the preservation, repair, and renewal of creation.

These six theses, taken as a whole, govern the biblical prophets' understandings of God and the world, and together they form the basis for hope that is both godly and realistic. From a prophetic perspective, that is two ways of saying the same thing. They enable us to embrace hope that is rooted in the concrete relational structure of the world that God has made and is still making, as exilic Isaiah declares:

> The One who forms light and creates darkness,
> who makes *shalom* and creates evil—
> I YHWH am doing all these things.
> (Isa. 45:7)

It is significant that the verbal forms here are all present participles; creation is God's constant activity, the perennial and everfresh ground for all God's work. The Hebrew word that best sums up that concrete relational structure may well be *ṣĕdāqâ*, the word Joel uses to characterize God's reason for giving the early rain: "He gives you the early rain for *ṣĕdāqâ*" (2:23). The word is often rendered "righteousness, vindication," but its scope is broader than those words normally suggest to us; it denotes a healthy relationality among creatures, between creature and Creator. So here I translate "right-order," recalling Margaret Barker's suggestion that the word connotes something very close to our notion of sustainability (see p. 88). Joel's vision would seem to give strong substantiation to that suggestion, which is so apt for this generation's reading of the Prophets.

Works Cited in Chapter 4

Barker, Margaret. *Creation: A Biblical Vision for the Environment*. London: T & T Clark International, 2010.

Bauckham, Richard. *The Bible and Ecology: Rediscovering the Community of Creation*. Waco, TX: Baylor University Press, 2010.

Berry, Wendell. *The Long-Legged House*. Washington, DC: Shoemaker & Hoard, 2004. First published 1969 by Harcourt, Brace & World.

Conrad, Edgar W. *Fear Not Warrior: A Study of 'al tîrā' Pericopes in the Hebrew Scriptures*. Brown Judaic Studies 75. Chico, CA: Scholars Press, 1985.

Davis, Ellen F. *Scripture, Culture, and Agriculture: An Agrarian Reading of the Bible.* Cambridge: Cambridge University Press, 2009.

Fretheim, Terence E. "The Earth Story in Jeremiah 12." In *Readings from the Perspective of Earth*, edited by Norman C. Habel. The Earth Bible 1. Cleveland: Pilgrim Press, 2000.

———. *God and World in the Old Testament: A Relational Theology of Creation.* Nashville: Abingdon Press, 2005.

Heschel, Abraham Joshua. *The Prophets: An Introduction.* 2 vols. New York: Harper & Row, 1962.

Hopkins, Gerard Manley. "As Kingfishers Catch Fire." http://www.poetryfoundation.org/poem/173654.

Marlow, Hilary. *Biblical Prophets and Contemporary Environmental Ethics.* New York: Oxford University Press, 2009.

———. "Justice for All the Earth: Society, Ecology, and the Biblical Prophets." In *Creation in Crisis: Christian Perspectives on Sustainability*, edited by Robert S. White. London: Society for Promoting Christian Knowledge, 2009.

McFague, Sallie. *The Body of God: An Ecological Theology.* Minneapolis: Fortress Press, 1993.

Smith, Mark S. *The Early History of God: Yahweh and the Other Deities in Ancient Israel.* Grand Rapids: Eerdmans, 2002.

Stockitt, Robin. *Restoring the Shamed: Towards a Theology of Shame.* Eugene, OR: Cascade Books, 2012.

Strawn, Brent A. "On Vomiting: Leviticus, Jonah, Ea(a)rth." *Catholic Biblical Quarterly* 74:3 (2012): 445–64.

Wilbur, Richard. "Advice to a Prophet." http://www.poets.org/viewmedia.php/prmMID/15485.

Wright, Christopher J. H. *God's People in God's Land: Family, Land, and Property in the Old Testament.* Grand Rapids: Eerdmans, 1990.

———. *Old Testament Ethics for the People of God.* Leicester: InterVarsity Press, 2004.

CHAPTER 5

Destroyers of the Earth

Prophetic Critiques of Imperial Economics

Behind every prediction of disaster there stands a concealed alternative.
—Martin Buber, *Prophetic Faith*, 134

Might is that which makes a thing of anybody who comes under its sway. . . .
Only [the one] who knows the empire of might and knows how not to respect it
is capable of love and justice.
—Simone Weil, "Iliad," 153–54, 181

It's so much easier to purchase the world.
—Norman Wirzba, oral communication,
October 25, 2012

The Great Economy and Little Economies

The prominent agrarian writer Wendell Berry recounts an early conversation between himself and farmer/biologist Wes Jackson, in which the two of them were laboring to envision and name an economic system that, in contrast to the industrial economy, would not be destructive in its basic design and principles. Berry proposed "that an economy based on energy would be more benign [than one based on money] because it would be more comprehensive," but Jackson disagreed.

"Well," I [Berry] said, "then what kind of economy *would* be comprehensive enough?"

111

He hesitated a moment, and then, grinning, said, "The Kingdom of God." (Berry, *Home Economics,* 54)

And so they agreed: the kingdom of God (Berry adopts the
term "the Great Economy" for more general use) is an indispensable economic model, in that "it includes principles and patterns
by which values or powers or necessities are parceled out and
exchanged" (*Home Economics,* 57). Any "little economy"—that is,
a human economy—may succeed and endure only to the extent
that "it justly and stably represents the value of necessary goods,
such as clothing, food, and shelter, which originate ultimately in
the Great Economy." When economies and cultures fail to recognize the Great Economy or kingdom in which all value originates,
"they make value that is first abstract and then false, tyrannical,
and destructive of real value" (61). Berry judges that all industrial
economies fail in precisely that way; therefore they are a form of
banditry, in which the only goal and hope is to get away with as
much as possible for as long as possible, before the inevitable reckoning comes.

This conversation between two contemporary figures whose
work is sometimes called "prophetic" provides a point of entry into
one aspect of the Bible's prophetic traditions, which are wholly oriented to the question of how humans are faring as members of the
Great Economy, to what extent they are living within its limits, and
what are the consequences of their failure to do so. It is hard to
think of a single passage in the prophetic books and even in the
Bible as a whole that does not in some way bear upon that question.
In connection with this central orienting concern, biblical prophets
have much to say about the various "little economies" that they are
called to confront.

In this chapter I focus on the two most fully developed economic
critiques in the Bible, John's graphic exposé of Roman commerce
in the book of Revelation and, underlying that exposé, Ezekiel's
several oracles against Tyre. Both these extended passages show
the real cost and the ultimate unsustainability of two mercantile
economies that enriched themselves by scouring virtually the whole
Mediterranean world. As we shall see, these two prophets speak at
112   various points in terms that we would recognize as having ecological
import. This is because both Ezekiel and John have a moral vision
that is wholly theocentric, focused on God's sovereignty over all

human enterprises and exercises of power, as well as over earth and heaven, that is, creation. The ecological dimensions of their visions point to the prophetic discernment that exploitative economies are unsustainable because they are fundamentally at odds with God's will as it is being worked out in and through the created order.

Revelation has justly been called the "climax" of biblical prophecy (Bauckham, *Climax*). John is consciously writing "prophecy" (Rev. 1:3) for the church, and what he writes is largely styled as a thoroughgoing and imaginative rereading of Hebrew Scripture, especially though not exclusively its prophetic witness, from Moses through Daniel. Richard Bauckham observes, "Revelation, as the culmination of the biblical prophetic tradition, is peculiarly able to transcend its original context of relevance" (*Theology*, 154); it gathers up and brings into a new context the prophetic themes and perspectives that preceded it. One of those is the naming and denunciation of brute force, and John's Revelation is acknowledged to be the acme of that tradition in its denunciation of "the beast" that represents the military and political power of the Roman Empire. Since Rome is never named throughout the book, the beast may come to represent "Empire with a capital *E*," power that is seemingly global and beyond effective opposition, as it manifests itself in other places and times. John may be seen as making a distinctive contribution to the prophetic critique of one aspect of imperial power, namely, its inhumane and destructive economic practices. This is a central element of his prophetic eschatology, although it has received relatively little scholarly or popular attention.

So that the direction of my argument is not misunderstood, I say at the outset that I do not understand or treat prophetic eschatology as simply a representation of the end of the world, in an absolute sense. It is true that John looks to a future consummation of the created order, in which the purified church and all the nations are gathered under the sovereignty of the Creator God and the Messiah, whose victory has already been won (Rev. 7:10; 11:15–16; 12:10–12; 15:4). The Risen Christ is himself "the first and the last, *ho eschatos*" (1:17; 2:8; 22:13). Significantly, John's vision does not end with the obliteration of the earth and the "rapture" of a faithful remnant into heaven, à la Hal Lindsey or Tim LaHaye and Jerry Jenkins. "If anything, it is God who is 'raptured' down to the Earth to dwell with people in a wondrous urban paradise (Rev. 21.3; 22.3). The plot of Revelation ends on Earth, not heaven, with

113

the throne of God and the Lamb located in the center of the city (Rev. 22.3)" (Rossing, "Alas for Earth," 191).

It is notable that the Greek adjective *eschatos* denotes not only a temporal end ("the last") but also "the farthest" edge or boundary of some spatial area. Accordingly, a work of biblical eschatology such as John's might well be seen as *a view from the edge*. Revelation is a representation of the known world, wholly dominated by Rome, as it looks from the social, spiritual, and geographical margin: the island of Patmos, where John resided as an exile. In view of his knowledge of Jerusalem and Hebrew (he writes in a semiticized Greek style), as well as the fact that he cites Hebrew Scripture continually and perhaps often unconsciously, John was most likely a Palestinian Jew who had fled his own country following the Jewish Revolt (66–73 CE).

John writes as a displaced person, if not necessarily a prisoner. Although there is no firm support for the common view that Patmos was a prison island or a refuge for those who had been legally banished, he implies that his presence in that place is in accordance with his "partner[ship] in the affliction and sovereignty and endurance in Jesus" (1:9). In other words, Patmos is a place from which he can participate in a community of Jesus' "slaves" (1:1), which—however small and diffuse it may be—is consciously taking a stand outside the sovereignty of the Roman Empire. It is no coincidence that one of the most perceptive modern studies of Revelation was written by South African Allan Boesak, reflecting the years of struggle against apartheid and his own prison experience. The edge (*eschaton*) is a place where the pretensions and deceptions of power can be exposed, where power that seems beyond opposition can be ironized or parodied, for those who can read and hear. What is more, the edge is the place where a concealed alternative can be revealed. This is the ultimate aim of prophetic eschatology: the disclosure of the divine intention for our world, which is already visible to those whose eyes are healthy enough to see the divine inbreaking (cf. 3:18), even as the regnant power makes every effort to distract and conceal.

In what follows, I approach Revelation as one would excavate a tel, an archaeological site of multiple layers: beginning at the top, in one small area, and digging down into the substrata. I begin with a few verses in a couple of chapters and from there dig into the layers of earlier prophecy on which John is building and of which he seems to expect some among his readers to be aware. Without bearing

114

in mind both those literary substrata and the historical situation in which John writes his prophecy to the churches in the imperial province of Asia, we are bound to misunderstand his message. The different results of such misunderstanding are amply evidenced in the contemporary church. On the one side, the "liberals" dismiss the book as a dangerous rant. On the other, some "conservatives" read it as a detailed diagram of the future, the end of the world, and thus completely miss John's own focus on alerting us to the dangers of accommodation to the power-wielding culture or empire in which we are currently immersed. On both sides, the church loses the benefit of the final prophecy in the Christian canon. We may begin to gain that benefit by recognizing that precisely the quality of "eschatological hyperbole" (Bauckham, *Theology,* 155) is what enables Revelation to speak to us, in our own political and economic circumstances, as vibrantly as it did to John's first hearers.

John's bold, imaginatively rich, yet culturally specific parody of the "global economy" of the Greco-Roman world may stimulate contemporary readers to see new aspects of the "little economy" in which we are all immersed. Globalization, the process of worldwide economic integration, both vertical and horizontal, has over the last few decades become the dominant cultural, political, and even biological force; it now leaves untouched no aspect of life on our planet. That new "biosocial" phenomenon—decentralized, transnational, its demands and its reach confined to no discrete territory—may well be the contemporary manifestation of imperial force that some now identify as Empire, with a capital *E* (see Hardt and Negri, *Empire*).

Commerce as Fornication

The core of John's economic exposé appears in Revelation 17 and 18. Rome's destructive and ultimately self-destructive economic practices are represented first symbolically in the portrait of "Babylon, the mother of whores" (17:5), and then schematically in a surprisingly detailed description of the merchant ship and maritime disaster that follows closely in chapter 18.

Chapter 17 marks a crescendo in John's indignant rhetoric, when one of the seven angels summons him to witness "the judgment of the great prostitute seated over many waters, with whom

115

the kings of the earth fornicated" (17:1). The whole development of the fornication image is highly distasteful, and deliberately so, in the manner of many parodies. I would discourage preachers from adopting the metaphor, yet I cannot agree with Brian Blount's suggestion that the "seer makes a vicious rhetorical turn that bludgeons women with a sweeping hammer of misogynism" (*Revelation*, 309). It is crucial to recognize both the object of John's rhetoric and why he chose this particular image.

A basic characteristic of John's rhetorical strategy is to adapt the language of the Hebrew Prophets in ways that his audience can recognize and understand, as John leads them in applying prophetic logic to the current situation. For anyone familiar with the Hebrew Scripture, his opening image evokes Jeremiah's lengthy climactic prophecy of the downfall of Babylon, who "dwells beside [or, 'over'] many waters" (Jer. 51:13). That is the first of many signals that the focus of attack is not women as such but rather a city or empire. Cities were most often represented in the feminine in the ancient world; their names were treated as grammatically feminine, and often they were associated prominently (though not exclusively) with a goddess. Here John is swinging his verbal hammer against "Roma," the feminized and divinized image of the imperial city.

An early decree of Augustus Caesar gave Rome the official status of *dea*, "goddess"; her elegant image appeared on coins; statues were erected in many temples around the empire. In the late first century, many cities in Asia and elsewhere in the Mediterranean, including at least four cities addressed by John—Sardis, Ephesus, Pergamum, and Smyrna—all demonstrated their patriotism with temples dedicated to *Dea Roma*. Her image, altars dedicated to Caesar and Rome, and other symbols, at once imperial and cultic, were prominent in hundreds of port cities. Sea trade was thus a quasi-religious activity, but more subtly so than the military, and so many Christians viewed commerce as a more acceptable profession (see Kraybill, *Imperial Cult*, 90–101). In this regard, it is apt to note that Paul's hosts in major port cities included Lydia, the dealer in purple textiles at Philippi in Macedonia (Acts 16:14–15), and at Corinth, Priscilla and Aquila. The latter sailed with Paul to Ephesus—from one major commercial center to another—where he left them (Acts 18:19), presumably to conduct business as well as to evangelize among fellow Jews (cf. v. 2) and perhaps others. Nelson Kraybill identifies them as "missionary/trades-people" whose

116

"most natural sphere of influence would have been among customers and other merchants" (*Imperial Cult,* 95).

Maritime trade may have been the life of some loyal Christians in the mid-first century, but a few decades later, John repudiated it entirely as an option for Christians (see Rev. 13:16–17 and 20:4). That is why he uses the strongest rhetoric possible, exposing Rome as "the great prostitute" sitting enthroned over the waters of the known world. The elegant lady Roma, often depicted seated on a throne, was to be seen (and handled) in every port, on coins or in statuary. If John sees "her" as a prostitute or a whore (the word *pornē* covers both options), he is doubtless scandalized that loyalty to Rome was not coerced from the imperial center but rather offered voluntarily by the provinces, in order to secure their share of the privilege associated with the much-vaunted *Pax Romana.* An ancient Greek graffito discovered in Ephesus, the leading city in the province of Asia, offers good indication of how the imperial center was perceived: "Rome, the one who reigns over all, your power will never end!" (see Kraybill, *Imperial Cult,* 57).

A prostitute cannot coerce but hopes to attract, and one as richly decked out as the *pornē* John "reveals" has obviously been successful; "the whole earth went marveling after the beast" (Rev. 13:3). When John wrote those words in the late first century, the imperial economy in Asia had accelerated to a new level. Among the seven cities where John addresses the church, five—Smyrna, Pergamum, Sardis, and Laodicea, in addition to Ephesus—ranked among the top ten commercial centers of the province. An inscription from Halicarnassus in Asia, which hails the emperor Augustus as "savior of the whole human race," celebrates the benefits of the *Pax Romana* thus: "Land and sea have peace, the cities flourish under a good legal system, in harmony and with an abundance of food, there is an abundance of all good things, people are filled with happy hopes for the future and with delight at the present" (quoted in Bauckham, *Bible in Politics,* 89). In John's eyes, at least, Christians were prominent among the happy customers of the *pornē* that was Rome, and their satisfaction was purchased at the price of idolatry. That is the problem this prophet seeks to address.

Although John portrays the prostitute as richly dressed, she is tattooed or branded on her forehead, like an enslaved sex worker (Blount, *Revelation,* 143, 315): "Babylon the great, the mother of whores and of the earth's abominations" (17:5). Of course, John did

117

not invent the image of fornication to characterize a nation's behavior. He inherited it from Israel's prophetic tradition, and so literarily speaking, this new "Babylon" is not so much the mother as the daughter of whoring nations. However, in biblical tradition whoring is not the metaphor by which Babylon is remembered. Rather, she is the great devastator (Ps. 137), the furious crusher and merciless reducer of nations (Isa. 14:6, 12). The distinction of being known as the prostitute among the Gentile nations belongs to Tyre, the leading city of Phoenicia, which was famed not for its warring but for its incomparable wealth. Tyre "piled up silver like dust and gold like the mud in the streets" (Zech. 9:3).

The massively wealthy island city maintained a vast trading network over a period of centuries, through much of the first millennium BCE. Like other small kingdoms in the Levant, including Israel and Judah, Tyre had to bow to the imperial might of (successively) Assyria, Babylon, Persia, Greece, and eventually Rome. Yet on the whole it prospered during this period. Tyre had the wealth to recover repeatedly from disasters both natural (earthquakes) and military, especially the devastating siege of Alexander, who took the island by building a causeway from the mainland. Visiting the city in the reign of Augustus, the geographer Strabo writes of its many-storied houses, more impressive even than Rome's; the natural and cultural historian Pliny speaks of it as "the mother-city" from which sprang others, ranging from mighty Carthage in North Africa to Cadiz in southern Spain (Jidejian, *Tyre*, xvii). In John's time, Rome had absorbed Tyre's commercial network; its trade region was approximately the same as had been Tyre's at its height, from the ninth to the sixth centuries BCE. Rome was at once the greatest land power ("Babylon") and the greatest sea power ("Tyre"), and that is how John represents "her."

It is unsurprising, perhaps almost inevitable, that John names the great city that threatens the faithful "Babylon." Writing in the coded style of underground literature, he never names the city Rome directly, but the equation is easily drawn. Rome and Babylon were known to all and hated by every Jew as the twin devastators of Jerusalem and destroyers of the temple. However, Tyre is less notorious in biblical tradition, and so John's indirect evocation of it is surprising and therefore telling of a crucial and sometimes subtle aspect of imperial domination. Through the several prophetic oracles against Tyre—Isaiah, Amos, Joel, Zechariah, and

118

above all Ezekiel inveigh against it—the specifically *economic* critique of Empire appears in its purest form. John's picture of Roman economics draws heavily upon those oracles, amplified by Isaiah's and Jeremiah's oracles against Babylon. Viewed against this scriptural background, John's portrayal of Rome appears like a pendant—ornate, carefully crafted, gorgeous and appalling at the same time—suspended from the long strand, slender yet strong, of prophetic denunciations of the economics of Empire.

The island city of Tyre appears early in the story of the kings of Israel. For building the temple, King Hiram of Tyre provided Solomon with valuable timber (cedar and cypress) from the nearby forests and gold acquired in trade, as well as skilled craftsmen. In exchange for those luxuries, Hiram received the essential agricultural products his own land could not produce, grain and olive oil (1 Kgs. 5:10–11 [24–25 Heb.]; cf. 9:11–14, concerning Hiram's acquisition of agricultural land from Solomon). The two kings cooperated on shipbuilding and launched a trading venture from the Red Sea port of Eilat, thus expanding the network for both (1 Kgs. 9:26–28). A century or so later this alliance went sour, originally perhaps because of competition between Israel and Tyre over major trade routes (Aubet, *Phoenicians,* 87). Amos refers to Tyre's having "forgotten a covenant of kindred [peoples]" (1:9; cf. Ps. 83:5–9 [4–8E]).

It is likely that John took the idea of representing Rome as a whore from Isaiah's lengthy oracle against Tyre, where she is named "a forgotten prostitute," who will return to her trade as soon as she gets the chance, and "fornicate [with] all the kingdoms of the earth on the face of the arable-land" (Isa. 23:16–17). That image of economic promiscuity is not easily forgotten. However, it is undoubtedly Ezekiel who provided the most direct inspiration for John's distinctly economic exposé of Rome. The sixth-century prophet's extended, detailed, metaphorically rich and therefore memorable portrait of Tyre is the fullest economic critique of Empire in the Old Testament.

Commerce without Morality: The Deadly Sin of Tyre

119

Ezekiel's oracles against Tyre are a prominent part of the lengthy series of oracles (chaps. 25–32) against Judah's neighboring states, anticipating that they will suffer, along with the house of Israel, at the hands of Nebuchadnezzar and the Babylonian army. And from Ezekiel's highly theocentric perspective, it is evident that "Nebuchadrezzar . . . king of kings" (Ezekiel follows Mesopotamian practice in his spelling of the king's name, as well as in the royal title; see Greenberg, *Ezekiel*, 532) is only the front man for YHWH:

> Therefore thus says the Lord YHWH: I am set against you, Tyre, and I will raise up against you many peoples, as the sea raises up its waves, and they will destroy your city-walls of Tyre and wreck her towers, and I will scrape her rubble off her and leave her a glaring rock-surface; she will be a place for spreading fishnets in the middle of the sea. (Ezek. 26:3–5a)

Ezekiel envisions "all the princes of the sea" (v. 16) raising a lament at the disaster, which is styled as an unleashing of the primeval waters, once constrained so that dry land might appear. Now "Deep" (cf. Gen. 1:2)—Hebrew *těhôm*, cognate with Tiamat, the Mesopotamian goddess of the primeval ocean—engulfs Tyre, which sinks into "the Pit" where the human dead are found (Ezek. 26:19–20).

In fact, Tyre was not finally destroyed until the end of the thirteenth century of the Common Era, some two millennia after Ezekiel first anticipated its reduction to bare rock. Although Nebuchadnezzar laid siege to it for thirteen years and deposed its king, he did not pillage the city, let alone raze it, as Ezekiel's later oracle acknowledges (29:17–18; see Greenberg, *Ezekiel*, 540). But even if the lengthy diatribe is not historically accurate on that one point, it is nonetheless deeply telling of Tyre's place in the ancient world, specifically with respect to a major cultural shift that began to take place during the Assyrian period and had lasting significance for that region and, in time, for the whole world.

Tyre was the essential agent in the emergence of a new kind of economic system, a mercantile economy based on the circulation of precious metals (silver and gold), which gradually replaced a simpler, more subsistence-oriented system in which goods were bartered (Aubet, *Phoenicians*, 83). Moving large quantities of metal overland is very difficult, but with their expertise in shipbuilding and sailing, the Phoenicians were able to procure silver from southern Spain and Anatolia (Turkey) and transport it, along with

120

precious woods and other exotic materials, within a trading circuit
that stretched across the whole breadth of the Mediterranean and
east to Mesopotamia, as well as south to Africa and Arabia. Ezekiel
captures Tyre's international reputation and the source of her prosperity in these few lines:

> Tyre, you have said, "I am a perfect beauty."
> In the midst of the seas are your borders;
> your [ship]builders perfected your beauty.
> (Ezek. 27:3–4)

The famed Phoenician carved ivories adorned Israelite palaces and great houses (Amos 3:15); ivories, vessels of gold, silver,
and bronze, and gold jewelry with filigree and delicate granular
decoration, all from Phoenician workshops, have been discovered
in Mesopotamian tombs and palaces. As the principal producer
and purveyor of luxury merchandise throughout the region, Tyre
enjoyed economic protection over a long period, beginning with
the Assyrians in the ninth century (Aubet, *Phoenicians*, 79–96). No
wonder Ezekiel envisions the princes sitting in deep mourning,
"appalled" that Tyre has perished, "horrified" at the disappearance
of the city that supplies them with status symbols (Ezek. 26:16–18).

The propagation of memorable metaphors is one of the most
powerful rhetorical devices in the biblical prophets' tool kit, a crucial means whereby they bend their hearers' minds to entertain radically different perceptions of reality. Evidently Ezekiel was known
among his contemporaries as a phenomenal "metaphor-monger"
(*měmaššēl měšālîm*, Ezek. 21:5). Certainly his depiction of Tyre as
a merchant ship (27:1–36) is one of the most sophisticated uses of
metaphor in the whole prophetic corpus. Through his imagination,
the island city that calls itself "a perfect beauty" (v. 3) becomes a
perfectly beautiful ship (v. 4), loaded with rich goods and plying
"great waters"—until "the east wind breaks [her] in the heart of
the seas" (v. 26). The hearer whose mind is attuned to the Exodus
account, as was Ezekiel's own, recognizes that this is the same God-
driven wind that once carved a path through the sea for the Israelites (Exod. 14:21) and left Pharaoh's army dead in its wake.

The ship "Tyre" is built and outfitted with materials from multiple districts on two or three continents: fir from Lebanon for the
mast (Ezek. 27:5; on the identification as fir, see Greenberg, *Ezekiel*,

549), oak from Bashan for oars and ivory-inlaid cypress from the island of Cyprus for the planking (v. 6), dyed Egyptian linen for the sails and blue and purple cloth from the coastland of Elishah (Carthage?) for decorative coverings or sunshades (v. 7). The whole picture is drawn in vibrant color (27:7, 16, 24), and that in itself is notable, since color is mentioned with relative infrequency in the Bible. In the Old Testament, most references to blue and purple pertain to the hangings of the tabernacle (Exod. 25:4; 26:1, etc.) or temple (2 Chr. 2:6, 13 [7, 14E]), and occasionally to the trappings of royalty (Esth. 1:6; Jer. 10:9). These colors were rare, because the dyes required to produce them, made from the glandular secretions of murex mollusks of several species, were fabulously expensive. Eight thousand mollusks had to be harvested and slaughtered to produce one gram of violet or red-purple dye.

The Phoenicians, and especially the artisans of Tyre, had brought to perfection the art (whose secret is still not entirely known) of extracting and blending the dyes (Jidejian, *Tyre*, 149–59). That is why the Greeks named this people "Phoenicians," from the word *phoinix*, "purple" or "crimson"—shades that to this day remain the hallmark of luxury. In order to maintain their distinctive source of wealth over centuries, the "Purple-people" committed themselves to an extractive economy, which could be supported only by vast resources, both natural and human. Beginning in the Iron Age and continuing through the Roman period, the search for new murex beds was one strong impetus for Phoenician colonization of coastal regions as distant as Spain and the Atlantic coast of North Africa (Odell, *Ezekiel*, 351). Great heaps of murex shells, still visible into modern times, marked the location of the colonies, as well as of Tyre itself.

If the dyed cloth was judged to be beautiful, the process of producing it was not. Diving for mussels and processing them was both labor intensive and dangerous. The geographer Pausanius, writing in the second century of the Common Era, tells of a Greek village where more than half the village was involved in harvesting murex (Odell, *Ezekiel*, 351). Pliny questions the taste for outrageous luxury—in his day purple dye was almost as costly as pearls, the most precious of jewels—that could "justify" the human risk of deep-sea diving (Jidejian, *Tyre*, 149–53). The Greek word *phoinix* was associated with the color of blood; one might suppose that purple dye was an ancient equivalent of the "blood diamonds" that have figured so prominently in modern colonial (and postcolonial) economies, or the ores such as radioactive cobalt, mined by African teenagers at the risk of life, and "consumed" by communications technologies utilized primarily by the comparatively wealthy around the world. As we shall see, John's "revelation" of Roma's corruption is drawn in purple and scarlet and marked with blood.

Following the outfitting of the gorgeous vessel (27:4–11), Ezekiel takes us into the hold and displays the array of trade goods taken from all over the known world (27:12–23). Like the twentieth-century poet John Masefield in his poem "Cargoes," the prophet delineates a whole culture simply by naming a merchant vessel and its trading route, and itemizing the cargo. But if Masefield offers a romanticized picture of ancient Mediterranean culture—with the "quinquireme of Nineveh . . . rowing home to haven in sunny Palestine," loaded with "sandalwood, cedarwood, and sweet white wine" (*Salt-Water*, 124)—Ezekiel's cargo list points subtly to the high human cost of the goods in the hold of the ship. Immediately following the precious and heavy metals that lead off the list (v. 12), our mind's eye is drawn to human beings (*nepesh 'ādām*, v. 13) who are listed and treated as simple trade goods. Their bodies are being marketed to peoples of Asia—Javan, Tubal, and Meshech—seemingly in exchange for bronze- or copperware. The prophet Joel adds an important detail about the Phoenician slave trade that Ezekiel may have expected his audience to know: the Ionians (= the people of Javan) were buying captives from Jerusalem and Judah! Joel's oracle against Tyre makes explicit the element of divine vengeance on their behalf:

> Quick as can be, I visit your payback on your heads,
> since you took My silver and My gold,
> and My greatest treasures you brought into your palaces,
> and the Jerusalemites and Judeans you sold to the Ionians.
> (Joel 4:4–6 [3:4–6E])

Ezekiel's list of trade items, with its artificial alternation of terms—"dealers" and "traders," "imports" and "exports"—makes for difficult reading, but the cumulative effect is to convey clearly that the whole world is trading with and through Tyre; she is the universal and indispensable "dealer for the nations" (Ezek. 27:3). Judah and Israel figure in the list only in passing, as suppliers of agricultural commodities, some of them high-end specialties:

123

"wheat of Minnit," oil, honey, balm (27:17). Submerged thus in the "global" network, Israel and Judah appear to have achieved their vaunted and ultimately self-destructive desire to "be as the nations, as the families of the earth, in serving wood and stone" (20:32). From Ezekiel's perspective, the house of Israel has enslaved itself in a mercantile system that renders it insignificant, all but invisible, and at the mercy of the merciless. Margaret Odell draws a telling analogy with the cost of participation in our contemporary global economy: "The labor-intensive production of purple-dye, which only the wealthy could afford; the production of cash crops to feed appetites grown accustomed to novelty and luxury; and the promise of full partnership in a world of increasing wealth all have their counterparts in the modern world of sweatshops, agribusiness, and multinational corporations" (*Ezekiel*, 354).

The diatribe against Tyre ends with two shorter oracles (Ezek. 28:1–10, 11–19) directed against its (unnamed) ruler. The two are closely related in their depiction of a godlike being, wise, wealthy, and beautiful, whom YHWH brings down from what had seemed to be a place of total security. The fall of the godlike being is ironically represented as a desecration: "Will you really say, 'I am a god,' before your killers? But you are human and not god, in the hand of those who desecrate you" (v. 9; cf. v. 16). At the same time, the fall is the just punishment for the king's desecration of his own "holy precincts" because of "the iniquity [*'ewel*] of [his] trading" (v. 18).

The theme of the toppling of the godlike because of their iniquity appears also in Psalm 82, in words that are strikingly similar to Ezekiel's oracle:

> God takes a stand in the divine council;
> He renders judgment in the midst of divine beings:
> "How long will you judge iniquitously [*'āwel*],
> and show favor to the wicked?
> . . . .
> I myself had thought you were divine,
> and children of the Most High, all of you.
> And yet like humans you will die,
> and as one of the princes, you will fall."
>
> (Ps. 82:1–2, 6–7)

Whether the king of Tyre did claim divine status in Ezekiel's time is uncertain (see Greenberg, *Ezekiel*, 577), but that is beside the point, which is rather the condition of the ruler's "heart." That word occurs a total of nine times in the two oracles (Ezek. 28:2 [4x], 5, 6 [2x], 8, 17). The first few verses establish it as thematic for the whole:

> Because your heart is haughty and you say, "I am a god; I dwell in the dwelling-place of gods, in the heart of the seas"—but you are human and not god, though you set your heart like the heart of gods. . . . Through your great wisdom and through your trading you have increased your wealth, and your heart is haughty because of your wealth. Therefore thus says the Lord YHWH, Because you have set your heart like the heart of gods, therefore I am about to bring against you aliens, the fiercest of nations. (vv. 2, 5–7a)

In the metaphorical physiology of the Bible, the heart is the organ of moral discernment, including religious discernment; it denotes what we would call the moral character of an individual or a nation. In these oracles Ezekiel probes also the "inmost self" (v. 16) of the king, who in his person represents the national character of Tyre. It becomes evident that if pride is the root of their sin, its fruit is overt evil: "Through the abundance of your trading they filled your inmost self [*tôkĕkā*] with violence, and you sinned. And I saw you desecrated, [unfit] for the mountain of God, and I banished you" (v. 16). Thinking back to the cargo list in chapter 27, we recall that slavery was one form of Tyre's characteristic "violence" (*ḥāmās*, 28:16). The reputation of Phoenicians as greedy, ruthless traders in goods and human lives is corroborated by Homer's *Odyssey*. Eumaeus, a swineherd serving on the estate of Odysseus's father, Laertes, tells that he was born a prince until he was captured in childhood by those "mariners renowned, greedy merchant men, with countless gauds in a black ship" (*Odyssey*, book 15, *Works of Homer*, 239).

As punishment for Tyre's lawlessness and self-desecration, YHWH makes fire burst out in their midst (or "inmost self"); "it will consume you, and I will make you into ashes on the ground in the eyes of all who see you" (Ezek. 28:18). As Greenberg points out, fire is in the Priestly tradition the punishment decreed for desecration (Lev. 21:9). However, Ezekiel's image of the destruction of Tyre by fire bursting out in her midst may also reflect some knowledge of the hot-dye process used by the purple industry, as it was practiced along the Mediterranean coast at Israelite or Philistine sites such as Dor and Ashkelon. Since the process required that fires burn for days, the danger of fire was notorious (see King and Stager, *Life*, 162). Ezekiel envisions Tyre utterly consumed, annihilated forever (28:19) by the very fires that fuel her iniquitous economy.

The whole picture of economic domination that emerges from Ezekiel's extended diatribe should be set alongside one part of Ezekiel's final vision of the future God intends for the house of Israel. That vision of the people restored to their own productive land and reconciled with God is important in the context of this study, because it points to a state of well-being that comprehends every aspect of life, including economics and even what we would call ecology. That final vision echoes one distinctive phrase from the denunciation of Tyre, thus signaling the connection and contrast between the two prophetic pictures. As ruined Tyre will be "a place for spreading fishnets in the middle of the sea" (26:5), so will the whole Dead Sea shoreline be "a place for spreading fishnets" (47:10), when the waters are "healed" (v. 9), fish of all kinds become abundant, and trees produce every edible fruit year-round (v. 12). The vision is fantastic, not attainable through merely human effort, and yet it shows also the most basic practical concern for human welfare. This is expressed in one small, almost incongruous detail in the picture of the sweetening ("healing") of the Dead Sea region: "Its swamps and its marshes shall not be healed; they will be given over to salt [production]" (v. 11). Genuine prophetic vision must answer to real material need.

Set side by side, the diatribe against Tyre and the final vision reveal the contrast between two economic systems. On the one hand, there is the unrighteous and godless economy of Empire, the "little economy" that is already doomed, however powerful it may appear to be. On the other hand, there is "the Great Economy" of a world created and healed by God, which alone guarantees long-term human flourishing. Such flourishing is possible only when land and people and nonhuman creatures flourish together, in intricate systems of interaction. The contrast between the two underscores the modern, prophetically informed insight: "The Earth is sufficient for everyone's needs but not for everyone's greed" (Boff, *Cry*, 2, paraphrasing Mahatma Gandhi).

126

Rome, Mistress of Desires

Some seven centuries later (approximately 95 CE), this vision of
the fall of Tyre informed the vision of another prophet, whose
cast of mind so evidently resembles that of Ezekiel, above all in
his "archival" habit of bringing forth images out of the tradition
and setting them in new contexts. Although Tyre is not named (and
neither is Rome), it is nonetheless unmistakably present in the
purple- and scarlet-robed image of "the great city who exercises
sovereignty over the kings of the earth" (Rev. 17:18) through her
trading in luxuries (18:11–14) and ultimately, through selling herself, as "the mother of whores" (17:5). The whole picture is a mosaic
of allusions, both scriptural and cultural. Maybe none of his audience would have caught all of them, and perhaps some would have
caught few. Yet it would have been hard for anyone in his original
audience to miss the point, for John was a gifted and outspoken
rhetorician, doubly equipped with vivid images from Israel's prophetic tradition and also with images that were readily intelligible
in the context of Greco-Roman culture.

John is taken up "in the spirit," like Ezekiel (Ezek. 3:12, 14;
8:3; 11:1, 24; 37:1; 43:5), and an angel enables him to see "a woman
seated on a scarlet beast, filled with blasphemous names, having
seven heads and ten horns. And the woman was robed in purple
and scarlet, and gilded with gold and precious stones and pearls.
She held a golden cup in her hand, filled with abominations and
the impurity of her fornication" (Rev. 17:3–4; similarly 18:16). The
image is a parody of imperial Rome, the stately goddess represented
as a wealthy whore. Dressed in the colors reserved for the aristocracy or the ultrarich, "she" is Roman culture, riding on the back of
the beast of imperial political and military power (see Rev. 13). The
golden cup in her hand recalls Jeremiah's metaphor for Babylon:

> Babylon is a golden cup in the hand of YHWH, inebriating the
> whole earth;
> the nations have drunk from her wine, and so nations act insane.
>
> (Jer. 51:7)

Jeremiah and John both show Babylon intoxicating the nations,
but John adds a further dimension: "I saw that the woman was

drunk from the blood of the saints and from the blood of Jesus' witnesses. And seeing her, I was completely astounded" (Rev. 17:6).

The picture of the garishly robed woman stands out in our mind's eye; the color purple appears in Revelation only in association with Babylon. By contrast, the robes of those who stand before the throne of God and sing praises are washed white in the blood of the Lamb (7:14). Moreover, there is a sharp contrast between this picture of the new Babylon and the image of the new Jerusalem, "the bride, the wife of the Lamb" (Rev. 21:9), who is represented, first anthropomorphically, dressed in "pure white linen," which "is the righteous deed of the saints" (19:8), and then as the city "herself," built of transparent gold, with jasper and jewels for its walls and gates (21:11–21). These two "portraits" are the most opulent pictures in the book; thus the "little economy" that is Babylon/Rome is revealed as the distorting-mirror image of "the Great Economy," Jerusalem, perfect in its beauty and true wealth. As with Tyre, so-called Babylon's pretension to godlike perfection and beauty (Ezek. 27:3–4; 28:12) is a snare to the nations and proves fatal to itself.

John's self-representation as the astonished narrator, an established technique in ancient rhetoric, slows us down as we encounter the beast that "was and is not and is to come" (Rev. 17:8). Allan Boesak, speaking out of his own experience in the struggle against apartheid, observes that "the actual existence of so much evil does take one's breath away. . . . Indeed, this is the *mysterium iniquitatis*" (*Comfort and Protest*, 117). Another contemporary angle of vision on John's perplexity might come from Walter Brueggemann's comment on a related text, the king of Tyre's claim to be "a god sitting in the seat of the gods" (Ezek. 28:2). Reflecting on that "recital of hegemony," Brueggemann speaks of the "deep vexation" felt by people whose social location is less privileged, and their "wonderment about how to maintain any local, rooted identity in the face of invasive, seemingly irresistible Coca-Cola and inescapable Microsoft" (*Texts that Linger*, 61).

The very fact that "the great city" (Rev. 17:18) is never specifically named as Rome leaves the portrait open to history; the Empire it represents "was, and is not, and is to come." Prophetic vision is neither escapism nor (in the first instance) prediction; it is, as Boesak observes, "insight into history," exposing "a condition that will reveal itself again and again in other times and other situations" (*Comfort and Protest*, 93). The tragic reappearance of such "perfect

128

evil" is reflected in Boesak's comment on this passage: "There is truth in the words we spoke to the apartheid regime on 16 June 1986: Your life shall be like the life of Ahab and the life of Jezebel. Your fate shall be the fate of Babylon, which is called Egypt. Which is called Rome, which is called Pretoria" (116).

Beginning with the angelic announcement, "Fallen, fallen is Babylon the Great" (Rev. 18:2; cf. Isa. 21:9), Revelation 18 is a series of funeral dirges (cf. Ezek. 26–28) that contrast the acute grief of those who had come under the spell of the city's mercantile "sorcery" (v. 23; cf. Isa. 47:12) with the joy of the prophets and apostles, on whose behalf God has executed judgment against her (v. 20). John follows Ezekiel in delineating the culture by means of a lengthy cargo list:

> And the merchants of the earth weep and grieve over her, because no one buys their merchandise any more: merchandise of gold and silver, and precious stones and pearls, and fine linen and purple-cloth and silk and crimson-cloth, and everything of citron wood and every ivory product and every product of precious wood and bronze and iron and marble, and cinnamon and cardamom and incense, including myrrh and frankincense, and wine and olive oil and fine flour and grain, and cattle and sheep, and horses and carriages and chattel-slaves [literally, "bodies"], that is, human souls. (Rev. 18:11–13)

The cargo list of twenty-eight items offers a thumbnail sketch of Roman society, where the superrich might spend the equivalent of five or six million U.S. dollars on one citron-wood wine table (Aune, *Revelation*, 1000). It also highlights political and military power (horses and chariots), as well as the stuff of ordinary life: wine, oil, and grain were the dietary staples for everyone. Probably few Romans would have considered the final item on the list to be a luxury. Slave labor was the essential energy supply for the Roman economy; it fueled agriculture, mining, and every other form of industry, as well as every household. Slaves, called *sōmata* ("bodies") in the market, "were treated much like livestock" (*Revelation*, 1002). That status befits their placement here, beside the domestic animals owned by ordinary people, as well as the horses and chariots belonging to the rich.

Strategically, John places those enslaved bodies in climactic position in the list of commodities. Clarice Martin calls "this slam

129

on Rome . . . one of the most emphatic critiques of Roman ideology in Revelation—namely, that it is an empire that enslaves human souls" ("Polishing," 100). By naming them specifically as *psychas anthrōpōn* ("human souls, lives"), John counters the dominant ideology, derived from Aristotle, that slaves are by nature "defectively souled," functioning chiefly as "soulless bodies," like tools or domestic animals (Martin, "Polishing," 89, 100). His rhetoric restores humanity and an inner life to (among countless others) the 97,000 Jewish prisoners enslaved in the great revolt against Rome (Aune, *Revelation*, 1003), some of whom might even now be in the churches that hear his message.

Immediately after mention of the "bodies" that keep the economy going, the heavenly voice (or John) turns directly to the audience and names the second thing that fuels this economy: the unceasing, passionate craving for more expensive stuff. "And the fruit, your soul's desire, is gone from you, and all the glitter and glamour is lost to you, and will never ever again be found" (Rev. 18:14). Thus John leads his audience and us to the recognition that desire is primarily a cultural disposition, and only derivatively an individual propensity. It is a key manifestation of the character of a society as a whole, or the deformation of its character. Here the language of intense craving and extreme distress (18:9, 11, 15, 19) suggests a society suffering from addiction, a disease that is not only fatal to the host culture (Babylon/Rome) but also destructive to all the other cultures that the "great city" colonizes, beguiles, exploits, and gradually, inexorably, drains. Such a view of Rome may lurk behind the extravagant oration delivered by the famed Asian orator of the early second century, P. Aelius Aristides, to the imperial court in Rome, praising the empire's commercial prowess:

> Here is brought from every land and sea all the crops of the seasons and the produce of each land, river, lake, as well as the arts of the Greeks and barbarians. . . . So many merchant ships arrive here, conveying every kind of goods from every people every hour and every day, so that the city is like a factory common to the whole earth. It is possible to see so many cargoes from India and even from Arabia Felix [the South Arabian Peninsula], if you wish, that one imagines that for the future the trees are left bare [*gymna*] for the people there and that they must come here to beg for their own produce if they need anything. (*Regarding Rome*, 11–12, *Works*, 2:75)

130

Is Aristides a completely satisfied customer of the Roman imperium (or "emporium")? Or does he speak as a colonial who has experienced some of the humiliation and harshness of having one's land denuded to fill Roman ships? Robert Royalty argues that "Aristides' fundamental self-identification as a Greek subverts his praise of Rome" (*Streets*, 119). Reading between the lines of his over-the-top description of Roman commerce, we might see an acknowledgment (however well concealed from his royal audience and perhaps from himself) of loss that is cultural, economic, and also ecological.

The truth is that the Romans, like the Greeks before them, vigorously and radically transformed the Mediterranean landscape (McNeill, *Mountains*, 72–73). They devoured forests for fuel, agriculture, shipbuilding, and other construction, including siege works. The Jewish historian Josephus, in his account of the savage attack on Jerusalem and Judah in reprisal for the Jewish Revolt, uses the same word as Aristides to describe the Romans "stripping bare" (*gymnoō*) the forests around Jerusalem, as they "reduced to desert wilderness [*erēmoō*]" the once-fertile countryside (*Jewish War* 5.264, 6.6–7; see Rossing, "River," 211). Nonetheless, if Josephus and Aristides harbored any negative thoughts about Roman hegemony, in speaking and writing for imperial audiences, they smothered them with praise. Both had made their accommodation to the empire and prospered greatly as a result.

There is a complete contrast between them and the prophet on Patmos, who had likely escaped the very scene of destruction that Josephus describes. John fights against accommodation, for himself and for his audience, with no holds barred. Taking his stand with the witnesses to Jesus, who offer lavish praise only in worship of the sovereign God and the Lamb (Rev. 7:12; 11:17; 15:3–4; 19:6–8), he hears the voice from heaven that issues the call, "Come out, my people, out from her, so you may not be partners in her sins!" (Rev. 18:4; cf. Jer. 51:45). Like Josephus and Aristides, John uses the language of stripping and desertification, but not with reference to occupied or colonial lands. Rather it is the richly dressed whore who is suddenly "made a wilderness" (*erēmoō*; Rev. 17:16) and stripped "naked" (*gymnos*)—by none other than the beast, which now turns on the one it lately supported, in the manner of many pimps. In the somewhat less metaphorical language of chapter 18, "the great city . . . is made a wilderness" (v. 19; cf. v. 17)—the complete inversion

131

of Rome's image of itself as the city that propagates countless more cities throughout the world. The scene seems to have been inspired by both historical experience and Hebrew Scripture: on the one hand, the Roman destruction of Jerusalem and Judea, and on the other, Isaiah's oracle against the original Babylon, which declares "Fallen, fallen is Babylon!" (Isa. 21:9). Likely John had in mind that oracle's unusual title, "On the wilderness of the sea" (21:1), a metaphor that he applied vividly to the (anticipated) collapse of the new Babylon.

John's exposé of the iniquity of the commercial enterprise of Babylon/Rome appears in climactic position in the book, shortly before the revelation of the new Jerusalem. As we have seen, the two opulent cities are distorting-mirror opposites; the description of each points to the other, and highlights the difference. We must view them together, as mutually exclusive alternatives. John bends all his rhetorical skill toward enabling us to recognize that the first city is deadly and doomed, and we must "come out" (Rev. 18:4) if we are to inhabit the future in *this* world that God intends. Yet if the specifically economic dimensions of John's vision have received relatively little attention from Christians in our time (certainly much less than his *purported* vision of the end of the world), perhaps that is because many of us do not know how to view our own economic behavior as John views the dominant economic paradigm of his time: from the edge, that is, the eschaton.

William Cavanaugh's theological analysis of contemporary consumer culture may help us to develop what John would certainly regard as an essential prophetic skill: connecting economics and eschatology in a responsible way. Observing that consumerism is itself a powerful system of moral formation, Cavanaugh suggests that it has affinities with the great faith traditions in that, paradoxically, consumerism "trains us to transcend the material world." For while the consumer spirit dwells on material things, "the thing itself is never enough. Things and brands must be invested with mythologies, with spiritual aspirations. . . . Above all, they represent the aspiration to escape time and death by constantly seeking renewal in created things. Each new movement of desire promises the opportunity to start over" (*Being Consumed,* 48). We are formed (or de-formed) to want one thing after another, and Cavanaugh's most penetrating theological insight is that precisely through that kind of formation in desire without satisfaction, we lose the ability

132

to hope in God. Thus "consumerism is the death of Christian escha-tology. There can be no rupture with the status quo, no inbreaking kingdom of God, but only endless superficial novelty" (93).

Cavanaugh's analysis of the contemporary predicament of many Western Christians comes close to echoing John's vision of the two cities, when he observes that, to those whose moral forma-tion derives from consumerism, "the witness of the martyrs to living the kingdom of God in the present becomes a curiosity: How could someone be so committed to one particular thing as to lose his life for it?" (*Being Consumed*, 93–94). Developing his thought, we might say that martyrdom—something that John holds up before his audience as a legitimate and even essential part of Christian experience—is something other and far more than resignation to death. Rather, it is the ultimate expression of active resistance to a tragic world of idolatry, of endless wanting and taking, and the resulting scarcity. Martyrdom is thus one traditional and perennial element in the complex of "edgy" Christian attitudes and behaviors that keep eschatological hope alive.

Eschatology and Ecology: The Sea Is No More

John, like Ezekiel, concludes his book with a new vision of the cre-ated order as it is reordered by God, following a great purging of the earth and the reassertion of God's sovereignty. Ezekiel's cul-minating vision (Ezek. 47:1–12) clearly stands behind John's pic-ture of "the river of the water of life," with fruit-bearing trees on either bank, and their leaves for healing. John goes beyond Ezekiel in specifying that this is the tree of life, and the healing is "for the nations" (Rev. 22:1–2). It is beyond the scope of this study to con-sider all that John envisions about the destruction of the old order, including the destruction of "those who destroy the earth" (11:18), in order to make way for this new one. I conclude by focusing on just one element of that picture, John's observation that "the sea is no more" (21:1). This part of John's vision is understandably distress-ing to some ecologically sensitive readers. Playing on the Hebrew word for "deep ocean" (*těhôm*), Catherine Keller locates John in a posited "tehomophobic tradition" of biblical thought, which, she maintains, identified the sea "with the death-tainted, threatening chaos of creation" ("No More Sea," 184).

133

Reading the sea as a symbol of chaos is common among biblical scholars, and that reading is apt in a number of literary contexts in both Testaments. However, it does not explain the disappearance of the sea here. I shall argue that it is in fact an economic statement, a statement about sovereignty. In both substance and literary form, John's assertion *hē thalassa ouk estin eti* ("the sea is no more") belongs to his vision of the collapse of Babylon/Rome as a great sea-trading empire; it signals and epitomizes the disintegration of the empire's political and cultural dominance. A contextually sensitive reading shows that, far from being part of a tradition that is phobic with respect to any aspect of the created order, the envisioned disappearance of the sea is a strong affirmation of life, as it is divinely given and sustained.

The phrase *ouk . . . eti* ("no more") marks this event as the final moment in the empire's collapse. It is a near echo of the recurrent phrase *ou mē eti,* "no more," which occurs six times at the conclusion of chapter 18, where the prophet itemizes the ordinary good things—musicians, artisans, the sound of the millstone, lamplight, voices of bride and groom—that will cease when "the great city" itself is "no more" (Rev. 18:21–22). Even a quick reading of Revelation shows that John favors numbering things by seven—the number denoting completeness—or its multiples. There are seven churches, eyes, horns, trumpets, bowls, plagues, etc.; the cargo list (18:11–13) includes 28 (= 4 x 7) items. So when this careful rhetorician stops at just *six* iterations of "no more," anyone who is counting might well await the final toll in the death knell for Babylon/Rome. And when, two chapters later, the seventh "no more" sounds, the effect is shattering. Gone is the vast sea that the Romans proudly called *Mare Nostrum,* "Our Sea," the maritime highway that was indispensable to their political, military, and economic imperialism.

John's vision of the vanished sea would speak powerfully to his audience, located as they were on the islands and coastlands of the Roman province of Asia. From their perspective, Rome was the "beast rising out of the sea" (13:1); Roman power always materialized in the form of naval and merchant ships coming over the western horizon. The sea was the essential medium without which "the great city" could never have conquered the whole Mediterranean Rim (and beyond) through both warfare and trade. In light of that social and geographic reality, it is evident that "the sea is no more" is the very opposite of a statement of human presumption.

134

It directly refutes the imperial claim to possess the work of God's hands: "Our Sea." Against that blasphemous claim, John asserts God's absolute and exclusive sovereignty over every aspect of the created order. Gone is the maritime horizon over which imperial ships sailed, their holds filled with the wealth of Asia and Africa, including live human bodies. Barbara Rossing, who has pioneered an economically and ecologically sensitive approach to Revelation, calls the similar heavenly proclamation of woe upon earth and sea (12:12) "a cosmic cry for an Earth free from Roman exploitation and dominance" ("Alas for Earth," 191).

The disappearance of the sea thus follows in a long line of radical biblical statements about God's sovereignty over creation in the face of human evil. These include the flood story in Genesis, the plague narrative and the crossing of the sea in Exodus, as well as multiple prophetic oracles that portend drastic reordering of what we moderns call the "natural" world. From Genesis to Revelation, the prophetic imagination displays harsh divine judgment upon those who misuse the creatures, the works of God's hands, and thus dishonor the Creator.

"The sea is no more" is an extreme instance of John's signature eschatological hyperbole, yet the dictum has a close parallel in another contemporary piece of literature from the Greco-Roman world. The Fifth Sibylline Oracle was written by an anonymous Egyptian Jew who, like John on Patmos, burned with indignation against "Babylon, golden-throned and golden-shod" (*Sibylline Oracles*, v. 434). Strikingly, this poet shares with John a fantastic "geophysical" and eschatological imagination:

> In the last time the sea shall be dry,
> *and no more [kouketi] shall ships sail to Italy.*
> (vv. 447–48)

Late in the twentieth century, postmodern theorists rediscovered that geography is a social construct and not a simple matter of "facts on the ground" (see, for example, Yi-Fu Tuan, *Space and Place*; Lefebvre, *Production of Space*). However, these two poets had understood that already in the first century. John of Patmos and the composer of the oracle both recognized that "the sea" as claimed by the Romans was a human construction; the empire had drawn a map of the world that reinforced its claim to sovereignty over three continents and convinced many or most of the verisimilitude

135

of that map. But these two poetic writers and visionaries expose the arbitrariness of the construct. As Paul Minear observes, far from being otherworldly and "spacelessly transcendent" in his thinking (*I Saw,* 277), John (along with the poet of the oracle) was challenging hearers to see the world they inhabited as wholly contingent on God's action. They dared to proclaim the disappearance of the sea as a signal that even now God is planning or inaugurating a radically new world order, one in which the power base for the destructive and godless "little economy" of Babylon/Rome literally (if imaginatively) evaporates.

All this makes clear how it is that John's vision pivots on his recognition that "the sea is no more." Immediately thereafter he sees "the holy city, the new Jerusalem, coming down out of heaven from God" (Rev. 21:2). As part of that vision, John hears "a great voice from the throne" announcing a second and climactic series of six phenomena that are "no more" (*ouk eti*): no more is death, mourning, crying, or pain (21:4); no more is any accursed thing (22:3); no more is night (22:5). This, then, is the structure of the final chapters of Revelation: two cities, economies, and sovereignties that exist in fundamental opposition to each other—"Babylon" and the new Jerusalem—are delineated, each by a series of six-plus-one; "the sea is no more" stands as the point of connection and overlap between them. Thus the eclipse of the sea constitutes at once the *last* of the seven "no mores" marking the end of accursed empire and the *first* of the seven "no mores" constituting the blessedness of the heavenly empire come to earth. The world turns on John's dictum, "The sea is no more."

I have argued that the disappearance of the sea fits into John's vision and its first-century context, as a uniquely powerful symbol of divinely given life over the imperial forces of destruction and death. Nonetheless, that symbol is unlikely to convey any such positive meaning in our own time, when the seas and oceans of the whole world increasingly experience humanly engineered attacks, "accidental" though some of them they may be. Oil spills and gushes, trawling and overfishing, rising sea temperatures and sea levels, vastly increased acidity, dead zones and superstorms—these are tragic and fearsome actualities that threaten to change, compromise, and diminish the life of the sea as humans have always known it.

John's metaphor of the evaporated sea cannot be applied uncritically to new situations. Nonetheless, the creativity and freedom with which the prophets use metaphor in order to expose the imperialistic forces they confront presents us with a challenge: What symbols might be encouraging and healing for our time, capable of asserting divine sovereignty in the face of the "empire of might" that (as Simone Weil said) we are obliged to *dis*respect, if we are to be just? Against imperialistic claims to the earth's "resources," what symbols might convey the essential prophetic assertion: "Earth and sea are not at your disposal"?

John himself offers one image that could serve us well. In the new realm that God is bringing to earth, immediately following the second series of seven things that are "no more" (Rev. 21:1–4), "the One seated on the throne said, 'Look, I am making all things new. . . . I myself will give to the thirsty from the spring of the water of life—without charge!'" (vv. 5–6). This is a metaphor with a pedigree. John, fluent in the language and imagery of the Hebrew Bible, here combines images belonging to the tradition. First, from Lamentations, the lament of the defeated Jerusalemites: "We drink our own water for a price" (Lam. 5:4); and following upon that, the divine promise heard through exilic Isaiah: "Everyone who is thirsty come to the water!" Anyone who has no money will receive water—and wine and milk—without cost (Isa. 55:1). A second tradition underlying John's metaphor comes from Psalms: the "fountain of life" that originates with God and is experienced in God's presence (Ps. 36:9 [10 Heb.]; cf. also Zech. 14:8). In the semi-arid zone of the eastern Mediterranean, fresh water is the indispensable symbol and indeed evidence of God's power to give and sustain life, a power that ultimately belongs to God alone.

The heavenly voice in Revelation continues: "The one who conquers will receive these things as an inheritance," a sure sign of membership in God's immediate family (Rev. 21:7). As Robert Royalty points out, inheritance (in contrast to commerce), and particularly a landed inheritance, "was the most respectable way to gain a fortune and raise one's status in antiquity. The Christians inherit landed property, a city of gold and jewels. Those who conquer' gain not only heavenly wealth but *respectable* heavenly wealth through respectable means" (*Streets*, 223). Christians on every rung of the social ladder would have understood that John is stripping Babylon/ Rome and its devotees of any prestige that mere commercial wealth

137

might have brought, while conferring status on those who belong to God's household, slaves and exiles though they might now seem to be.

Revelation reaches its rhetorical climax in this passage, where for the first time in the whole book a word is heard directly from the One seated on the throne—and before that throne, probably not incidentally, is something like a sea, crystalline in its perfect transparency (Rev. 4:6). The point is clear: The things essential for life cannot be commodified. They are priceless in God's Great Economy, regardless of what the puny mercantile economy of Babylon may say. Accordingly, these needful things must be cherished, preserved with the utmost care, and shared as a common good among rich and poor alike. This is a word that speaks powerfully and disturbingly to us.

In the first decade of the third millennium, the status of fresh water emerged as a highly vexed issue. Should water be regarded as a common good or as a commodity to be privatized and traded on the open market? In early 2001, the president of Azurix, Enron's water subsidiary, declared that she "would not rest until all the world's water had been privatized" (Barlow, *Blue Covenant*, 63). However outrageous the statement may be, it marks a critical moment in history. Who could have even conceived of such a thing before the full onslaught of globalization as a comprehensive economic, political, militarized, and even geophysical phenomenon? By the end of that first decade, the global water market had revenues of $508 billion and was growing at 6.4 percent per year; *Fortune* magazine suggested that water is "the gold of the 21st century" (Moore, "Beating," 28), with abundant opportunities for corporations that can figure out how to beat the coming water shortage. The year before *Fortune* issued that statement, the United Nations General Assembly made a historical declaration representing a very different view of water. In July 28, 2010, it declared safe and clean drinking water and sanitation as a human right essential to the realization of all other human rights. Resolution 64/292 was approved by 122 nations, in the face of the fact that one-third of the world's growing population currently lacks access to such basic water services, and further, "as much as 40 percent of food production comes from . . . unsustainable water sources," rivers and aquifers that are pumped at rates far exceeding replacement rates (Gleick, "Facing Down," 19–20).

138

Although forty-one nations abstained from voting, the U.N. declaration nonetheless may be judged a crucial step toward the sort of global water covenant for which Canadian activist Maude Barlow calls. She envisions three components to "the Blue Covenant": *water conservation*, to protect water supplies for the sake of the earth and all its species; *water justice*, to promote solidarity "between those in the global North who have water and resources and those in the global South who do not"; and *water democracy*, in which all governments would acknowledge "that water is a fundamental human right for all" (Barlow, *Blue Covenant*, 156). We can be quite certain how Ezekiel and exilic Isaiah, the psalmist and John on Patmos—indeed every prophet and poet of the Bible, all of whom lived in the semi-arid region of the eastern Mediterranean—would counsel us to view and act upon this issue of water security, which may well be "the most underappreciated global environmental challenge of our time" (3). Likely it is no coincidence that the penultimate divine statement in the entirety of the Christian Bible is about water: "And let whoever is thirsty come, and whoever desires, receive the water of life—without charge!" (Rev. 22:17). No doubt John is speaking metaphorically, but woe to us if we "diminish" (cf. 22:19) or dismiss those words of John's prophecy as *idle* metaphor!

Works Cited in Chapter 5

Aristides, P. Aelius. *The Complete Works*. Translated by Charles A. Behr. Leiden: E. J. Brill, 1981.

Aubet, Maria Eugenia. *The Phoenicians and the West: Policies, Colonies, and Trade*. Cambridge: Cambridge University Press, 1993.

Aune, David E. *Revelation 17–22*. Word Biblical Commentary 52C. Nashville: Thomas Nelson Publishers, 1998.

Barlow, Maude. *Blue Covenant: The Global Water Crisis and the Coming Battle for the Right to Water*. Toronto: McClelland & Stewart, 2007.

Bauckham, Richard. *The Bible in Politics*. Louisville, KY: Westminster/John Knox Press, 1989.

———. *The Climax of Prophecy: Studies on the Book of Revelation*. Edinburgh: T & T Clark, 1993.

139

————. *The Theology of the Book of Revelation*. Cambridge: Cambridge University Press, 1993.

Berry, Wendell. *Home Economics*. New York: North Point Press, 1987.

Blount, Brian. *Revelation: A Commentary*. New Testament Library. Louisville, KY: Westminster John Knox Press, 2009.

Boesak, Allan A. *Comfort and Protest: Reflections on the Apocalypse of John of Patmos*. Philadelphia: Westminster Press, 1987.

Boff, Leonardo. *Cry of the Earth, Cry of the Poor*. Translated by Phillip Berryman. Maryknoll, NY: Orbis Books, 1997.

Brueggemann, Walter. *Texts that Linger, Words that Explode*. Edited by Patrick Miller. Minneapolis: Fortress Press, 2000.

Buber, Martin. *The Prophetic Faith*. New York: Harper & Row, 1949.

Cavanaugh, William T. *Being Consumed: Economics and Christian Desire*. Grand Rapids: Eerdmans, 2008.

Gleick, Peter H. "Facing Down the Hydro-Crisis." *World Policy Journal* 26:4 (Winter 2009/10): 17–23.

Greenberg, Moshe. *Ezekiel 21–37*. Anchor Bible 22A. New York: Doubleday, 1997.

Hardt, Michael, and Antonio Negri. *Empire*. Cambridge, MA: Harvard University Press, 2000.

Homer. *The Complete Works of Homer*. New York: Random House, 1950.

Jidejian, Nina. *Tyre through the Ages*. Beirut: Dar el-Mashreq Publishers, 1969.

Keller, Catherine. "No More Sea: The Lost Chaos of the Eschaton." In *Christianity and Ecology*, edited by Dieter Hessel and Rosemary Radford Ruether. Cambridge, MA: Harvard University Press, 2000.

King, Philip J., and Lawrence E. Stager. *Life in Biblical Israel*. Louisville, KY: Westminster John Knox Press, 2001.

Kraybill, J. Nelson. *Imperial Cult and Commerce in John's Apocalypse*. Journal for the Study of the New Testament Supplement Series 132. Sheffield: Sheffield Academic Press, 1996.

Lefebvre, Henri. *The Production of Space*. Oxford: Blackwell, 1991.

Martin, Clarice. "Polishing the Unclouded Mirror: A Womanist Reading of Revelation 18:13." In *From Every People and Nation: The Book of Revelation in Intercultural Perspective*, edited by David Rhoads. Minneapolis: Fortress Press, 2005.

Masefield, John. *Salt-Water Poems and Ballads.* New York: Macmillan, 1944.

McNeill, J. R. *The Mountains of the Mediterranean World: An Environmental History.* Cambridge: Cambridge University Press, 1992.

Minear, Paul S. *I Saw a New Earth: An Introduction to the Visions of the Apocalypse.* Washington, DC: Corpus Books, 1968.

Moore, Tara. "Beating the Coming Water Shortage." *Fortune,* October 17, 2011.

Odell, Margaret S. *Ezekiel.* Macon, GA: Smyth & Helwys, 2005.

Rossing, Barbara R. "Alas for Earth! Lament and Resistance in Revelation 12." In *The Earth Story in the New Testament,* edited by Norman Habel and Vicky Balabanski. Earth Bible 5. London: Sheffield Academic Press, 2002.

———. "River of Life in God's New Jerusalem." In *Christianity and Ecology,* edited by Dieter Hessel and Rosemary Radford Ruether. Cambridge, MA: Harvard University Press, 2000.

Royalty, Robert M., Jr. *The Streets of Heaven: The Ideology of Wealth in the Apocalypse of John.* Macon, GA: Mercer University Press, 1998.

The Sibylline Oracles, Thesaurus Linguae Graecae. Irvine, CA: Thesaurus Linguae Graecae, 1996–.

Tuan, Yi-Fu. *Space and Place: The Perspective of Experience.* Minneapolis: University of Minnesota Press, 1977.

Weil, Simone. "The *Iliad,* Poem of Might." In *The Simone Weil Reader,* edited by George Panichas. New York: McKay, 1977.

CHAPTER 6

Witnessing in the Midst of Disaster

The Ministry of Jeremiah

Pessimism and optimism are both forms of arrogance. We have no right to stop hoping.

—Wes Jackson, personal communication, April 6, 2013

For Christian readers especially, the book of Jeremiah is the center of gravity of the whole prophetic tradition in the Bible. More than any other book of the Christian canon, Jeremiah points both backward and forward along the whole stream of biblical prophecy from Moses to Jesus. He is the prophet who most closely resembles Moses, the father of all prophets. This is evident from the outset, when he balks at YHWH's call to what will be a ministry of some forty years: "I am not expert at speaking" (Jer. 1:6; cf. Exod. 4:10). Like Moses, Jeremiah continues to chafe at what his calling requires, and nonetheless, like Moses, he has a deep and abiding intimacy with God. So Jeremiah's story builds on Moses' story, and likewise Jesus' story builds on Jeremiah's. Jesus, like Jeremiah, challenges the religious and political authorities, most notably those in the temple; he echoes Jeremiah's words, that they have made it "a den of thieves" (Jer. 7:11; Mark 11:17 and pars.). As a result of such allegations, Jesus and Jeremiah are judged to be subversives; in due course, each of them becomes a prisoner of the state.

Jeremiah deserves special attention in any contemporary study of the Prophets, because he is a prophet who speaks to our time and

143

cultural situations in strong and unsettling ways. His voice comes to us out of wartime, sometimes out of prison; he speaks of cultural erosion and eventually the political collapse of the known world. Jeremiah offers the most direct prophetic witness, promulgated over decades, as Judah and Jerusalem approach and descend into the hell of destruction and exile. With brutal honesty, he names the self-delusion, the idolatry that is bringing on the harsh judgment of God. Yet for all this, Jeremiah is a prophet and poet of stubborn, paradoxical hope, certain that beyond this present disaster lies the good future that God intends for the Judeans, the Jews. One of the boldest and most inventive poets ever to write in the Hebrew language, he creates unforgettable images of both devastation and restoration. His images speak to the "heart"—perhaps the nearest equivalent, in biblical terminology, to what we mean by "imagination"—and even to the gut. This prophet speaks for God in language that is literally visceral: "My guts [mēʿay], my guts; I writhe!" (Jer. 4:19); "My guts yearn for [Ephraim/Israel]" (31:20). Although the visceral character of Jeremiah's words is (regrettably) obscured by most translations, this feature of his poetry is an important indicator of his distinctive place within the prophetic canon. For Jeremiah is a witness to horror who never looks away, and thus he may teach us something of what it is to speak and act on God's behalf in the most grievous situations.

Witnessing to God's presence in the midst of horror is an inalienable aspect of ministry, a task that comes always unbidden and more often than we may care to admit. Episcopal priest Janet Vincent describes her experiences serving those engaged in the recovery efforts at ground zero in New York City in the immediate wake of the terrorist attack on September 11, 2001. The first day, she was asked to bless body parts that had been pulled from a pile of debris:

> I am spattered with mud and I can taste the grit in the air. The stench is awful. I wear my mask until someone speaks to me and I must answer. . . . I feel stripped of every comforting phrase, every bit of theology and any sense of purpose except to be there. The being there makes me feel sick. Just hold your ground, I think, don't vomit and don't turn away. It's my first inkling that I am a witness—that's my job. I never looked away. ("Worst of Times," 39)

In sum, Jeremiah shows us a practice that belongs at the core of ministry and likewise of prophetic witness: the practice of standing mud-spattered (see Jer. 38:6) amid the ruins of life—not just an individual life but the life of a people, one's own people—while speaking honestly to God and truthfully for God. Prophetic ministry and witness entails making God real, present, and necessary in situations that seem to deny that God exists, that God has any power in our lives, that God's will for us is not death but life.

Jeremiah is the longest of the prophetic books, and it is certainly the most confusing to read. The ordering of material is not chronological, nor can any clear topical arrangement be discerned. The book seems to draw to a conclusion several times (45:1–5; 51:59–64; 52:31–34), yet each time it pulls back from any sense of resolution; even the final hopeful (?) words about King Jehoiachin receiving honorable treatment in Babylon are greatly overshadowed by the immediately preceding notices of the slaughter and exile of thousands of Judeans (see 52:24–30; the whole chapter is a near duplicate of 2 Kgs. 24:18–25:20). Moreover, the diversity of material here is greater than in any other prophetic book: poetic oracles of doom and restoration, first-person prophetic laments, lengthy biographical narratives, dialogues between prophet and God, and other kinds of prose pieces—sermonic, epistolary—in a highly rhetorical style.

It has been common among modern scholars to distinguish several sources or streams of tradition, oral and written, and to dissect Jeremiah into redactional layers, often with the aim of identifying a simpler "original" text. However, newer approaches tend to view the book's untidy complexity not as an accident of its compositional history, but rather as a crucial part of its message— or rather "messages," which are sometimes radically contradictory. For instance, is Babylon a partner in God-given peace (chap. 29), or the ultimate enemy that God will destroy (chaps. 50–51)? According to L. Stulman and H. C. P. Kim, "Jeremianic dissymmetry" is engaging for readers and ultimately even hopeful, because it "takes seriously massive and unmanageable loss" and "honors a range of human responses to the horror of suffering" (*You Are My People*, 106).

From a theological perspective, the most deeply confusing and disturbing aspect of the book is that very different pictures of YHWH emerge, with no clear guidance as to which of them might be reliable. God persistently sends prophets to warn the people against disaster (7:25) and to test their ways (6:27); yet YHWH is also the One who sets up stumbling blocks in their way (6:21) and exposes them to sexual humiliation by their enemies (13:26). The people appeal to YHWH as "the Hope of Israel" (*miqwēh yiśrā'ēl*, 14:8; cf. 17:13), a phrasing which is in fact a pun; it could equally be translated as "Israel's water-pool," especially since it appears here in the context of a lament over a deep drought. Using another water image, Jeremiah decries those who forsake "the Fount of free-running [or 'living'] water" (17:13). Yet those positive images contrast starkly with Jeremiah's pointed accusation to the divine Face, that YHWH is like a streambed suddenly gone dry (15:18).

In view of such contradictions, Kathleen O'Connor characterizes the book as "a boiling pot of language" that "spills worlds of words into the ruptures of communal life" (*Pain and Promise*, 33). Drawing on studies of Holocaust survivors, she suggests, "The book's confused shape conveys the 'damaged mosaics of the mind, memories in pieces, memory creating a shadow over the normal'" (128, citing Lawrence L. Langer). Jeremiah's experience of God and the world resists any neat ordering as he "stammers toward the unsayable" (*Pain and Promise*, 137). There can be no settled or consistent theological message in the face of the previously unthinkable, the destruction of the holy city of Jerusalem and the covenanted throne of David. Nonetheless, the prophet makes it impossible to ignore YHWH, even when that might be the easier course, and perhaps the one that is safer, theologically speaking.

This chapter traces some of the key elements of Jeremiah's stammering, mud-spattered, yet artful prophetic witness, beginning with the elements of confrontation and castigation; Jeremiah's words expose and, for those (few perhaps) who have ears to hear, dismantle the religious delusion that grips the people as a whole. Second, and as a counter to delusion, Jeremiah names the dominant cultural experience of profound loss and suffering, articulating it fully through the laments that are a prominent feature of the first twenty chapters of the book. Through these cries and protests addressed to God, we can follow Jeremiah's own painful growth into his role as a prophet in the midst of chaos; he struggles mightily to understand YHWH's justice (12:1), YHWH's apparent unreliability (15:18), and his own apparently futile ministry (20:7). Naming confusion and loss fully makes it possible to lay claim to realistic hope, and so the third and fourth sections of the chapter treat Jeremiah's so-called Book of Consolation (chaps. 30–33). In the books of the Prophets, this constitutes the most full-orbed vision of a new social order. Jeremiah offers hope in terms that are identifiably those of his particular place and culture, and yet in their very concreteness they guide the work of envisioning hopeful change for our own world. The final section of the chapter points to the work of several contemporary artists—a painter, a poet, and a printmaker—who find in Jeremiah inspiration for their own creative work, and whose hopeful yet grief-stricken perspectives on the social order might themselves be judged prophetic.

Confronting Idolatry

YHWH sets Jeremiah up for a ministry that is fundamentally confrontational; he is to be "a fortified city, a column of iron, walls of bronze against the whole land, namely the kings of Judah, its ministers, its priests, and the citizens" (1:18). He confronts them with the most fundamental of all problems, the problem of God. Jeremiah speaks persistently of and to YHWH, in harsh castigations and strident laments. His unrelenting YHWH-talk isolates him (15:17) and at the same time brings him into constant conflict with everyone, from the king and the temple establishment down to his own kinfolk (12:6). He is completely out of tempo with his time and place, because he speaks of nothing but YHWH in the midst of an idolatrous culture and city (2:11–13, 17–18, 19, 25, etc.), to a people assiduous in their practice of religious self-delusion:

> For your gods are as many as your towns, Judah,
> and you have set up altars to Shame [Boshet, a mocking name for
>   Baal],
> as many as the streets of Jerusalem—altars to make sacrifice to Baal.
>   (11:13)

> And they built shrines for Baal to burn their children in the fire—
> burnt offerings to Baal!—which I [God] had never commanded,
> never decreed; it never even occurred to me. (19:5; cf. 7:31)

In spite of their religious delusions and atrocities, Jeremiah has some pity for the people he (or God speaking through him) repeatedly calls "my daughter-people" (4:11; 6:14, 26, etc.); the term

147

denotes both their vulnerability and his own unbreakable affiliation with them. Jeremiah has no "critical distance" from the people whose suffering he sees and foresees so clearly: "Because of the shattering of my daughter-people, I am shattered" (8:21). By contrast, he dissociates himself entirely from the religious professionals, against whom he regularly turns his most bitter denunciations:

> How can you say, "We are wise, and YHWH's Instruction [*torah*] is in our hands"?
> But here, for the sake of deception it has acted, the lying pen of scribes!
> The wise shall be put to shame—broken and captured.
> Here, they reject the word of YHWH, and wisdom—what is that to them?
> Therefore I shall give their wives to others, their fields to dispossessors,
> for from small to great, all seek their own profit.
> From prophet to priest, all enact deception.
> They treated the wound of my daughter-people superficially,
> saying, "*Shalom*/health, *shalom*/peace, prosperity"—but there is no *shalom*.
> They have behaved shamefully, for they have committed atrocities—though they feel no shame at all; they do not know how to experience humiliation.
>
> (8:8–12; cf. 6:13–15)

The final lines are pointed in their condemnation: The opinion leaders, priests and prophets, behave shamefully yet are incapable of feeling any shame. Elsewhere (14:3–4) Jeremiah portrays the *appropriate* shame and humiliation felt and expressed by those at the opposite end of the social scale. When a terrible drought scourges Judah, the common workers (i.e., those with little social power) cover their heads in shame—not out of personal guilt but on behalf of the whole people. They are astute enough to recognize the drought as a sign that human behavior has thrown the whole world, indeed the natural order itself, far out of kilter. By contrast, the religious leaders are morally inert, and deadly in their blandishments: "*Shalom, shalom.*" They are incapable of recognizing the Source of the problem, as well as the Source of possibility for a different future, namely YHWH.

148   In short, the nation's leadership lacks the wit to fear what—or rather, the One who—should be feared:

They have not said in their hearts, "Let us fear YHWH our God,
the One who gives rain—early and late rain in its season,
who keeps for us the weeks appointed for harvest."
Your iniquities have turned these things away,
and your sins have deprived you of what is good.
For the guilty are found among my people;
one of them watches as (in) a hunter's-blind.
They set a trap; human beings they catch.
Like a basket full of birds, so are their houses full of deception.
On that account they have waxed great and enriched themselves;
they are fat and smooth. They even went beyond wicked deeds.
They would not try a case—the case of the orphan, so they could
    prosper,
and the plea of the vulnerable they would not hear.

(5:24–28)

These words resound powerfully in many parts of our global society, where the gap continues to widen between the comparatively few who are rich in monetary and social capital, and the very many who lack both. Jeremiah points to the social tragedy that involves everyone, regardless of whether they are directly involved in acts of oppression ("wicked deeds"): a justice system that provides no representation or recourse for the "vulnerable" (*'ebyônîm*, traditionally, "the needy"). These are the countless people who have no one to argue their case when they are wronged or to seek amelioration for them when they fall into desperate straits.

As Jeremiah sees, the religious establishment and the general public are not discontent with the situation:

The prophets prophesy in delusion,
and the priests rule beside them—
and my people, they love it this way.
But what will you do at its end?
(5:31)

The false prophets' utter dismissal of God as the One who directs events is summed up in just two Hebrew words: *lō'-hû'*, "Not He" (Jer. 5:12a). So inept are they at reading the current situation that they cannot even see the threat posed by the Babylonian army: "Sword and famine we shall not see" (5:12b). With a tragic and ultimately fatal irony, the opinion leaders of the community reckon that the sole threat to be eliminated is Jeremiah, the one whom YHWH has sent

149

in one last attempt to turn the nation around. "And they said, 'Come, let's devise a scheme against Jeremiah, for instruction shall not fall away from the priest, nor counsel from the wise, nor the word from the prophet! Come, *let's strike him down with the tongue*, and we won't listen anymore to all his words!'" (18:18; emphasis added). The language here is telling: it is their tongue against his. The religious leaders above all others know that words publicly promulgated are dangerously powerful and must be controlled, if they are going to succeed in manipulating the masses to their own political ends. Jeremiah announces that "Judah's sin is inscribed with an iron stylus" (17:1); this is the instrument used for permanent, public inscriptions on stone or metal, at the direction of the bureaucrats whom he opposes. He sets himself against the co-opting of wisdom by scribes who wield a "lying pen" (*'ēṭ šeqer*, 8:8). The prevalence of falsity in Judah's public sphere is implied by repeated use of the word *šeqer*, "deception, delusion, falsehood," which appears thirty-seven times here, more frequently in Jeremiah than in any other book of the Bible.

Accordingly, the potential danger of this one prophet's unregulated words and performances is clear to Pashhur the priest, who, as chief official at the temple, organizes all major public ceremonies. He recognizes that Jeremiah threatens the state precisely in its assumed role as official interpreter of reality. Pashhur may be the first to mark him as a public enemy, when he puts him in stocks at the city gate (20:2), as punishment for dramatic performances such as the one Jeremiah enacted in the great Valley of Ben-Hinnom just outside the city walls. In this place where children were sacrificed as burnt offerings, supposedly for the defense of the city, the prophet had smashed a clay jug, announcing that this is how YHWH would smash the city itself (19:11). Jeremiah pitted divine words directly against the "counsel" of the opinion leaders: "And I shall empty out the counsel of Judah and Jerusalem in this place, and make them fall by the sword before their enemies, and by the hand of those who seek their lives. And I shall give their carcasses as food for the birds of the sky and the beasts of the land. And I shall make this city a desolation and an object of hissing; everyone who passes by will be appalled and hiss over all its [deadly] blows" (19:7–8). In his seditious prophetic imagination, awesome Jerusalem is already reduced to an object lesson; hissing is a prophylactic gesture, to ward off communication of its dreadful fate (cf. Lam. 2:15).

If propaganda is the manipulation of public opinion through words, images, symbols, and ceremonies that disguise more than they disclose, then this prophet is "the model antipropagandist" (Austin Dennis, oral communication). In the last analysis, to be a prophetic antipropagandist is to be an honest theologian. Jeremiah speaks of and for a God who is fully sovereign over history, summoning nations and armies against Judah (5:15–19; 6:1–9, 18–23, etc.), and at the same time is utterly involved in its sufferings. It is often difficult to distinguish the voices of Jeremiah and YHWH. Which of them, for instance, wishes for the capacity to weep and never stop (8:23 [9:1E])? Often it is assumed to be Jeremiah, yet a few verses later, the Hebrew text ascribes to God these words: "Over the mountains I take up weeping and wailing" (9:9 [10E]; for the mountains as a place of idolatrous worship, see 3:23). English translations often follow the ancient Greek version, modifying the divine first-person statement to an imperative, addressed to the Judeans: "Take up weeping." However, there is a strong case to be made for divine weeping, here and elsewhere (see also 9:17 [18E]), as one component of a complex response to treacherous behavior, indeed fierce attack by the people whom YHWH calls "my household, . . . my Heritage, . . . the love of my life" (12:7–8). God is no more immune to the pain of tortured love than is Jeremiah; neither has any emotional distance from the people whose infidelity and doom are so evident.

This paradoxical connection between Deity and people—seemingly indissoluble, yet often strained to the breaking point—means that (to use blunt language) it is in YHWH's self-interest to provide true religious teaching and thus open an avenue whereby at least a remnant of the people may return to their God. Here YHWH offers a reinterpretation of what it is to be a wise interpreter of divine Instruction:

> Thus says YHWH:
> Let not the wise person boast of wisdom, nor the powerful boast of
> power,
> nor the rich of riches.
> Rather in this let the boaster boast: understanding and knowing me,
> for I, YHWH, perform covenant-loyalty, justice, and righteousness in
> the land [or, on the earth]—for in these I delight.
> (9:22–23 [23–24E])

151

More than any other prophet, Jeremiah underscores the need for honesty and profound humility among "opinion leaders" in every time and place. A contemporary prayer seeking guidance "for those who influence public opinion" accords with Jeremiah's notion of the kind of leadership needed in the public sphere:

> Almighty God, you proclaim your truth in every age by many voices: Direct, in our time, we pray, those who speak where many listen and write what many read; that they may do their part in making the heart of this people wise, its mind sound, and its will righteous; to the honor of Jesus Christ our Lord. *Amen.* (*Book of Common Prayer,* 827)

This prayer could be offered *by* church leaders for (say) journalists and politicians, and equally *on behalf of* such "opinion leaders" as pastors, preachers, and teachers, who are entrusted with the responsibility of speaking and writing about who God is and what true faithfulness might entail.

Jeremiah's Laments: The Felt Reality of Loss

There are dimensions of God that are only released into the world through the witness of suffering.
—Peter J. Storey, personal communication,
Duke Divinity School, November 2, 2010

Idolatry, delusion in the things of God, leads inevitably to loss. This is the core message of Jeremiah, and his is overwhelmingly a book about loss. The essential dynamic of the book may be seen in light of Walter Brueggemann's observation that "the prophetic-pastoral task is to provide a script of imagination whereby folk can linger in our loss and then be done with the loss in order to move on" (*Practice,* 84). Yet the image of "lingering" is inadequate to describe Jeremiah's fierce energy. Rather, he grips us and forces us down with him into the hell of Jerusalem's impending and then realized doom. If we really hear him, Jeremiah makes us feel the reality of massive loss in all its dimensions.

His is the Joban voice among the prophets; poem after poem dwells on and in the totality of loss, even to the point of tedium—so that we ourselves feel the immobilizing grind of misery. The Joban poet might well be Jeremiah's near contemporary, working at the

152

same time and with the same theological concerns as the writers who compiled the book of Jeremiah, probably in the generation following the destruction in 586 BCE. The most specific point of similarity between the two traditions is that Jeremiah and Job both curse the day of their birth (Jer. 20:14–18; cf. 15:10; Job 3:1–26); they are the only two in the Bible to do so. It is not possible to say with certainty whether one poet depended on the other, or if they independently took up a theme already long established in the literary traditions of the ancient Near East (see Lundbom, *Jeremiah 1–20*, 869). In any case, these two books raise some of the darkest doubts voiced within the Bible about the suffering that inevitably comes to those who are "enticed" (!) into God's service (20:7). The first twenty chapters of Jeremiah are punctuated with strident laments such as these:

> Yes, you [God] know! O YHWH, remember me and take account of me!
>
> . . . .
>
> Know that it is on your account that I endure ridicule.
>
> . . . .
>
> I have not sat in the company of the rowdy, living it up;
> Because of your hand, I have sat alone. Yes, you have filled me with indignation.
> Why is my pain endless and my wound incurable, defying healing?
> Certainly you have been to me like a deceptive stream,
> waters that cannot be relied upon.
>
> (15:15, 17–18)

Jeremiah models the kind of frank speech to God that might be recognized as one mark of genuine prophetic utterance; thus it is instructive for all those who would serve God truly.

Telling what it is to be a prophet as Judah descends into hell, he disabuses us of the notion that if our ministry brings us agony, then we must have missed our vocation. Likewise, Jeremiah's laments and even accusations addressed to God strip us of a common pretext for idolatry; if we heed him, then we cannot in good faith claim that a God who has disappointed our most fervent hopes is on that account unworthy of worship.

The books of Jeremiah and Job would seem to have emerged 153 as part of Judah's agonizing process of coming to terms with collapse and exile. These two books stand together in the canon as the lengthiest and most thorough explorations of the winding path through the mixed landscape of suffering, endurance, and—erratically, eventually—hope, hope that lasts and does not disappoint. This is of course the path that Paul traces in the Letter to the Romans: "Suffering produces endurance, and endurance produces character, and character produces hope" (5:3–4). It is hard to imagine that the apostle could have written those words without having the characters of Jeremiah and Job as part of his own scriptural heritage.

Like Job, Jeremiah the antipropagandist is a searingly honest theologian and pray-er, never doubting that God is fully implicated as both the Source of his suffering and the Judge of his prophetic performance. Again like Job, Jeremiah is occasionally self-centered, intemperate, and inadequately informed about the character and ways of YHWH. One of the most instructive aspects of the deeply textured presentation of this prophet is that it shows how much he has to learn in order to bear true witness. In one self-revealing moment, Jeremiah accuses YHWH:

> You have surely deceived this people and Jerusalem,
> saying, "It shall be well [shalom] for you"—yet the sword touches
> [n-g-'] the throat!
>
> (Jer. 4:10)

However, YHWH's response, which includes a partial echo of Jeremiah's accusation, makes it abundantly clear that the nation has in fact deceived itself:

> Proclaim against Jerusalem:
> Watchers are coming from a land far away; they will lift their voice
> against the cities of Judah.
> Like keepers of fields they are all around her, for it is against me that
> she rebelled—an utterance of YHWH.
> Your ways and your deeds have done these things to you;
> this is your evil—how bitter! For it touches [n-g-'] your heart.
>
> (4:16–18)

The divine correction is essential from the standpoint of prophetic integrity. For a moment at least, it seems that Jeremiah has overempathized with the people whom he and God call bat-'ammî, "my daughter-people" (4:11). To the extent that he loses sight of their self-deception, and thus in a real sense the nation's self-destruction, he compromises his own vocation to represent God.

154

Jeremiah must learn to live in acute tension: feeling the excruciating pain of impending disaster, and at the same time acknowledging the justice of divine punishment for this beloved yet wayward people. For such learning, the practice of prophetic lament is crucial. Lament is not aimless whining, but rather a search for meaning and direction. It is the means by which Jeremiah comes to terms with what it is to be YHWH's prophet in this increasingly hopeless situation. Chris Rice and Emmanuel Katongole comment insightfully on the nature of lament:

> To lament is to see, stand in, describe, and tell the truthful story about the brokenness around us and in us. To lament is to learn to refuse to be consoled by easy explanations or false hopes. Lament is bringing our analysis into conversation with God and learning to pray with urgency. Lament is . . . a journey into seeing what God sees and feeling what God feels. ("Christian Vision," 8)

No prophet surpasses Jeremiah in giving direct and forceful expression to divine pathos, God's pain and indignation:

My guts, my guts, I writhe—the walls of my heart!
My heart pounds within me; I cannot be silent.
For the sound of the trumpet I hear, the blast of war.
Disaster follows after disaster—for the whole land is wrecked.
Suddenly my tents are wrecked—my fabric, in an instant.
How long shall I see the battle-standard, hear the sound of the
    trumpet?
For my people are foolish; they don't even know me!
They are witless children; they are not insightful.
They are skilled in doing evil, but they don't know how to do good.
(4:19–22)

This visceral cry might be attributed to Jeremiah, or even to (personified) Judah and Jerusalem, but there is good reason also to attribute it to YHWH, sandwiched as it is between two marked divine utterances (4:17–18, 22), with no explicit change of speaker. The ambiguity here and elsewhere is doubtless a deliberate effect, evoking what the poet Daniel Berrigan calls "a harmony of grief so subtle, measured, true" (*Jeremiah*, 108). Because it cannot be assigned with certainty to any one speaker, the cry signals that both Deity and prophet must live in the same anguished tension between the pull of love and the demands of justice.

155

Perhaps the most enduring theological significance of Jeremiah's laments is to sever decisively the link between suffering and personal sin. As Jeremiah himself recognizes, he suffers precisely because God relies on him (Jer. 15:15–17); for him as for Job, suffering is both a mark and a consequence of faithful service (20:8–9). Jeremiah's laments thus attest to his prophetic authority, constituted in part by his inability to turn away from either God or the people he loves, despite his bitter experiences with both. Paradoxically, the laments also qualify him to speak a word of hope to his people. Clustered in the first part of the book, they may be seen as preparing a foundation for the well-articulated vision of hope that emerges later, in the Book of Consolation (chaps. 30–33). The paradoxical yet essential relationship between lament and hope is illumined by J. Christiaan Beker:

> Whenever we divorce the experience of suffering from our projects of hope, *suffering* itself loses its inherent relation to hope and becomes instead a form of inactive, introverted, resigned, or despairing suffering.
> Conversely, whenever we divorce hope from suffering, *hope* disintegrates either into a wishful "Dreamsville" . . . or into an egocentric project of survival, a hope "fenced in" and "protected" from the reality of suffering in the world. (*Suffering and Hope*, 115)

Jeremiah's laments are indirect testimony that the hope he articulates is a genuine word from God, in contrast to the "lying vision and worthless divination" (Jer. 14:14; cf. 23:16, 25) of those who "prophesy" out of an egotistical imagination.

Laying Claim to Hope

In the monastic tradition, the highest form of sanctity is to live in hell and not lose heart. (Gregory Boyle, *Tattoos*, 86)

The prophetic trajectory in the Bible tends toward hope, the kind of difficult yet realistic hope that is born of a full reckoning with the dimensions of infidelity and disaster. This trajectory toward hope is evident in the framing of the canonical section designated Prophets. Likely it is more than coincidence that the whole corpus of writing prophets (Isaiah to Malachi) opens with lament over

156

alienation and ends with hope of reconciliation. The divine lament about YHWH's own rebellious children (Isa. 1:2) has its final positive counterpart in a divine vision of the hearts of parents and children brought together through adherence to "the Torah of Moses my servant" (Mal. 3:22–24 [4:4–6E]). Likewise, elements of hope emerge in most individual books of the Prophets. Uniquely in Jeremiah, however, the trajectory toward hope is evident from the outset. He is charged "to uproot and to tear down and to annihilate and to destroy, and to build and to plant" (Jer. 1:10). The four verbs of destruction would seem to govern the first twenty-eight chapters of the book, as Jeremiah works to dismantle the delusion that is widespread in Judah and Jerusalem. However, when those six verbs are reiterated in the Book of Consolation, the emphasis is decidedly on the final two: "And it shall be, just as I watched over them to uproot and to tear down and to destroy and to annihilate and to do harm, so I shall watch over them to build and to plant—an utterance of YHWH" (31:28; cf. 31:4–5). In this book, as in the prophetic canon as a whole, the long-term goal of prophecy is represented as the transformation and renewal of a people and a culture. Three elements in particular are central to Jeremiah's vision: *a genuine and healthy community*, built on the twin foundations of *a renewed and deepened faith* and *a sustainable local economy*, a land-based economy composed of small family farms. Each of those elements is interrelated and multidimensional, and all of them speak directly to the needs of church and society in our own time.

The worshiping community is a key concept in Jeremiah's vision. Speaking of Jacob/Israel, he says,

His children shall be as in the past,
and his community ['*ēdâ*] will be established before me.
(30:20)

The notion of community is overused in our society, perhaps especially by the advertising industry. In its parlance, one joins a "community" by buying a certain product or piece of real estate, always expensive and deliberately exclusive—that is, the community is gated, either literally or metaphorically. By contrast, the community that Jeremiah envisions is in its very essence a community of outcasts: "For 'Outcast' they named you: 'That Zion—no one cares about her!'" (30:17).

157

This new community is radically inclusive, certainly by ancient standards. In Jeremiah's God-given "dreams" about the restoration of Zion's people (31:26, perhaps evoking Ps. 126), most prominent among them are those who would normally be considered weak, or deprived of God's favor:

> And I will gather them from the far reaches of the earth—
> among them the blind and the lame,
> the pregnant together with the one in labor—
> [as] a large congregation they will come back here.
>
> (31:8)

Kathleen O'Connor comments perceptively on the connection with the gospel:

> For Christians, Jeremiah's new society evokes and anticipates Jesus' teachings about the poor and the lowly, his practices of welcoming and eating with tax collectors and sinners, of healing the sick and raising the dead. . . . Jeremiah tells the believing community who matters to God, who are the creative contributors to the future, who are the salt of the earth. These are the ones who anticipate Jesus' revelation of God in his own body, broken for us. (*Pain and Promise*, 155)

The fact that pregnant women and those in labor are conspicuously present among the returnees is also significant; these are "wounded survivors beginning life anew, broken yet fertile" (O'Connor, "Jeremiah's 'Prophetic Imagination,'" 68). In its emphasis on female generativity, the passage points to another poetic image, in 31:22b: "For YHWH has created a new thing on earth: a female surrounds a strongman" (or "a landowner," cf. Mic. 2:2).

This, Jeremiah's most enigmatic image, stands in its ambiguity, with no explication. The word "female" (*nĕqēbâ*), related to a verb meaning "pierce," might suggest both sexuality and vulnerability. Is it an image of the land itself (cf. 6:23), or of its women, or of the ancestor Rachel who lost her sons (cf. 31:15)—the female once stricken, now surrounding and protecting sons and sustaining them on their own soil? A comment of Cheryl Sanders may illumine both these images of female generativity in Jeremiah's vision of a revitalized community. She observes that "the process of transformation in which God engages us ends, not with our being reborn in the

Spirit, but rather with our *giving birth*, giving new life to others" (lecture, Duke Divinity School, May 28, 2013).

The community of returnees is dedicated to reenfranchisement. Those who are in the yoke of slavery will be cut loose, "and foreigners will never again enslave them, but they will serve YHWH their God, and David their king, whom I shall raise up for them" (30:8–9). A king from the house of David is an important part of Jeremiah's vision of restoration (cf. 23:3–6), just as Davidic kings— specifically those who succeeded to the throne after Josiah, whom the prophet greatly admired—were central to the nation's demise (22:22–23:2). Yet despite the considerable attention (positive and negative) he gives to kings, Jeremiah, like most biblical prophets, has no "secular" political vision; he ignores the ordinary functions of governance. His vision of kingship was likely inspired by the traditions that underlie the book of Deuteronomy; these seem to have come to prominence in Judah during the reign of Josiah, as reflected in the story of the discovery of "a scroll of the Teaching [*torah*] in the house of YHWH" (2 Kgs. 22:3–23:27). Like Deuteronomy, Jeremiah ascribes to the king no "secular" duties such as war making or empire building. Properly construed, the royal role is simply to provide religious leadership: the king studies Torah (Deut. 17:14–20) and "draws near" to God, presumably in sacrificial worship (Jer. 30:21). Thus through their sovereign the people may be restored to genuine relationship with God: "You shall be my people, and I—I will be your God" (30:22). This is a reiteration of what God promised Moses in Egypt (Exod. 6:7); Jeremiah here envisions a son of David who will be more like a new Moses, capable of restoring the covenantal relationship that seems to have broken down beyond repair.

Another evocation of the Mosaic covenant appears in the familiar and (for many Christians) most beloved image of covenantal renewal in the Bible:

> Look, days are coming—an utterance of YHWH—when I will make with the house of Israel and with the house of Judah a new covenant, not like the covenant that I made with their ancestors in the day I seized them by the hand to bring them out of the land of Egypt—my covenant which they violated, and yet I had been a husband/master to them!—an utterance of YHWH. For this is the covenant that I will make with the house of Israel afterward,

159

[in] those days—an utterance of YHWH: I will put my Teaching [Torah] within them and on their heart I will write it, and I will become their God, and they shall become my people. They shall no longer teach each other, one his neighbor and another his kin, saying "Know YHWH!" For all of them shall know me, from the littlest of them to the greatest of them—an utterance of YHWH—for I will forgive their iniquity, and their sin I will no longer remember. (Jer. 31:31–34)

Whether the passage comes from Jeremiah or a later hand has been much debated, although there is no reason to dismiss the possibility of Jeremianic authorship, most probably in the period immediately following the fall of Jerusalem (Lundbom, *Jeremiah Closer Up*, 26). Indeed, it is hard to imagine that such a radical theological statement is purely the creation of the Deuteronomists, who are widely supposed to have preserved Jeremiah's words and put them in book form some time after the prophet's death. One would imagine those traditionalists to have been more careful than to invent a statement that can too easily be read as questioning the adequacy of the Sinai covenant, which they themselves upheld so strongly.

A much more important matter than authorship is the theological significance of the passage, which has indeed been frequently and even tragically misunderstood. It has been common among Christians through the ages to see the passage as rendering the Sinai covenant obsolete, replacing it with a completely different covenant, in which Jews have chosen to have no part (Lundbom, *Jeremiah 21–36*, 479–82). This supersessionist view is flatly contradicted by the succeeding verses, in which God solemnly declares that if the divine ordering of the heavenly bodies should even be annulled, only then "would the seed of Israel cease to be a nation in my presence" (31:36).

It is also possible to misunderstand the passage by taking it too literally, so that the divine writing directly on the heart makes obedience unproblematic, in the sense that "the whole process of God's speaking and man's [*sic*] listening is to be dropped" and "the rendering of obedience is completely done away with" (von Rad, *Old Testament Theology*, 2:213). It is better to work with Jeremiah's statement as a poetic image, which evokes and reverses another of his images, namely that of Judah's sin "engraved with a diamond tip on the tablet of their heart" (17:1). He now sees God erasing

160

that tablet and rewriting it, with God's Teaching replacing sin as the marker of this people's identity. The point, then, is not that disobedience will be impossible, and therefore obedience deprived of any real meaning. On the contrary, willing, trustful obedience will become a genuine possibility, perhaps for the first time since Sinai.

In a careful treatment of this passage, Karl Barth speaks helpfully of the "freedom of obedience" (*Church Dogmatics,* IV/1:33). The logic bears a resemblance to that of the apostle Paul. We can become so alienated from God and ourselves that, unless God takes the initiative to annul our alienation, our acts of will are ineffectual: "I can will what is right, but I cannot do it" (Rom. 7:18 NRSV). God's gracious action negates "the unfaithfulness of Israel, but not the faithfulness of God Himself, nor His covenant will in relation to His people" (*Church Dogmatics,* IV/1:34).

Although Jews have generally considered that this promise is to be fulfilled only in the coming messianic age, they proleptically enact its realization. In many communities, the most exuberant celebration of the Jewish year is Simchat Torah, "the joy of Torah," when people dance through the night with Torah scrolls, just as Jeremiah dreamed for his people:

> They shall come and shout for joy on Zion's height,
> and glow about the goodness of YHWH:
> over the grain and over the new wine and over olive oil,
> and over the young of flocks and cattle.
> And they themselves shall be like a well-watered garden,
> and they shall be sickly no more.
> Then young women shall rejoice in the dance,
> and young men and old as well.
> And I will turn their mourning into gladness;
> I will comfort them and give them joy out of their sorrow.
> (31:12–13; cf. 30:19; 31:4)

A contemporary reading of Jeremiah's new covenant vision from East Africa shows how it speaks with startling relevance to a society that, like ancient Israel and Judah, is severely torn by both external war and violent animosities among tribes. Reading in the context of the Democratic Republic of Congo, Old Testament scholar Bungishabaku Katho makes the grammatical point that the "heart" (*lēb*) on which Torah is written is a singular noun with a plural pronominal suffix: "their heart." From this he concludes, "It will be a community matter, a corporate mind and heart. . . . The writing of the torah in the heart will create solidarity in the community" ("New Covenant," 116–17). In contrast to other passages in Jeremiah, where references to "neighbors" and "kinfolk" point to practices of deceit and hostility (9:3–5; 12:5–6; 34:15–16)—even YHWH has only "wicked neighbors" (12:14)!—Jeremiah 31:34 "talks about a learning community, a transformed community, a community that is willing to know the Lord's way together and to grow together" (117). For Katho, the prophetic vision challenges the prevalence of "ethnic Churches," in which tribal identity trumps Christian identity, but it also offers hope. His comment speaks forcefully not only to African Christians, but also to churches in the West, divided as they are along ethnic, economic, and ideological lines: "I understand the internalization of the torah in the community of the new covenant as the value principles that will structure the people's thought, guide their action, and form their world-view. . . . If we want change in our nations, we must let Biblical principles and values guide our thinking, our mentality and our action" (119).

Giving Hope a Place

Found your hope, then, on the ground under your feet. (Wendell Berry, *Leavings*, 93)

Taken by itself, the new covenant written on the heart might be seen as presenting a *utopian* vision of the future—a future that is literally "nowhere." So it is not incidental that following closely thereafter is a lengthy, detailed narrative (32:1–44) that gives the future a *topos*, an identifiable location and shape, and this constitutes the third element of Jeremiah's vision of renewal: a sustainable local economy composed of small landholders. That is the significance of the story (32:1–44) of Jeremiah's acquisition of a field in his village of Anathoth on behalf of his cousin Hanamel, who has evidently fallen into straits and been forced to sell off the family land, or some portion of it, as collateral for a debt. (Peasant farmers in the ancient world were subject to taxes that often amounted to a third of their income, or more, and severe debt encumbrance, even slavery, was therefore common.) The right and obligation to redeem the land and thus keep it within the family falls to Jeremiah, as the nearest

162

male relation, or perhaps as the next in line when others have refused. The year is "the tenth year of Zedekiah" (32:1), that is, 587 BCE, a year before the fall of Jerusalem; the second and final siege of the city is under way, and the surrounding countryside is under Babylonian control. Practically speaking, it is foolish to acquire a field a few miles to the north, the direction in which Nebuchadrez-zar's army is encamped, and especially since Jeremiah has received this word of YHWH: "I am about to give this city into the hand of the king of Babylon, and he will take it, and Zedekiah king of Judah will not escape from the hand of the Chaldeans" (32:3–4). For preaching that message, the prophet has been confined to the court of the guard, part of the palace compound, the site where he now contracts his foolish business of obedience to this new word of YHWH (v. 8).

So while in confinement, in the face of the invading army, and not without protesting to God (vv. 16–25), Jeremiah draws up a legal document, summons witnesses, weighs out the silver to acquire land that is worthless to him as an individual, and has the deed of purchase put in a sealed container (vv. 9–14). It is the most detailed biblical account of any legal transaction. Thus Jeremiah becomes a "redeemer" (*gōʾēl*), the legal term for one who restores arable land to the family unit that depends on it for survival. The action foreshadows what YHWH will in time do for the whole people (vv. 15, 42–44). If the term "redeemer" came to be a primary epithet for YHWH, likely first in the period of the exile (Isa. 41:14; 43:14; 44:6, etc.), that is because land redemption was understood to be a theologically significant action. From a biblical perspective, arable land—the most important element of the Israelite economy—is not simply a commodity, "real estate." There exists no clear bibli-cal or documentary evidence of the sale of land in Israel until 515 BCE, a generation after the exile (see Domeris, *Touching*, 132). Rather, arable land was held and parceled out by a clan or village or extended family as the resource base for sustainable life, genera-tion to generation. The Bible consistently represents arable land as an inalienable trust from God, a tangible sign of the covenant—in contrast to landless townhouses, which could be sold outright (see Lev. 25:30).

Jeremiah's redemption of family land is paradigmatic of Israel's redemption; in a concrete legal transaction, at the local level, he enacts the restoration that other prophets envision. The

163

redemption of land in chapter 32 is in a sense the answer to the traumatic vision of the land's decreation (4:23–26). Jeremiah, who has no children of his own, acts for the sake of the future, knowing that the children and grandchildren will surely pay for what this generation allows to be destroyed (32:18). Even as he protests the illogic of what God requires of him—when siege ramps have already been laid up against the walls of Jerusalem (32:24–25)— the prophet lays a personal claim to God's promise to "bring the seed of the house of Israel from the land to the north and from all the lands to which I banished them, and they will return to their own arable-land [*'ădāmâ*]" (23:8; cf. 32:37). In the final verses of the chapter, the most elevated religious rhetoric—"one heart and one way to fear me," "everlasting covenant" (32:39–40)—intermingles with the legal particulars of deeds and witnesses and silver (v. 44). As Daniel Berrigan observes, the one sheds light upon the other:

> In the understanding of Jeremiah (and of Yahweh as well), a modest sign goes far and deep into reality; it touches matters high and low, divine and human, the spiritual and the visible. . . . It is as though a divine husbandman were planting healing realities in minds blinded and polluted by the smoke of battle. A small slice of geography takes the guise and import of prophecy itself—a small relief in a viciously factitious world of pricings and sell-outs, of betrayals and treacheries, of greed and disregard! Cling to the field with all your might! (*Jeremiah*, 140)

This story of redemption in Anathoth gives the future a *topos*, a location, for Jeremiah's audience of sixth-century Judeans. But does a culturally specific vision of land redemption have any meaning for us—non-Israelites living in the twenty-first century, in many or most cases urbanites? The biblical notion of land as a trust from God, belonging to a community or to a family through generations rather than to an individual, runs contrary to notions of private property predominant in North America, at least. Nonetheless, this notion and Jeremiah's vivid account speak to issues that concern us directly, whether we know it or not. Jeremiah speaks about investing in the future through responsible care of land and systems of land tenure that keep arable land in the control of communities committed to caring for the land on which their lives depend—in Berry's terms, they "found [their] hope on the ground under [their] feet." Read in our own social and historical context, Jeremiah 32 speaks against the mounting danger of the so-called global land rush. Large-scale purchase or leasing of arable land by corporations and (often foreign) investors constitutes one of the greatest long-term threats to food security, adequate employment, and environmental sustainability worldwide, especially in Africa, Latin America, the former Soviet Union, and Southeast Asia. (A useful source of well-researched and readable publications on the issue of land grabbing versus land sovereignty is the Institute for Food and Development Policy, also known as Food First.)

North American corporations, as well as individuals, universities, and even churches, are widely invested in a system of land control and food production that depends upon scarcity to be "profitable." In a 2012 article on commodities investing, Steve Schaefer—writing for *Forbes*—advised readers to heed the counsel of "famed value investor Jeremy Grantham," who is now committing 30 percent of his portfolio to "resources," including forestry and farms. Grantham reasons that this is a wise strategy, since we are "about five years into a chronic global food crisis that is unlikely to fade for many decades, at least until the global population has considerably declined from its likely peak of over 9 billion in 2050"—that is, until some of those billions have starved to death. "So," Schaefer asks, "how can you profit from these trends?" and answers his own question with a list of "five appetizing choices," namely investment options in multinational industries producing tractors, meat, and chemical inputs for agriculture, as well as a market vectors firm. With chilling frankness, the original print article was titled "Hunger Games."

Land grabs by investors are possible and even attractive in poor regions because they exploit existing inequities of power and serve to consolidate power further. The positive challenge, Eric Holt-Giménez suggests, is to build community power through "a proactive strategy that advances alternative land and livelihood projects while building broad alliances that protect vulnerable communities from resource dispossession. It also requires community vigilance against the political, economic, and infrastructure changes that precede land grabbing. It requires a strategy for territorial land sovereignty" ("Land Grabs," 3). For all the social and economic differences between the twenty-first century and the sixth century BCE, that suggestion fits well with Jeremiah's vision of a nation

165

of healthy agrarian communities, exercising sovereignty over their own land, with just, indigenous leadership. I think of a young man in South Sudan saying to me just a few years ago: "For us, agriculture is the only alternative to war."

Artful Prophecy, Prophetic Art

> The hell of the artistic imagination, one might argue, is the only real point of departure to create today. (Fujimura, *Refractions*, 125)

Jeremiah is a prophet and poet of wartime, an artist whose verbal images—searing, poignant, shocking, hopeful—have entered into the core lexicon of our faith and even our common language: "Does the leopard change its spots?" (13:23); "The heart is perverse above all things" (17:9); the temple as "a den of thieves" (7:11); "Rachel weeping over her children . . . for they are not" (31:15). Moreover, Jeremiah's biography as shaped (presumably) by the Deuteronomists is itself a work of art; the narrative presentation makes him a persona, the most fully rendered character of all the prophets. Alone among them, he is fully *imaginable* to us. A key to seeing how Jeremiah speaks to our own time may lie in the idea that the prophet was an artist, whose war-torn life and work generated artful theological reflection in the form of this book. His words and experience of God are illumined by comparison with those of other artists of wartime and other forms of social chaos. Specifically, the book of Jeremiah may be illumined by contemporary artists who consciously work, as Jeremiah does, out of a clear sense that God has laid upon them the opportunity and responsibility to create through the descent into hell, and likewise out of its depth.

One Christian artist who frequently acknowledges his debt to the biblical prophets, especially Isaiah and Jeremiah, is Makoto Fujimura, an American master of Nihonga (traditional Japanese painting), an art form that begins with grinding mineral pigments by hand. In September 2001, his studio and his family's home were each within a few blocks of what would become, on the eleventh day of that month, ground zero of a terrorist attack on New York City. A few months before that event, he had written the following for a Santa Fe art exhibition called "Beauty without Regret":

166

Art cannot be divorced from faith. . . . Death spreads all over our lives and therefore faith must be given to see through the darkness, to see through the beauty of "the valley of the shadow of death."

Prayers are given, too, in the layers of broken, pulverized pigments. Beauty is in the brokenness, not in what we can conceive as the perfections, not in the "finished" images but in the incomplete gestures. Now, I await [*sic*] for my paintings to reveal themselves. Perhaps I will find myself rising through the ashes, through the beauty of such broken limitations. (*Refractions*, 12)

Three years later, on September 11, 2004, Fujimura wrote,

The power of art is to convey powerful personal experiences in distilled language and memorialize them in a cogent manner. . . . Art may be at times the only true memory we own in our experience of disintegration. Art may even point to a greater redemptive plan beyond "the life and death" of each of our melodies. . . . In the fallen realities of our days, God continues to affirm our creative responses to the darkened horizon, and by naming the indescribable, we may yet rediscover our hope to endure yet another dark day. (*Refractions*, 39)

Twice since writing this, Fujimura's life and art have been directly touched by new experiences of mass destruction: first the tsunami on March 11, 2011, in Japan, where he had studied and was formed as a young artist, and then Hurricane Sandy, which flooded his New York gallery and destroyed much of his work in 2012. He has responded to both disasters with series of images, "elegies" in painted form. He was working on the series dedicated to the victims of 3/11 in Japan when Hurricane Sandy hit and wiped out some fifty works; when he repainted the series, titled "Walking on Water," he wrote, "Thus, the process of painting [has] now become, literally, a way to 'walk on water'" (http://www.makotofujimura.com/works).

Having painted and written through so much large-scale destruction, Fujimura now describes his whole creative and intellectual project under the rubric of "culture care." Through his art, through his writing and speaking—some of it in church-related settings—and even (recently) through vegetable gardening, he works to counter the cosmetic notions of beauty that dominate our culture by emphasizing that the only source of beauty is divine love, which is often present to our world in the form of self-sacrifice. "Anytime we isolate beauty from truth and goodness, we may end up

167

with an idol. . . . [Christ] is the transformative presence in culture, because he created toward and through his love for us" ("Beauty in Culture").

Fujimura acknowledges that he is frequently drawn to read Jeremiah, especially its laments (personal communication, October 28, 2013); other readers of that biblical book may be helped by his lived understanding of how artistic responses to profound loss may lead, through prayer, toward beauty and hope. Certainly Fujimura's words about creating out of a truthful awareness of the presence of divine love and beauty in the midst of suffering complement the insight of biblical scholar Kathleen O'Connor about the particular form of literature that the book of Jeremiah is, namely, "a work of resilience, a survival manual, a literary anthology, and a work of theological art. It is not a factual history of events, as if that could be told. It is an emotion-soaked set of testimonies that plunge into overwhelming catastrophe and transform it, that the nation might not perish but be reborn as God's people" (*Pain and Promise*, 135). The God whom Jeremiah reveals is "blazing, angry, emotional, muted, weeping, furious, and always yearning for the beloved. Jeremiah's God desires love, gives love, brings new life, and reconceives the nation. . . . Jeremiah's God is the living God" (137)—and not an idol.

Among contemporary artists, the Jesuit priest Daniel Berrigan may give unique insight into the character of the prophet whose words and life have so profoundly shaped his own. Berrigan is a prolific poet, like Jeremiah, as well as a lyrical biblical commentator, but the stronger resemblance between them is that both are what we now call activists—subversives, from the perspective of the state. As a result, both have spent substantial time in prison and sometimes in hiding (see Jer. 20:2–3; 32:2; 33:1; 36:5, 19; 37:15–16; 38:6–13, 28). As with Jeremiah, Berrigan's life is itself a primary text, a form of his art. Starting in 1967 and continuing over more than twenty years, and in prayerful community with his brother Philip and other priests, seminarians, nuns, grandmothers, and other people of faith, he performed many acts of nonviolent civil disobedience, protesting the war in Vietnam, the proliferation of nuclear weapons, and U.S. policies and involvement in Central America.

168

As graphic enactments of a message, some of these public protests would rank with the sign acts of the biblical prophets: pouring their own blood on draft files and burning them with homemade napalm, to dramatize an alternative to soldiers burning children; pouring blood and hammering nuclear missile heads at the General Electric Weapons Plant in King of Prussia, Pennsylvania (1980). The latter action, which was paradigmatic of many others, became known as the "Plowshares Eight" action. Eight Christians, formed into a community of prophetic action through disciplined practices of Scripture study and prayer, used household hammers on nuclear missiles to enact Isaiah's and Micah's vision (Isa. 2:4; Mic. 4:3) of beating weapons into implements useful for the business of daily living. Of their core motivation, Berrigan wrote, in a 1982 Jesuit conference address, "We want to test the resurrection in our bones. To see if we might live in hope, instead of in the *silva oscura*, the thicket of cultural despair, nuclear despair, a world of perpetual war. We want to taste the resurrection. May I say we have not been disappointed" (*Testimony*, 225).

If we try to imagine how Jeremiah might have appeared in the eyes of his contemporaries, we might discover a close approximation in this tough, imaginative, eccentric (by the norms of our culture), and utterly convicted priest, a man well acquainted with Scripture and the "near despair called hope" (*Testimony*, 144).

Berrigan explains how this costly, shared commitment to nonviolence grew to be a point of orientation for a diverse community of Christians. He defines the nonviolent person (and by extension, the community) "in biblical terms," as "a prophetic nucleus of political movement . . . , the person who believes that history has a future" (*Essential*, 64). He recounts how this particular prophetic community and the political movement it generated arose out of a rereading of both history and Scripture: "We were talking about the meaning of nonviolence in history and the relevance of the Sermon on the Mount. We tried to be real about the real state of humanity with regard to violence and then to suggest the hope that underlies a history of violence in a prophetic movement which does not declare this history is final, or is fully human" (60–61).

The nonfinality of "this history," the fact that all human arrangements are radically contingent on the will of God—this is what Jeremiah declared to Judah's kings and religious leaders, when he announced that because they had failed to listen to God, the palace, the temple, the people, and the whole land would be brought to ruin (Jer. 7:13–14, 33–34; 22:5). In words that especially evoke

169

the thought-world of Jeremiah, Berrigan identifies the nonviolent person as the one who "can save normal times from their idolatries—neglect of the poor, growing bourgeois selfishness, weapons of war," and further, as one who "sees life in terms of a choice toward change" (*Essential*, 64).

Berrigan's address to the jury at the 1981 Plowshares Eight trial articulates a sense of inevitability, indeed of coercion, that recalls Jeremiah's laments about his own experience of God's relentless demand:

> The statement we would like to present to you is this.
> We could not *not* do this. We could not not do this! We were pushed to this by all our lives. . . .
> When I say I could not [not] do this, I mean, among other things that with every cowardly bone in my body I wished I hadn't had to enter the GE plant. I wish I hadn't had to do it. And that has been true every time I have been arrested, all those years. My stomach turns over. I feel sick. I feel afraid. I don't want to go through this again.
> I hate jail. I don't do well there physically. But I cannot not go on, because I have learned that we must not kill if we are Christians. . . . And I am supposed to be a disciple. . . .
> So at some point your cowardly bones get moving, and you say, "Here it goes again," and you do it. And you have a certain peace because you did it, as I do this morning in speaking with you. (189)

In 1999, Berrigan reflected on twenty-five years of writing on the Hebrew Bible, including the Major and Minor Prophets. In contrast to his experience of being "pursued by a demon or a fireball," he notes a species of biblical commentators who are "cautious taxidermists and diggers . . . Safe, sure, and ultimately deadly, the motto of their efforts went something like: 'The text is the text is the text.' . . . This brand of exegesis allowed for no point of contact or contrast" (*Testimony*, 33). Berrigan's own motto, expressed in a poetic line, is telling of his personal history, and of Jeremiah's as well: "Bodies belong where words lead" (32).

Among contemporary visual artists, printmaker Nikos Stavroulakis may be the one who has opened up the spirit and meaning of Jeremiah most fully. Although he has illustrated many characters and scenes and sayings (proverbs) in the Hebrew Scriptures,

170

Stavroulakis has given particular and sustained attention to Jeremiah. A series of thirty-one woodcuts were published in 1973, accompanying a new translation, the New Jewish Publication Society version. The sharp, strong, even harsh lines of woodcut make it an ideal medium for imaging Jeremiah. Jeremiah's call scene is far from sublime; the prophet crouches before the city walls, under the glaring sun, his head wrenched at an impossible angle, as a claw-like hand reaches toward him: "Herewith I put My words into your mouth" (Jer. 1:9 NJPS, 1985).

The images are dense, complex, and fragmented, like the book of Jeremiah itself; in the whole series of prints, there is only one unbroken expanse: the vast lightless sky that stretches over an indecipherable landscape, to illustrate Jeremiah's vision of the undoing of creation (4:23–28). Images such as these cannot be taken in at a glance; we are forced to enter into the confusion that is itself the experience the book conveys. Arms and hands, disembodied faces, leg and foot are jumbled together, with wings and beaks hovering above—and again, the glaring sun: "The carcasses of this people shall be food for the birds of the sky and the beasts of the earth, with none to frighten them off" (7:33 NJPS, 1985). One image depicts people worshiping in a densely patterned space, with palm branches, faces, and hands uplifted—and gradually the eye traces out a horned calf standing on an altar. "All the remnant of Judah who came to the land of Egypt to sojourn there shall learn whose word will be fulfilled—Mine or theirs!" (44:28 NJPS, 1985).

Not every image is literal: serpents are huge coils, besieging the walls of Jerusalem: "Lo, I will send serpents against you" (8:17 NJPS, 1985); their tongues rise like flames, and the city is burning—a common theme in this series.

A Jew born to a Cretan father and a Turkish mother, educated in American Catholic schools and university, Stavroulakis is also a cultural and political historian who has written about the destruction of cities and peoples in modern Europe, from the Holocaust to Sarajevo; his woodcuts make such destruction graphic. When Jeremiah redeems the field in Anathoth, he does it against the background of Jerusalem in flames, their light making visible the bodies scattered on the ground: "And the Chaldeans who have been attacking this city shall come and set this city on fire and burn it down" (32:29 NJPS, 1985). Jeremiah, who looks younger and more vulnerable than we might imagine him, clutches his head in horror.

171

In the final image, an unidentifiable man—any "of the common citizens who were inside the city" (52:25) at the time when it was taken—is being pelted with stones; he topples backward, holding up his hands to protect his face, in vain. The series of images, like the book of Jeremiah itself, stops suddenly, with no resolution. Stavroulakis allows his series to end in the manner of so many events of war, whether among nations or tribes or street gangs, with yet another violent death. The reader of his images, of Jeremiah's text, and of the daily news is left suspended in the midst of history, repeating (consciously or not) the wish or the prayer of Jeremiah:

If only my head were water and my eyes a font of tears,
so I could weep day and night for the slain of my daughter-people.
(Jer. 8:23 [9:1E])

Works Cited in Chapter 6

Barth, Karl. *Church Dogmatics.* Peabody, MA: Hendrickson, 2010.

Beker, J. Christiaan. *Suffering and Hope: The Biblical Vision and the Human Predicament.* Grand Rapids: Eerdmans, 1994.

Berrigan, Daniel. *Daniel Berrigan: Essential Writings.* Selected by John Dear. Maryknoll, NY: Orbis, 2009.

———. *Jeremiah: The World, the Wound of God.* Minneapolis: Fortress Press, 1999.

———. *Testimony: The Word Made Fresh.* Maryknoll, NY: Orbis, 2004.

Berry, Wendell. *Leavings.* Berkeley, CA: Counterpoint, 2010.

The Book of Common Prayer . . . according to the use of The Episcopal Church. New York: Church Hymnal Corporation, 1979.

Boyle, Gregory. *Tattoos on the Heart: The Power of Endless Compassion.* New York: Free Press, 2010.

Brueggemann, Walter. *The Practice of Prophetic Imagination: Preaching an Emancipating Word.* Minneapolis: Fortress Press, 2012.

Domeris, William Robert. *Touching the Heart of God: The Social Construction of Poverty among Biblical Peasants.* New York: T & T Clark, 2007.

Fujimura, Makoto. "Beauty in Culture." Video of a talk by Makoto Fujimura, available at Q: Ideas for the Common Good. http://www.qideas.org/video/beauty-in-culture.aspx.

———. Makoto Fujimura Web page. http://www.makotofujimura.com/works/.

———. *Refractions: A Journey of Faith, Art, and Culture.* Colorado Springs: NavPress, 2009.

Holt-Giménez, Eric. "Land Grabs Versus Land Sovereignty." *Foodfirst Backgrounder* 18:4 (Winter 2012–13): 1–3.

Institute for Food and Development Policy (Food First). http://www.foodfirst.org.

Katho, Bungishabaku. "The New Covenant and the Challenge of Building a New and Transformed Community in DR Congo: A Contextual Reading of Jeremiah 31:31–34." *Old Testament Essays* 18:1 (2005): 109–23.

Lundbom, Jack R. *Jeremiah Closer Up: The Prophet and the Book.* Hebrew Bible Monographs 31. Sheffield: Phoenix Press, 2010.

———. *Jeremiah 1–20.* Anchor Bible 21A. New York: Doubleday, 1999.

———. *Jeremiah 21–36.* Anchor Bible 21B. New York: Doubleday, 2004.

O'Connor, Kathleen M. *Jeremiah: Pain and Promise.* Minneapolis: Fortress Press, 2011.

———. "Jeremiah's 'Prophetic Imagination': Pastoral Intervention for a Shattered World." In *Shaking Heaven and Earth*, edited by Christine Roy Yoder et al. Louisville, KY: Westminster John Knox Press, 2005.

Rad, Gerhard von. *Old Testament Theology.* 2 vols. New York: Harper & Row, 1965.

Rice, Chris, and Emmanuel Katongole. "A Christian Vision of Reconciliation." *Divinity* (Duke University), Spring 2012.

Schaefer, Steve. "How to Make Money Off the Drought: Fertilizers and Food." *Forbes,* September 10, 2012. Online: http://www.forbes.com/sites/steveschaefer/2012/08/22/how-to-make-money-off-the-drought-fertilizers-and-food/.

Stavroulakis, Nikos. *The Book of Jeremiah: A New Translation.* Philadelphia: Jewish Publication Society, 1973.

Stulman, Louis, and Hyun Chul Paul Kim. *You Are My People: An Introduction to Prophetic Literature.* Nashville: Abingdon Press, 2010.

Vincent, Janet. "The Worst of Times: Sharing Faith through Tragedy." *Virginia Seminary Journal,* Fall 2012.

CHAPTER 7

The Difficulties of Revelation

Prophecy as Risk, Challenge, and Gift

> *Nine-tenths of wisdom lies in listening;*
> *It almost matters more than what you see.*
> *The other tenth is knowing when to sing*
> *The truth, all-daring, pure audacity.*
> —Wilmer Mills, *Audare/Audire*;
> unpublished

> *In the twenty-first century, prophetic imagination concerns redeciding about images that generate attitude, conduct, and policy. In all such circumstances, it is redeciding about life or death.*
> —Walter Brueggemann, *Practice*, 43

Many North American Christians take a paradoxical attitude toward prophecy. In the so-called mainstream churches, probably most would regard with suspicion any notion that the prophetic spirit is abroad and active in the church—that is, that prophecy does not belong exclusively (and safely) within the covers of the Bible. Yet at the same time, the descriptor "prophetic" is now widely applied (and by some of those same people) to any person or statement or movement judged to be promising and "progressive," whether or not any explicitly religious dimension is present. If contemporary Christians are lax or confused about what might constitute a genuinely prophetic disclosure, in this we may not differ entirely from the cultures that the biblical writers address and represent: ancient Israel and the Greco-Roman world. Indeed, both Testaments acknowledge that reliance on the spirit of prophecy to know the will or action of   175

God is inherently risky, if also necessary. From a biblical perspective, prophetic activity is often, perhaps invariably, attended by uncertainty and disagreement (some of it violent) about the genuineness of any words or actions purported to be from God.

As the Bible consistently represents it, prophetic disclosure entails uncertainty for both the prophet and the audience, in several respects:

1. Genuine prophecy—the revealed word or the commanded action—is given, not produced (although Paul does urge the Corinthians to strive for that gift; 1 Cor. 14:1). It is contingent upon the inbreaking of God's spirit, experienced in the social order. The prophetic word is a "happening," as the formulaic Hebrew phrasing suggests: "And the word of YHWH was [or 'happened'] to Elijah the Tishbite" (1 Kgs. 21:17, 28; cf. Jer. 1:11; 33:19, 23; Ezek. 1:3; Jonah 1:1; 3:1; etc.)

2. Prophecy is not philosophy; it deals for the most part with neither eternal verities nor strict logic—although the prophetic message may endure for ages, and prophetic thinking is not illogical. Rather, prophecy deals chiefly with the contingent, the historical, with socially conditioned events in the life of nations, a people, a congregation. The prophet's primary role is to interpret a given moment or movement in history, and, guided by the spirit of God, to point to where current human practices are heading. The "news" the biblical prophet brings is often of a kind that is bound to be resisted by those in power and perhaps by the majority of the people, and the truth of the revelation may be neither immediately self-evident nor verifiable in the near term.

3. The prophetic event is contingent upon the agency of a human person who can serve as a clear channel for such inbreaking. Some biblical accounts (Elijah, Jeremiah, Jonah) indicate that the true prophet must learn to be such a channel. Moreover, in many cases, the calling to prophesy publicly seems to be occasional, not lifelong. Prophets with a long history of public recognition (e.g., Isaiah, Jeremiah) may be the exception rather than the rule. So the reliability of prophets and their performances must regularly be assessed anew. As we shall see in this chapter, even a prophet sent by God may be mistaken, at least for a time, about the truth that comes from God. Therefore the person so charged and likewise the audience for whose benefit the divine disclosure is given must also engage not only in *envisioning* but also in constant *critical*

176

evaluation. As the poet Wilmer Mills suggests, perhaps "nine-tenths" of both activities is based more on listening than speaking. The disciplined work of envisioning and evaluating entails the virtues of trust in God and courage (traditionally known as "fortitude"), both to speak and to accept a given revelation as from God, even though no objective proof exists.

These several elements of uncertainty mean that a prophetically oriented faith such as Israel's must continually contend with the difficulty of knowing what God has revealed. In our multifaith culture, it is important to recognize that this biblical view of prophecy contrasts starkly with that of Islam, which regards the Qur'an as a wholly reliable, direct, and complete communication of the divine will and word, given through the final prophet, Muhammad. Moreover, the Qur'an and Islam affirm that every true prophet before Muhammad, including Noah, Abraham, Moses, David, Job, and Jonah, as well as Jesus, was morally impeccable, a perfect servant of God and thus a clear channel for divine revelation. (The final chapter of this volume treats this and other points of connection and difference between Christianity and Islam as two faiths grounded, directly or indirectly, in the prophetic traditions of the Bible.)

The biblical writers are alert to these various forms of difficulty and give them searching treatment within the prophetic corpus itself. Most notable in this respect is the Deuteronomistic Historian, master craftsman of the prophetically focused account of Israel and Judah found in Joshua through Kings. That extended narrative, which incorporates a number of older stories and story cycles, serves an important function within the biblical canon, even if its role as a distinctly *prophetic* narrative is obscured for most Christian readers. Known in Jewish tradition as Former Prophets, the narrative complex immediately follows Torah in the Jewish Bible. The first of two large sections of the prophetic corpus, Former Prophets prepares the way for reading with deeper comprehension the Latter Prophets (Isaiah through Malachi). However, in the Christian ordering of the canon these two sections are separated by nine or ten books (Chronicles through the Song of Songs); thus the thematic and theological connections between them are less evident.

We may also note a significant literary contrast between the two sections: Former Prophets is composed primarily of narrative texts, and Latter Prophets primarily of poetic texts. In this there is a

177

similarity to the literary form of Torah, where the highly developed narratives of Genesis and Exodus 1–19 precede the more lapidary forms of the commandments and instructions, which dominate the rest of Torah. In both Torah and Prophets the effect of this ordering of two different genres is the same: narrative latitude allows our thinking to develop around key themes before we encounter them again through literary forms (poetry or "legal" material) that are terse and often highly ambiguous. Narrative provides the verbal space and the carefully articulated contexts that enable us to reckon with theological difficulty and thus mature as theological thinkers. To reapply the terms of the apostle Paul, biblical narrative may be the "milk" that precedes the "meat" of less accommodating literary forms (cf. 1 Cor. 3:2).

The focus of this chapter is on the milk. It begins with studies of three lengthy prophetic stories from the Deuteronomistic History. Perhaps all of them were adapted from earlier sources, and the Historian has given them prominence in its extended account of prophets and kings. In this context, the several stories show prophets engaging with the government-religious-military establishment in mutual support or in hostile confrontation, and also prophets encountering other prophets, often in contests over the truth of the word spoken. The common theme of these carefully crafted narratives is the difficulty of knowing where the power and will of God may be pointing in any given situation. In each, the uncertainty of divine revelation is experienced by parties in very different social locations and also with different relations to YHWH: the lone man of God, far from home, who confronts Jeroboam I with a divine decree at Bethel (1 Kgs. 13); the king, abetted by 400 prophets, who reluctantly summons the rogue prophet Micaiah son of Imlah (1 Kgs. 22); and everyone in 2 Kings 6 except Elisha, that is, those who do not see what the prophet sees: the king, the prophetic protégé, and the Aramean enemy force.

The final text treated here is Paul's First Letter to the Corinthians—not a narrative but nonetheless a vivid account of early Christian life in community; Margaret Mitchell describes the Corinthian correspondence as "a kind of epistolary novel" (*Paul, the Corinthians*, 6). It is addressed to and depicts a community in which the prophetic spirit is very much abroad; Paul is seeking to help these new Christians to live in the gospel truth, by the difficult blessing of prophetic charism.

178

The Risk and Cost of Truth (1 Kings 13)

In a world in which falsehood is powerful, the truth is paid for with suffering. (Pope Benedict XVI, Homily at the First Vespers of the Feast of Saints Peter and Paul, Rome, 2008)

Certainly one of the most disconcerting stories in the Bible is the tale of the nameless man of God from Judah who comes to Bethel "by the word of YHWH" (1 Kgs. 13:2), there to utter a decree of doom against the great sacrificial altar. For the Deuteronomistic Historian, Jeroboam's founding of the Bethel cult ten miles north of Jerusalem was an invention "out of his own heart" (1 Kgs. 12:33), with no religious legitimacy. Its sole purpose was political: drawing Israelites away from worship at the temple (12:26–30). Thus Bethel epitomizes the apostasy of the northern kingdom, and the "portent" brought about by the man of God—the cracked altar and the spilt ashes of sacrifice (13:3, 5)—signals its demise. Jeroboam himself is presiding over the sacrifice as this disaster unfolds; he stretches out his hand to have the man seized, and it instantly withers. The man of God prays for him, and the hand is restored. Desiring to secure the cooperation of this powerful wonder-worker, the king invites the man of God to dine with him, but he staunchly refuses: "If you gave me half your house I would not come with you and I would not eat bread and not drink water in this place, for so he commanded me by the word of YHWH" (13:8–9). Rejecting food and water is the prophetic sign that supports YHWH's rejection of "this place."

The public confrontation with the king sets the stage for the real drama, which subsequently unfolds between the man of God from Judah and "a certain old prophet living in Bethel" (13:11). On his own initiative, the old man pursues the man of God as he begins to make his way home; he literally turns the (presumably) younger prophet around on the road with a purported oracle:

I too am a prophet, like you, and an angel spoke to me by the word of YHWH, "Bring him back with you to your house, so that he may eat bread and drink water." He deceived him. And he went back with him and ate bread in his house and drank water. And it happened while they were sitting at the table: the word of YHWH came to the prophet who had brought him back . . . , "Because you rebelled against the mouth of YHWH and did not keep the commandment that YHWH your God commanded you

179

> . . . , your corpse will not come to the grave of your ancestors."
> (13:18–23)

One prophet deceives another, presumably with the hope that if the Judean's sign act of refusing food and drink in Bethel is reversed, then his proclamation of doom may be annulled. The less experienced prophet accepts as new revelation the report from his elder of what an angel supposedly said. The man of God will shortly die for his gullibility, but even while they are still seated at the table, his role as the reliable channel for the divine disclosure passes to the other. On his second departure from Bethel, "a lion found him on the road and killed him, and his corpse was cast aside on the road" (13:24). The death of the man of God is not an attack but an execution; the lion does not eat him but rather guards the corpse and the riderless donkey. Travelers bring word of this remarkable tableau—another divinely orchestrated sign—and once again the old prophet comes after the man of God and brings him back to Bethel, this time to lay him in his own grave. The man of God is eliminated, yet also honored in his death and beyond.

Three centuries later, King Josiah of Judah, the great religious reformer in the Deuteronomistic tradition, comes to Bethel to destroy the shrine, unwittingly accomplishing what was decreed long before by the nameless man of God from Judah. Afterward, seeing the carefully marked grave of the two prophets and hearing their story, he leaves their bones in peace—although bones from all the other graves are burned on the altar to defile it (2 Kgs. 23:15–18).

It is possible, though unsatisfactory, to read the story as a simple moral tale, with a single clear message. So, for instance, Simon DeVries says that here Scripture offers "the clearest test" of true prophetic disclosure: radical obedience. Thus he draws a possible inference for contemporary ministry: "The preacher-prophet must be so committed to the transcendent truth of what he proclaims that his very own life is affected by it" (*1 Kings*, 174). Yet this is a surprisingly flat lesson to draw from a story that leaves us with large unanswered questions: Does the old prophet consciously lie to the man of God? Is he a false prophet, "the mere professional" who serves the interests of the king rather than God (Barth, *Church Dogmatics*, II/2:402)? Or is he acting out of what he takes to be a God-given chance to turn around the oracle of doom and save his city? Why does God not send a lion after the old deceiver before he reaches the man of God, or at least send him on the wrong road? And why does God use him to undeceive the man of God only *after* the latter has committed an apparently unforgivable violation? Why is there no redemption for the faithful servant who errs in innocence?

A story that leaves so much to the reader's moral imagination should not be reduced to a truism. A reading such as DeVries's may reflect the common view that the Deuteronomistic Historian is a doctrinaire theologian with a straightforward (i.e., unimaginative) understanding of sin begetting direct retribution. However, that judgment is belied by the prominence of such a carefully wrought yet untamable story within the History, where it is set as a frame around almost the entire account of the divided monarchy. Thus it serves as an introduction to the (mostly) disastrous history of kings and prophets, including the independent men of God who often stood against them, and it raises questions about God's ways with prophets that are not easily, if ever, resolved. Karl Barth is surely right when he observes, "'Perplexity' is much too weak a word for the authors and editors of texts like these" (*Church Dogmatics*, II/2:393).

It is better to read this disconcerting story with a view to what it may reveal about the unique difficulty of the prophetic vocation and prophetic faith altogether, as the Bible sets it forth. I suggest five nonexclusive lines of interpretation, which certainly do not exhaust the possibilities for this passage:

1. *It asserts the reliability, the persistence, and ultimately the irresistibility of the word of God.* This may be the best way of understanding the structural role that the story in both its parts plays within the Deuteronomistic History. Positioned as a framing structure around the history of the divided monarchy, this is the most prominent of numerous instances of a literary and theological pattern that runs throughout Former Prophets and especially 1–2 Kings, in which an event is designated as the fulfillment of a previously cited prophetic word (cf. 1 Kgs. 14:10–13 and 17–18; Josh. 6:26 and 1 Kgs. 16:34; 1 Kgs. 17:13–14 and 15–16; 21:19 and 22:38, etc.). Uriel Simon comments perceptively, "From beginning to end the story dwells on a single theme—the fulfillment of the word of the Lord in its appointed time, after it transcends the weakness of its bearer and converts into affirmers those who would violate it. 'In its appointed time,' because its fulfillment, after the lapse of the

three centuries that separate Jeroboam from Josiah, is presented as added proof of its power" (*Reading*, 154).

2. *It confirms that the call to prophetic witness entails a burden, a responsibility, and a judgment that cannot be escaped.* The castigations of false prophets within the prophetic corpus are numerous and harsh (e.g., Jer. 23:9–40; Ezek. 13:1–23; Zech. 13:2–9), but even a true prophet such as Jeremiah is called more than once on the carpet before the divine throne:

> Do not break down because of them, lest I break you down before them. (Jer. 1:17)

> If you have run with foot-racers and they have worn you out, how will you do in the heat with horses? (12:5)

> If you come back to me, I shall take you back, and before me you will stand.
> If you sort out the precious from the worthless, you shall be as my mouth. (15:19)

Chastening is a mode of judgment, and the prophet stands under the judgment proclaimed. Yet Jeremiah has second and third chances, over a ministry that extends for decades. By contrast, the man of God is given only this one lost chance. With tragic irony, he is himself the first victim of the judgment he speaks— not Jeroboam or the priests of Bethel, all of whom the Historian regards as idolaters.

That the guilt of the man of God consists of no more than a single error in judgment (see point 4 below) is irrelevant to his immediate fate: "his subjective innocence is of no account when balanced against the objective damage caused when the sign is breached by the one who bore it" (Simon, *Reading*, 142). This story, unlike the Jeremiah tradition, gives no heed to the prophet's moral stature, subjective experience, and personal relationship with God. If the story has a protagonist, even a "hero," it is the word of God (cf. *Reading*, 136).

3. *It points to the suffering of the true prophet.* This is the first instance within the prophetic corpus of something that will become evident especially in the stories and poetry of Elijah, Jeremiah, and Second Isaiah, namely, the high, sometimes terrible cost the prophet pays as a witness to the truth. The man of God from Judah

182

bears a distant resemblance to the archetypal prophet Moses of the Priestly tradition, who is condemned to death outside the promised land of Canaan because at the waters of Meribah he failed to "trust in [YHWH] in order to manifest [YHWH's] holiness in the eyes of the Israelites" (Num. 20:12).

Yet as with Moses, the failure of the man of God, though personally disastrous, does not undo the truth of his witness. On the contrary, his death for the sake of clarifying and validating the word of YHWH is part of his witness, which in his life and beyond his death speaks with power to at least five identifiable audiences:

Jeroboam.

The deceiving prophet, who is apparently "converted" by the manner of his death and chooses to be fully identified with him in his own death.

The people of Bethel, who some 300 years later still remember the story of his true prophecy against the altar of Jeroboam.

Josiah, who leaves undisturbed the bones of the two prophets.

Later readers of the story, who through it come to an understanding of the suffering prophet whose witness remains true even after his ignominious death. These later readers might include the Isaianic poet of the Fourth Servant Song (Isa. 52:13–53:12), the New Testament writers struggling to understand the truth of the crucified Jesus' witness, and ourselves.

4. *It illumines the difficulty of knowing when God might have spoken a new word that challenges what we thought we knew.* The man of God accepted as new revelation the reported message from the angel calling him back to Bethel to accept hospitality there, and he proved to be wrong. Yet the prophetic corpus attests to the phenomenon of change or difference in divine messages, even with respect to what is at issue here, namely, making peace with enemies. Nahum inveighed against Nineveh and foretold its destruction, but then the serious fantasy that is the book of Jonah portrays a prophet unwillingly bringing that great city in its entirety to repentance—and thus proving to be the most successful prophet in Israel's history. Jeremiah writes to the exiles to seek the *shalom* of Babylon (Jer. 29:1–14), and then the book culminates with graphic, triumphal visions of its demise (Jer. 50–51). In a different kind of

183

life-and-death matter, which nonetheless bears some relation to the situation here, Abraham, the very first person designated a prophet (Gen. 20:7), receives conflicting divine commands: first to offer up Isaac, and then to put down the knife (Gen. 22). Everything depends on his recognizing that the word from God has changed.

So this is the question that the man of God must answer for himself—on the spur of the moment, on the run from the city (1 Kgs. 13:14) he has just damned, suddenly confronted with a different, purportedly divine message conveyed by a senior colleague: Could anything good come from Bethel? Was the threat against the altar perhaps a provisional truth, a dire warning that nonetheless might leave open the possibility of godly fellowship with this man? Barth observes that "he shows the abyss on whose edge . . . every man of God and every genuine prophet walks" (*Church Dogmatics*, II/2:399). Indeed, all those who try to order their lives by the word of God as we encounter it in Scripture walk at times at the edge of the abyss, knowing that God can speak a new word that overturns what we had previously understood, that God can call us into fellowship with those whose company we had previously feared (perhaps for good reason) would take us away from God. We take a risk whenever we say, "Yes, this is that moment; a new word, a new way has been revealed"—and yet sometimes we must take that risk, knowing we may be wrong.

5. *It shows the dynamism of the prophetic disclosure and thus challenges any simple dichotomy between true and false prophets.* The drama of the story lies in the surprising fact that the two prophets switch roles: the truth-teller is deceived, and the deceiver suddenly becomes a channel for truth, even in the midst of the fellowship meal that is itself the result of deception. The switch is not morally justified by gradual deterioration of character in the one or strengthening of character in the other. It simply happens, leaving us with the suspicion that the categories of true and false prophets may be much more porous than we are inclined to think: "All of us will always have something of the false prophet in us, wherefore we ought to speak humbly. We will mistake our own dreams for the word of God" (Niebuhr, *Beyond Tragedy*, 109). Both the fatal error of the man of God and the sudden change in the old prophet point to the need for modesty in religious disagreement, for recognizing that on both sides of the argument we may yet be surprised by God.

184

Prophetic Irony (1 Kings 22:1–38)

Following upon 1 Kings 13, this story represents a second public challenge to the king. In the first account, the central confrontation was between two prophets; King Jeroboam was a secondary figure. In 1 Kings 22 the primary antagonists are an otherwise unknown prophet, Micaiah son of Imlah, and the king. The 400 other prophets are the secondary "character," portrayed as a single group of yes-men for the king of Israel, who is named only once, as Ahab (22:20). The original identity of the king is debated; many scholars suggest that the Deuteronomistic Historian incorporated a once-independent account into the group of stories about prophetic challenges to Ahab, whom he represents as the epitome of royal opposition to the word of YHWH. (For a summary of the arguments for and against the historicity of the account within the Ahab cycle, see Sweeney, *I and II Kings*, 255–58.)

The two stories of prophetic challenge highlight different aspects of the king's authority. First Kings 13 portrays Jeroboam as head of the cult, who manipulates it for his own political purposes (1 Kgs. 12:26–33). By contrast, 1 Kings 22 treats the king's role as chief of the armed forces of Israel, and the central issue is one of perennial relevance up to our own day: the right of the head of state to declare a war that is not primarily defensive. Here the king seeks to provoke war after several years of nonaggression between the rival states of Aram (Syria) and Israel:

> And they "sat" for three years; there was no war between Aram and Israel. But in the third year Jehoshaphat king of Judah went down to the king of Israel. And the king of Israel said to his servant, "Do you realize that Ramoth-Gilead is ours—yet we are keeping still rather than taking it from the hand of the king of Aram?!" And he said to Jehoshaphat, "Will you come with me to war at Ramoth-Gilead?" And Jehoshaphat said to the king of Israel, "It is with me as with you, with my people as with your people, with my horses as with your horses." (22:1–4)

At Jehoshaphat's behest, prophetic counsel is sought. This is standard ancient Near Eastern practice in anticipation of battle, but now the king of Israel goes all the way, assembling all 400 of his prophets—except for one. Yet Jehoshaphat is not quite satisfied with their unanimous declaration: "Go up, so the Lord may give

[Ramoth-Gilead] into the hand of the king!" (22:6; cf. v. 12). So at his urging, the king of Israel reluctantly summons Micaiah son of Imlah to give an oracle.

In contrast to 1 Kings 13, the drama that now unfolds does not turn on the question of whether the genuine prophet knows what YHWH may be saying in any given situation. If Micaiah has any uncertainty on that score, it is momentary and inconsequential, whereas for the man of God at Bethel, mistaking the true message was fatal. The problem here is that so many religious leaders, "prophets," are duped, however willingly, into abetting the foolhardy schemes of the political leadership—and moreover, it is YHWH who dupes them! We are given a glimpse of the heavenly court of YHWH, where a spirit is charged to "beguile [p-t-h] Ahab, so he might go up and fall at Ramoth-Gilead" (22:20). A serious question arises, then, about how the true prophet can effectively challenge political manipulation of the prophetic word, if even the Deity is complicit in the manipulation. As we shall see, the story is told with a profound underlying irony, an irony that is itself "a mode of revelatory language" (O'Day, *Revelation*, 31).

When Micaiah is brought before the kings, it is not for private counsel. This is an elaborately staged public event: wearing robes of state, they sit enthroned before the city gate, surrounded by the prophetic minions. There is even a stage performance, a visual enhancement of the prophetic message by one Zedekiah son of Canaanah. The very name of this actor is ironic; from a Deuteronomistic perspective, following the lead of a "Canaanite" in the matters of God is a straight path to idolatry. Zedekiah "made himself horns of iron and said, 'Thus says YHWH: With these you shall gore Aram until they are finished'" (22:11). Ancient Near Eastern iconography suggests that he would have concluded the performance with a flourish, presenting the horned helmet to the king. Reinhold Niebuhr describes Zedekiah as "the first pulpit sensationalist engaged in the dubious practice of echoing popular prejudices and adding nothing to them but an excess of emotion" (*Beyond Tragedy*, 75).

Micaiah's first words are addressed to the king's messenger. In response to that functionary's advice to speak along the same encouraging lines as Zedekiah and the 400, Micaiah asserts his own loyalty to another Monarch: "As YHWH lives, what YHWH says to me, that I shall speak!" (22:14; cf. Balaam's nearly identical

186

declaration, Num. 22:38). Yet strangely, his very next words repeat those of the 400 prophetic yes-men: "Go up and have success!" (22:15, cf. v. 12)—counsel that he himself will shortly reverse.

One possible explanation for this puzzling contradiction is that the existing story is a complex blending of two originally different narratives. Simon DeVries's argument for A and B narratives may be summarized as follows (*1 Kings*, 263–72):

> A: An older narrative, dating from the late 9th century, in which the main prophetic conflict is within the mind of Micaiah. Although he may have no use for the king, he desires the deliverance of his people from the Aramean threat, and so he begins by encouraging a war of liberation. But the king's own response to that oracle opens Micaiah's eyes to the unfavorable vision that will shortly be realized: "I have seen all Israel scattered on the mountains, like a flock that has no shepherd . . ." (1 Kgs. 22:17; cf. Zech. 13:7; Ezek. 34:1–34; Mark 6:34).

> B: A later and more sharply negative reading of history, in which the chief contrast and conflict are between the authority of the king in Samaria and the sovereign authority of YHWH. Micaiah's vow to speak God's word only (22:14) comes from this later tradition.

Even if something like DeVries's historical analysis is correct (a point on which scholars are divided), the present story in all its complexity makes rich, though not easy, sense. An ironic double development may be traced through the interaction between Micaiah and the king of Israel: as the tension between those two antagonists deepens, so does prophetic insight, for both prophet and reader. The irony is that the king himself, for whose sake Micaiah is summoned, fails to gain any insight. Like Pharaoh, the quintessential royal opponent of the prophet in the Bible, he cannot hear—because of his hardness of heart—even when the divine word is made plain.

This dynamic is set in motion as soon as Micaiah meets the king face to face:

> And he came to the king, and the king said to him, "Micaiah, shall we go up to Ramoth-Gilead for war, or shall we desist?"
> And he said to him, "Go up and have success, and YHWH will give it into the hand of the king."

187

> And the king said to him, "How many times must I make you swear that you shall speak to me only truth in the name of YHWH?!"
>
> And he said, "I have seen all Israel scattered on the mountains, like a flock that has no shepherd, and YHWH said, 'These have no leaders; let them go back, each one to his home in safety.'"
>
> And the king of Israel said to Jehoshaphat, "Didn't I tell you, he will not give any good prophecy about me, but only bad?!"
>
> And he said, "Therefore hear the word of YHWH: I have seen YHWH sitting on his throne, and all the host of heaven standing beside him, on his right and on his left, and YHWH said, 'Who will beguile Ahab, so he might go up and fall at Ramoth-Gilead?'" (22:15–20)

It has been suggested (by those who read the story as a unified whole) that when Micaiah utters the first, apparently favorable oracle, his words are "dripping with sarcasm" (Brichto, *Grammar*, 191; cf. Moberly, *Prophecy*, 114), but this is unlikely. Open sarcasm addressed to the king in a public situation—indeed, in front of another king—would hardly have been tolerated. Yet the king of Israel, instead of banishing Micaiah or ordering his execution, gives him time to say more; he even acknowledges that the favorable oracle cannot be true. Micaiah is a wise speaker; to appreciate his skill in this interaction, it is important to note the important rhetorical difference between sarcasm and irony. Sarcasm is a weapon; it creates a no-man's land between two interlocutors or viewpoints, across which each views the other with hostility. By contrast, the more subtle speech mode of irony is a sharp tool, which has the potential for opening up a situation and creating new insights on both sides. Irony is a way of being "clear without being evident" (O'Day, *Revelation*, 9); it may induce change in a situation through creating intriguing incongruities that stimulate the moral imagination. Micaiah succeeds in being ironic without begin sarcastic, and thus through this exchange with the king he himself comes to see the situation differently.

Imagine, then, that Micaiah echoes the positive oracle of the 400 court prophets, but in a noncommittal tone, which contrasts sharply with their boosterism. His restraint is itself the clear evidence that his mouth has to some extent been forced. The incongruity between his words and his tone throws the king off balance, yet without provoking immediate censure or reprisal. Moreover,

188

irony begets irony: The king's adjuration for Micaiah to speak "only truth in the name of YHWH" is incongruent with his orchestration of the whole prophetic performance. Insincerely pious though it may be, it is also more probing than anything he has said before. He obliquely admits that no one—not himself, not even the prophet—controls the truth of God. Thus the king's admonishment opens Micaiah's mouth to speak a genuine prophetic vision, of leaderless, scattered Israel. This is a vision that the king cannot bear to hear, and so he turns away, to Jehoshaphat. By evoking YHWH's truth and then turning away from what he hears, the king elicits from Micaiah an even more unnerving vision, of the heavenly court. Now Micaiah points to the realm of power that trumps Ahab's puny dominion, and thus he discloses the reality of what is happening right now, in Samaria, where there indeed is a "beguiling spirit" at work: the king's own political and military ambitions, abetted by the court prophets.

The notion that YHWH would recruit a heavenly attendant to become, for a time, "a spirit of deception in the mouth of all his prophets" (22:22) is outrageous but not incomprehensible. Another divine oracle, uttered through Ezekiel against false prophets, helps us to understand the situation here: "The prophet, when he is beguiled and speaks a word—it is I, YHWH, who beguiled that prophet, and I shall stretch out my hand over him and annihilate him from the midst of my people Israel" (Ezek. 14:9). Ezekiel envisions a scenario in which Israelites are clutching their beloved idols, holding them before their faces as they go to the prophet to inquire of . . . YHWH! The point is that they are all self-beguiled; these inquirers get exactly the kind of prophet they deserve. The only kind of revelation they can hear is further beguilement, drawing them all on to their own destruction—and only thus is the infection contained. Those self-deceivers are destroyed for the sake of others, "so that the house of Israel may no longer wander away from me, and they shall no longer defile themselves with all their crimes, and they shall become my people, and I shall become their God—an utterance of Lord YHWH" (14:11).

The immediate effect of Micaiah's public vision reports is that everyone acknowledges in some way that the truth has now been spoken. Immediately Zedekiah "the Canaanite" strikes him and asks the telling question: "'How did the Spirit of YHWH pass from me to speak with you?' And Micaiah said, 'You are about to see, on that day when you go into a chamber within a chamber to hide'" (1 Kgs. 22:24–25). "A chamber within a chamber" in the city of Aphek is where the Aramean king Ben-hadad fled after defeat in battle (1 Kgs. 20:30); thus Micaiah implies that in the aftermath of an ill-conceived military campaign, the prophet who encouraged it will not be safe from his own people. But there may also be a crude and scathing double entendre in this answer, as Marvin Sweeney suggests: what Zedekiah takes to be the prophetic spirit (*rûaḥ*) within himself is actually another kind of "wind" (also *rûaḥ*), one to be expelled in a private setting (*I and II Kings*, 260)!

Now the king also sees the truth of the heavenly visions, at least at one level, although he takes extreme and futile measures to evade their realization. Micaiah is sent to the dungeon with the barest minimum of bread and water (1 Kgs. 22:27) until the king should return safely; Simon DeVries proposes that the superstitious king intends this as a physical means of stifling the power of Micaiah's prophecy during the battle (*1 Kings*, 268–69). Further, the king insists that Jehoshaphat of Judah wear royal robes in battle, while he wears the armor of an ordinary soldier. However, the Arameans have no illusions about who is responsible for this aggression; when they recognize Jehoshaphat on the field, they simply turn away (22:33). As it happens, an Aramean arrow finds a chink in the armor of the disguised Ahab, and so he dies, unheroically and according to the word of YHWH (22:38).

At sunset the cry goes forth among the Israelites: "Let each one return to his city, each to his own country" (22:36); thus the vision of the scattered flock (22:17) is fulfilled. Whether it is a cry of victory or retreat is uncertain, but that is beside the point. For all this pointed irony is targeted at one thing only: the death of the king who mocked God, crudely manipulating the prophetic establishment to legitimize his own expansionist aims. Apt here is Carolyn Sharp's observation about the "profound theological irony" embedded in prophecies of judgment: "Those who choose not to heed the prophetic word will be destroyed, thus proving the power of the very word they considered irrelevant or inefficacious" (*Irony*, 129–30).

However, this profoundly ironic story about the manipulation of prophecy is in the canon as a means of grace. Rereading this story more than seventy years ago, Reinhold Niebuhr perceived in it an "apprehension of the profound religious truth that God is not

190

simply the sum total of the highest social values" (*Beyond Trag-edy,* 82). Writing in the first half of the twentieth century, as "the American state is developing and increasing its powers," he urged the church to recognize itself as something more than a politically formulated community at prayer, whether it represents the political majority or minority. "The Christian Church must be and remain a fellowship of Christ; and Christ is the judge of the self-will and self-righteousness of every social group" (86–87).

It is instructive to read Niebuhr's words in conjunction with a recent comment of Walter Brueggemann, as he considers how a change in the social location of the church within the last genera-tion or two may affect its current capacity to function as a prophetic institution. Because the church has been effectively marginalized by well-established forces of secularization, he judges that "the old confrontational model of 'prophet versus established power'" is now outmoded. He concludes the discussion with this intriguing statement: "Given that social reality . . . , I suspect that whatever is 'prophetic' must be more cunning and more nuanced and perhaps more ironic" (*Prophetic Imagination,* xii). Although Brueggemann does not elaborate on what it would mean for the church to engage the wider society in "more ironic" modes, perhaps the story of Mic-aiah and the king of Israel can help us begin to imagine that. It is a tale for our time.

A Divine Comedy (2 Kings 6:8–23)

> The principle to be kept in mind is to know what we see rather than to see what we know. (Abraham Heschel, *Prophets,* xv)

This is another story of a prophet and kings in time of war between Israel and Aram, the main characters here being Elisha and (pre-sumably) Jehoram, son of Ahab—although neither the king of Israel nor the king of Aram is named. However, in this case there is no tense confrontation, nor any battle account. This story reads even less like military history than the rest of the stories in Kings, imaginatively wrought and theologically focused though they are (cf. 1 Kgs. 20 and 22; 2 Kgs. 3). This one, only lightly informed by historical particularities, is rather an aspirational account, a sort of hopeful dream of what good might come to Israel, were the

191

king really to listen to the prophet and act in positive response. This could be called a prophetic "comedy," in both senses of that genre designation. First, it is humorous; the irony here is cheerful, in contrast to the grim tone of the Micaiah story. Second (and in accordance with the classical definition of a comedy), it has a happy ending: because of the prophetically engendered action of the king, Aramean raiding parties stop attacking Israel (2 Kgs. 6:23). Admittedly, the happy ending of this story evaporates in the larger narrative context; war with Aram resumes in the very next verse (6:24), and a few verses later the king of Israel is calling for Elisha's head (6:31). The Elisha cycle consists of many loosely connected legends, longer and shorter, put together with no editorial attempt at full consistency.

In addition to its cheerful tone, this story of Elisha at Dothan is the mirror image of Micaiah's story in several ways. That story begins with the resumption of war after several years of peace; this one begins with war and ends with peace. There the king of Israel "hated" Micaiah (1 Kgs. 22:8) and summoned him only under duress; this prophet is a trusted adviser who has the ear of the king. In the earlier story the king of Israel was obdurate and died as a result of his inability to hear the prophetic word, but this is an all-but-isolated case of a royal success story among the rulers of the northern kingdom: a king who listens to the prophet and even changes course as a result. In Micaiah's story, the prophetic word is vindicated by the king's death in battle, which functions as a negative example for the reader's moral instruction, a warning against hard-heartedness. In this comedy, by contrast, we are drawn into the different but related perspectives of two people, Elisha's attendant and the king; we see the processes, both natural and supernatural, whereby they come to see the world as Elisha sees it and thus (for a narrative moment, at least) lose their fear of the enemy.

Seeing or not seeing clearly is a major theme of this story, which anticipates important prophetic passages and Gospel stories that highlight the theme of seeing or not seeing as a metaphor for spiritual perception (Isa. 6:9–10; Matt. 23:16–19; John 9, etc.). Along with this goes the related theme of knowledge: who knows what, and how it is known. The story opens with a security crisis in Aram; the heart of the king of Aram "was storming" (2 Kgs. 6:11) over a series of disastrous (for him) security leaks to the king of

192

Israel. He suspects a double agent within his court circle, but in fact the culprit is "the man of God," as Elisha is called by the narrator (6:9–10). One Aramean minister accurately reports the source of the leaks, but tellingly, he refers to "Elisha the prophet, who is in Israel" (22:12)—likely regarding prophethood as a governmental post rather than a divine appointment. The business of the story is to show that the political issues are epiphenomena; reality has another dimension that neither the Arameans nor even most Israelites can see.

"And [the king of Aram] said, 'Go and *see* where he is, that I may send and take him,' and it was reported to him, '*Here* [*hinnēh*], in Dothan!'" (6:13; emphasis added). This is the first of six instances of the verb *r-'-h*, "see" (cf. 6:17, 20, 21), and the first of four occurrences of *hinnēh*, the particle of vivid narration (cf. 6:15, 17, 20). The latter is used in both speech and third-person narrative to bring the audience immediately into the character's experience of fresh perception. The dense usage of both words within the space of a few verses moves readers through a changing "see-scape," in Burke Long's phrase (*2 Kings*, 86). Within the story, the evident dynamic force is not an oracle addressed to a prophet or a king, but rather Elisha's prayer. The first change takes place when God responds to his prayer that the eyes of his attendant (or apprentice prophet) may be opened, with the result that he sees "horses and chariots of fire around Elisha" (v. 17), vastly outmatching those of the Arameans' "heavy force" of the same (v. 14).

That visionary experience is the reification of Elisha's prophetic epithet, "the chariot of Israel and its horsemen," an honorific that he shares only with Elijah (2 Kgs. 2:12; 13:14). Both the epithet and the vision make the point that YHWH, working through the prophet, is Israel's true defense force. The psalmist uses the same image to make that affirmation:

> These [trust] in chariots and these in horses,
> but as for us, we shall call to mind the name of YHWH our God.
> (Ps. 20:8 [7E])

The fact that this part of the story is located in Dothan may reinforce the point that YHWH is the source of Israel's security. Dothan was a fortified city on the major route leading from Samaria into the Jezreel Valley, the country's most fertile region and also its major east-west passage. Located at the edge of the valley, Dothan

193

was the key point for controlling the king's access to the region most vital to the nation's agriculture, trade, and military security.

When Elisha prays a second time, it is with the opposite intention and effect; now "confused vision" befalls the Arameans (2 Kgs. 6:18). This is the same divine "bedazzlement" (*sanwērîm*) that frustrated another group of men bent on violence, the attackers of Lot's house in Sodom (Gen. 19:11). Having brought on the soldiers' confusion, Elisha promptly offers to guide them to the man they are seeking (himself), and he leads them straight into the royal citadel of Samaria. There he prays a third time, that their eyes might be opened—"and they saw, and here [*hinnēh*], [they were] in the middle of Samaria!" (2 Kgs. 6:20).

Up to this point the story is heroic and humorous, in a fairly predictable patriotic mode: Arameans are befuddled, and Israelites are given insight by the Israelite prophet. But now comes the surprising turn that makes this a serious story, a divine comedy:

> And the king of Israel said to Elisha, when he saw them, "Shall I strike, shall I strike, my Father?"
>
> And he said, "You shall not strike. Would you be striking those whom you captured with your sword and with your bow? Put food and water before them, that they may eat and drink and go to their master."
>
> And he prepared for them a great feast, and they ate and drank, and he let them go; and they went to their master. And the raiders of Aram did not continue any more to come into the land of Israel. (6:21–23)

Initially, the excited king sounds just like an unattractive child, eager to assert his power, even if it is not really his own. But then he not only takes correction from the prophet; he even goes beyond what his "father" requires. Instead of POW rations—food (or "bread") and water—he gives the enemy troops "a great feast."

An ancient audience would have viewed this as more than an arbitrary narrative embellishment. In a traditional, kinship-based society such as Israel's, receiving hospitality is a definitive moment in the process whereby outsiders become insiders. The king's hospitality is a marker of status at the highest social level, even a vehicle of social change (see MacDonald, *Not Bread Alone*, 142–64). Since the feast in Samaria is laid on at the instigation of Elisha "the man of God," in a real sense YHWH is its host. The

194

Isaiah tradition envisions YHWH giving a feast "for all the nations on this mountain" and wiping away "tears from every face" (Isa. 25:6–8); the psalmist sees YHWH's richly laden table as a place of safety and protection "in front of my opponents" (Ps. 23:5). This long scriptural tradition of YHWH as host to the vulnerable stands behind Mary's song, magnifying a God who "has filled the hungry with good things and sent away the rich, empty" (Luke 1:53). The book of Kings itself gives particular prominence to the provision of food as a marker of social change, with God presumably standing behind the change. Notably, the whole History concludes with a notice about the king of Babylon giving life tenure at the royal table to the king of Israel, who had long been in prison or under house arrest (2 Kgs. 25:27–30). Within the Elisha cycle, several other stories of God's miraculous provision of food to the needy through the prophet (2 Kgs. 4:1–7, 38–41, 42–44) serve as prolegomena to this story.

Perhaps one of the most intriguing aspects of this prophetic comedy is its implication that feeding enemies is one of the things that makes for peace. From a political and historical perspective, it is relevant that food and water insecurity has perennially been one of the chief causes of war, in the biblical world as in ours. By feeding the Aramean troops instead of following the common practice of publicly humiliating prisoners of war, the king of Israel may be signaling to "their master" (2 Kgs. 6:23) that essential resources can and must be shared among nations. Moreover, there is a distinctly theological dimension to the feeding of enemies, as the apostle Paul underscores in his Letter to the Romans, citing Scripture: "If your enemy is hungry, feed him; if he thirsts, let him drink. For in doing so 'you will heap fiery coals on his head'" (12:20; cf. Prov. 25:21–22). In a passage that urges the Roman Christians to "live at peace with everyone" (12:18), Paul evokes that enigmatic image, which has since ancient times been read as referring to a rite of repentance (see Waltke, *Proverbs*, 330–32). Similarly, the Letter to the Ephesians (chap. 4) emphasizes mutual kindness, forbearance, and forgiveness among those who might view each other as enemies, even within the body of Christ. David Ford comments on the significance of that apostolic instruction: "In a culture of great physical, verbal and structural violence it may be that gentleness is a virtue of prophetic power." Ephesians makes compassion and gentleness not "an optional extra," but a constitutive element of

195

Christian community—indeed one that is already realized, albeit in a "contingent realization," with massive historical and spiritual forces still arrayed against it (*Self and Salvation*, 136). Both the power of gentleness and its contingency are conveyed by the story in 2 Kings 6: at one narrative moment, Aramean prisoners feast in Samaria and war ceases (6:23), and then in the very next verse and the next historical moment, King Ben-hadad of Aram lays siege to the city (6:24).

The prophetic power of gentleness, as experienced in the Christian practice of feeding or eating with enemies, is expressed in this liturgical chant, which I once heard as a group gathered around the Communion table:

> We are here at the table of the Lord;
> we are not alone.
> We are here with our enemies.

On that particular occasion, we happened to be a multinational, multidenominational, multiethnic assembly. Yet often enough any group of Christians meeting at the Table where Lord Jesus is host could truthfully sing that chant.

Ford's notion that gentleness is a virtue with prophetic power may also suggest how this particular Elisha story may enrich our understanding of the Jesus tradition. Raymond Brown and others have argued persuasively that the Elisha cycle is a clear Old Testament antecedent for the accounts of Jesus' miracles. The older miracle tradition is set in a literary and theological context that "begins with Elijah's constitution of Elisha as a prophet and ends with Elisha's death and burial, which is the cause of a resuscitation of the dead" (Brown, "Jesus and Elisha," 99). They note that a miracle such as the multiplication of barley loaves (2 Kgs. 4:42–44 and John 6:4–14) forms a substantive link with the story of Jesus. But likewise, so does this story of the feeding of the Aramean army—a miracle in the sociopolitical rather than material sphere. Both traditions affirm that truly *seeing* the power of God at work through the agency of the man of God is the necessary condition for being delivered from fear and thus repudiating the "normal" punitive and vengeful behaviors that follow from it.

196

The sixth chapter of 2 Kings shows a young prophet's outlook changed because of Elisha's prayer, and a king's sovereign action redirected by his rebuke. In each case, the narrative character is able to receive the prophetic or divine disclosure and benefit from it, although one receives it by supernatural means and the other by (firm) appeal to reason. Thus this rare prophetic success story offers two different models of the dynamics of prophetic revelation. We now turn to another instance of prophecy working through the faculty of reason, in Paul's instructions to the Corinthians.

Prophecy and the Spirit's Way of Love (1 Corinthians 12–14)

In the New Testament, it is the apostle Paul who treats most directly the role of prophecy in the church. There is more exhortation than explanation in Paul's instructions to the Corinthian church on ordering its worship in anticipation of and response to the spiritual gift of prophecy (1 Cor. 14). He offers no theological rationale for this new phenomenon of the revealed word being given through the Spirit to the ethnically mixed community that is the body of Christ (12:27). Rather, Paul assumes that the members know as much as they need to know about the nature of prophecy, and his purpose is to encourage them all to strive for it (14:1) as the best of spiritual gifts. This is obviously a new way of viewing prophecy; one can hardly imagine such counsel coming from a weary and beleaguered Moses or Jeremiah, or the blistered lips of Isaiah.

Although Paul does not give even a cursory description of the contents of any inspired utterance, the overall picture that emerges is that prophecy is the gift, privilege, responsibility of speaking for God to God's people in the context of worship, with the expectation that others will "judge the soundness" (*diakrinō*, 14:29) of each utterance. This gift of the Spirit engages the faculty of reason, in both articulation and reception. (The verb *krinō*, "judge," with its compounds, appears some thirty times in the letter.) Set in the context of Paul's larger teaching for the Corinthians, his detailed instructions on the ordering of prophetic utterance in worship show that the aim is to enable the community to be what it is: nothing less than Christ's articulate body. The reality underlying that metaphor becomes perceptible through worship, when all participate in the exercise of spiritual gifts and disciplines, and especially spiritual judgment of prophecies.

197

In contrast to the stories of the man of God (1 Kgs. 13) and Micaiah ben Imlah (1 Kgs. 22), the predictive element of oracular prophecy plays no role in Paul's discussion. His understanding of divine revelation is more in line with certain elements of the Elisha story (2 Kgs. 6:8–23), in which the prophet enables others to perceive the powerful presence of God and thus to live differently in the world. "For I determined to know nothing among you except Jesus Christ, and him crucified" (1 Cor. 2:2); Paul's understanding and teaching about God's presence and self-revelation proceeds wholly from the prior event of the cross, "God's wisdom hidden in mystery" (2:7), whose meaning is still being unfolded. Therefore the proclamation of Christ crucified provides the depth dimension of prophetic utterance. If Paul's own preaching proves persuasive, this is not because of any conventional rhetorical argumentation but rather through "a display of the Spirit and of power" (2:4). That suggests why Paul accords prophetic utterance a central place in worship; the depth of the mystery, indeed the very implausibility of the wisdom of the cross is such that it must be continually probed, week after week, in the power of the Spirit. For him prophecy seems to occupy the place that many later Christian theologians would accord to the sermon, which is not even mentioned among the elements of worship that contribute to the edification of the congregation (14:26)! Giving prominence to prophetic utterance means welcoming the Spirit, which searches out the mind of God in Christ (2:10–13), to speak that mind for the benefit of the assembled body of Christ. Ensuring that prophecy is spoken and weighed in an orderly and "peaceable" fashion (14:29–33, 40) is a matter of bringing disciplined intentionality into the worship and common life of the church. Thus worship does not devolve into sentimental self-expression, and its true character as response to God is evident to everyone. Prophecy in Paul's understanding is profoundly relational, on both horizontal and vertical planes.

Unquestionably, Paul is drawing on scriptural traditions about prophecy in his lengthy discourse on the spiritual gifts (1 Cor. 12–14). He evokes the Moses tradition with the notion that even the work of prophecy is only provisional, preparatory to the experience of one day seeing God "face to face" (1 Cor. 13:12; cf. Exod. 33:11; Num. 12:8). When Paul envisions that an unbeliever will hear all members prophesying and declare, "God is really among you!" (14:24–25), he is echoing the evangelistic visions of

198

Zechariah (8:23) and Isaiah (45:14; cf. 2:2–3 and Mic. 4:1–2). He surely intends his readers to imagine such an experience as fulfilling Joel's vision of God's prophetic Spirit poured out on "all flesh" (Joel 3:1 [2:28E]). Yet at the same time, the picture of everyone prophesying stands in striking contrast with all actualized Old Testament models of prophecy, where the word is given through a particular individual, man or woman, designated as "prophet" or (occasionally) "man of God." Now, however, Paul is preparing the church for the spiritual gift of prophecy to be manifested through any member—potentially every member, over the course of time. Moreover, regardless of which individual may manifest that gift at any occasion, it is given for the immediate benefit of all: "Whenever you assemble, . . . you can *all* prophesy one by one, so that *all* may learn and *all* be encouraged [or 'comforted']" (1 Cor. 14:26, 31; emphasis added). Paul's consistent focus is on the whole community, endowed by the Spirit with numerous gracious *charismata*, including the articulation of wisdom or knowledge, faith, healing, miracles, discernment of spirits, and tongues and their interpretation (12:8–11). Elsewhere (1 Cor. 12:28–30; Rom. 12:6–8; cf. Eph. 4:11) Paul lists other gifts not named here, where the focus seems to be specifically on those manifested in the context of worship. Of these enumerated gifts, prophecy is the one that benefits the community most and can also bring outsiders to conviction; that is why everyone should be striving for it.

In most of our churches, Paul's careful instruction on prophecy (1 Cor. 14) is completely overshadowed by the justly famous passage extolling the "way" or "journey" (*hodos*) of love (*agapē*), which immediately precedes it (1 Cor. 13). Yet it is misleading to separate the two, for they constitute two of the three major sections of the discourse on spiritual gifts. Probably most contemporary Western Christians would be surprised and even confused by Paul's insistence that the regular and disciplined practice of prophecy belongs essentially to the church's way of love. Pursuing love and seeking the gift of prophecy are but two aspects of the same spiritual striving.

Paul is of course not writing about romantic love, nor even familial love; rather he is describing the kind of love that holds together the community in a "way" that is genuinely beneficial for each of its members. His notion of love conforms to usage of the word *agapē/agapaō* (noun and verb) in the Septuagint and other literature of Hellenistic Judaism, where it denotes the practice of the

199

faithful that earns favor with God (e.g., Wis. 3:9) or a political virtue that works for the common good (Philo, *On Virtues* 10; see Wilson, *Philo*, 64, 258–59). Taking his place in a literary, rhetorical, and theological tradition that views love as a *corporate* way or virtue, he begins his discourse on spiritual gifts with the playful yet serious discussion of what it means for the church to be a *body* (1 Cor. 12). Here again he draws on established political thought and language; in the rhetoric and literature of the Greco-Roman world, the body politic was the most common figure for social unity (Mitchell, *Paul and the Rhetoric*, 157–64).

Unity within the church is precisely the central issue in this discourse on spiritual gifts and within the letter as a whole. It is no coincidence that Paul uses the word "one" (*heis* and variants) more than thirty times as he constructs a careful argument, both theologically grounded and pastorally sensitive, for unity within the church in Corinth. What he advocates is not uniformity but a sturdy unity that can hold together members of that new church, who differ from each other in many ways: ethnically, culturally, economically. The need for a Christ-centered unity that can accommodate diversity commends this letter especially to our attention at this time in the church's life. Several aspects of the social context and character of the Corinthian Christians may be congruent with our own situations:

The multicultural character of Corinthian society. Strategically located on the narrow land bridge connecting the Peloponnese to the Greek mainland and commanding harbors to both the east and the west, ancient Corinth was the site of active commercial, cultural, and linguistic interchange. Refounded by Julius Caesar as a Roman colony in 44 BCE, here Italy met Asia and Jews met Gentiles, both Romans and Greeks. As a Greek-speaking Jew who was (likely) a Roman citizen, Paul seems to have been successful in reaching people across the social spectrum and maintaining a pastoral relationship with them over some years.

An economically mixed and socially fluid church membership. Many or most citizens in this relatively new colonial city were former soldiers or freed slaves or their children, seeking to climb the social ladder. A few were wealthy, and the church would have convened for worship in their villas, likely in subgroups. Archaeological evidence suggests that most large homes could have

200

accommodated a couple of dozen people—perhaps half the total membership. Paul writes to the Romans that one Christian, Gaius, was "host to me and the whole church" (Rom. 16:23; see Murphy-O'Connor, *Keys*, 183–89). However, when the members gathered to eat "the Lord's supper"—not a symbolic taste of bread and wine, but a real meal—those social and economic differences could be the source of humiliation for the less affluent members. It is notable that the teaching on spiritual gifts is immediately preceded by Paul's lengthy and sharp rebuke to the church for its inegalitarian and ultimately self-deluded (1 Cor. 11:20) "eucharistic" practices. Some of the poorer members, including slaves, were arriving late, tired and probably dirty after a long day of work. They would have had to find room to stand or squat in the atrium, the large public courtyard, while a few privileged members reclined comfortably in the elegantly decorated *triclinium*, the dining room. The result was that some had plenty of rich food and too much intoxicating drink, while others went hungry (11:21). Paul does not pull his punches about the disparity. In a memorable aphorism that echoes the terse rhythms of scriptural Proverbs he declares:

> The one eating and drinking judgment on oneself—
> [such is] the one who eats and drinks without discerning the body.
> (11:29)

Taking the Lord's body and blood in vain (11:27), oblivious to the needs of the real body that is the church, is ultimately a deadly business (11:30).

An intense spiritualism in a highly privatized mode. Richard Horsley makes the plausible suggestion that partly because so many Corinthians had only shallow roots in that new city, many sought security through public manifestations of gifts of the Spirit (*Wisdom,* 122). However that may be, a number of Christians were (in Paul's view) hyperspiritual elitists—competitive, contentious, and boastful (1:10–12; 3:1–4, 18; 4:6–7). Presuming themselves to be spiritually advanced—Paul mocks their claims to be "rich" and "kings" (4:8), which echo boasts that Cynic and Stoic philosophers made about their own wisdom (Hays, *First Corinthians,* 70)— they completely missed the core spiritual reality on which Paul insists: "Do you not know that you are God's temple and the Spirit of God dwells in you?"—in each case, a *plural* "you" (3:16; cf. 6:19).

201

God's Spirit cannot be claimed by any individual for her- or himself, "for in one Spirit we were all baptized into one body, whether Jews or Greeks, slaves or free, and all given to drink of one Spirit" (12:13). Extending the symbol of the waters of baptism, Paul speaks of "drinking" God's Spirit, active ingestion and incorporation for the sake of the whole body—a powerful metaphor in the hot, arid climate of the Mediterranean, where drinking pure liquids often makes the difference between health and illness, life and death.

First Corinthians may rightly be called "Paul's most contemporary letter" (Bailey, *Paul*, 21). His robust challenge to the Corinthian church to be what in fact it is (unless it be a sham)—the body of Christ, actively infused by the Holy Spirit—speaks directly to many aspects of our own experience in

a multicultural, economically stratified society, where congregations and even denominations are among the most racially and economically segregated of our social institutions;

a contentious religious environment, where exchanges among Christians constitute some of the most acrimonious rhetoric in the public square;

a time when institutionalized Christianity is widely discredited as self-involved and socially irresponsible, or simply found to be uninteresting, and therefore many in the (cultural) West now claim to be "spiritual but not religious";

a political environment where the church's effectiveness as a source of sustained challenge and moral guidance is incalculably reduced, in comparison to its influence a couple of generations ago.

In the past, some parts of the church have occasionally succeeded in "speaking truth to power" and stimulating massive social change (in the United States during the years of the civil rights movement and the Vietnam War, in South Africa during apartheid). But if in our time the church can no longer offer a credible, compelling, or even comprehensible prophetic witness to the larger culture, then perhaps it is time for us to heed Paul's different way of viewing prophecy. Could we exercise that spiritual gift on the small scale of a worshiping congregation, or possibly even a denomination—a larger scale, but still with lines of accountability? Our faithfulness in exercising the gift would be judged, in accordance with

Paul's standard, by the consistency of our efforts to "build up" the church (1 Cor. 10:23; 14:3, 4, 5, 12, 17, 26; cf. 2 Cor. 12:19; 13:10; Rom. 14:19; 15:2; 1 Thess. 5:11)—that is, to work for sound moral formation of Christians and selfless regard for others, indeed, for justice within the body of Christ.

Several necessary activities of congregations and denominational bodies would seem to provide regular opportunities for such "prophetic edification." A nonexhaustive list would include preaching, making an annual budget, discerning and pursuing a call to mission, choosing leadership, making decisions about ethical matters with respect to both clergy and laity. All of these often constitute occasions for dispute, self-righteousness, and bitter division within the church. However, we might view them from a fresh angle by bearing in mind the contrast Paul draws between the two spiritual gifts of prophecy and tongues. "For one who speaks in a tongue is speaking not to people but to God, for no one hears [with comprehension], for he speaks mysteries by the Spirit. But the one prophesying speaks to people [words of] edification, and encouragement, and comfort" (1 Cor. 14:2–3). Speaking in a tongue is privatized religious language; it does nothing to increase mutual understanding in the church. By contrast, prophecy builds community because it involves the public use of shared language. One person takes the risk of uttering in plain language what she believes to be the word of God, and then, with courtesy and humility, waits in silence for others to evaluate and speak in turn (14:29–30).

As is clear from Paul's constant references to the Christ and the cross throughout the letter (1:23; 2:2, etc.), the shared language of prophecy reflects a common story—a story that is no less countercultural in our society than it was in ancient Corinth. When Christians make mindful use of such unpopular terms as "repentance," "sacrifice," "sin," "faithful suffering," "temptation," and "cross," we take part in the continual retelling, application, and extension of the Christian story in our current circumstances. Thus we mark our experience and thinking with what Stanley Hauerwas calls "the Christian difference" (*Without Apology*, xx), which the dominant culture tempts us to overlook or underplay. Using that distinctive language in ways that others can hear with comprehension and the expectation of benefit is a sign of fellowship, an acknowledgment that both speaker and hearer belong to a tradition that is still alive.

203

When we speak courteously and "in words . . . taught by the Spirit" (1 Cor. 2:13), sincerely seeking to probe the mind of Christ (2:16), then we invite others to articulate what they hear from God, and edify us in turn.

One congregation known to me offers a rare contemporary example of Paul's instructions to the Corinthians taking on new life, even within a "mainstream" denomination. Several years ago, a global economic crisis moved the pastor to lead the congregation in a twenty-four-hour prayer vigil, to discern how they should respond, at local, national, and international levels. Each member was asked to spend one hour of that time in prayer, in the sanctuary, and to write down what they heard God saying. The congregation as a whole then "weighed" what was written, according to several criteria:

1. Is it "in order" (cf. 1 Cor. 14:40)—that is, can this word be received in the context of the life established by this faith community?

2. Is it congruent with the Scripture?

3. Does it speak to the hearts of the faithful in this place, at this time?

These three criteria point to the need for the prophetic word to be received in the context of the ongoing life of a faith community, grounded in the common resource of Scripture, and balanced with other aspects of its ministry. Some writings were judged by a fourth criterion:

4. Will it bear the test of time? Can we wait and return to weigh this word again?

This last criterion is not simply equivocation. It is a reminder that prophetic faith must be disciplined by the virtue of patience—an eschatologically oriented virtue grounded ultimately in the resurrection, in the Christian habit of remembering what God has done in Christ and waiting in trust for God to bring it to completion.

This final criterion, of durability over time, shows that the congregation had understood Paul's teaching about prophetic discernment. No sooner does the apostle complete his instructions on prophecy and spiritual gifts than he turns to an extended discourse on the resurrection, about which the Corinthians had been arguing (1 Cor. 15:12, 35). The juxtaposition is deliberate; thus Paul "transforms a subject of dispute into the very *telos* or goal which should govern all Christian decision making" (Mitchell, *Paul and the Rhetoric*, 283). With this reminder of "the good news . . . that you

204

received, on which you have also taken a stand, and through which you are also saved" (15:1), he points the Corinthians and every later generation of Christians to a firm "location" from which to listen for God and to each other in patience and trust. Decisions should be made, not in panic, but in openness to the fresh action of the Spirit and confidence in the future God intends.

In this chapter we have seen some difficulties of revelation: the risk to which the prophet is exposed as the first hearer and judge of the divine word (1 Kgs. 13), the likelihood that prophecy will be an occasion for political manipulation and self-delusion (1 Kgs. 22). We have seen also the potential for genuine political change to happen in response to prophetic prayer and instruction (2 Kgs. 6), and the shared responsibility of the whole faith community to weigh and judge what has been heard (1 Cor. 14). The next chapter will explore how the evangelist Matthew advances a prophetically informed understanding of discipleship, as a mode of life that enables the Christian community to bear the difficult responsibility of witnessing truthfully to God's revelation in Jesus Christ.

Works Cited in Chapter 7

Bailey, Kenneth E. *Paul through Mediterranean Eyes: Cultural Studies in 1 Corinthians*. Downers Grove, IL: InterVarsity Press, 2011.

Barth, Karl. *Church Dogmatics*. Peabody, MA: Hendrickson, 2010.

Benedict XVI. Homily at the First Vespers of the Feast of Saints Peter and Paul, Rome, June 28, 2008. http://www.vatican.va/holy_father/benedict_xvi/homilies/2008/documents/hf_ben-xvi_hom_20080628_vespri_en.html.

Brichto, Herbert Chanan. *Toward a Grammar of Biblical Poetics: Tales of the Prophets*. New York: Oxford University Press, 1992.

Brown, Raymond E. "Jesus and Elisha." *Perspectives* 12 (1971): 85–104.

Brueggemann, Walter. *The Practice of Prophetic Imagination: Preaching an Emancipating Word*. Minneapolis: Fortress Press, 2012.

———. *The Prophetic Imagination*. Minneapolis: Fortress, 2001.

DeVries, Simon. *1 Kings*. Word Biblical Commentary. Nashville: Thomas Nelson Publishers, 2003.

205

Ford, David. *Self and Salvation: Being Transformed.* Cambridge: Cambridge University Press, 1999.

Hauerwas, Stanley. *Without Apology: Sermons for Christ's Church.* New York: Seabury Books, 2013.

Hays, Richard B. *First Corinthians.* Interpretation Series. Louisville, KY: John Knox Press, 1997.

Heschel, Abraham Joshua. *The Prophets: An Introduction.* 2 vols. New York: Harper & Row, 1962.

Horsley, Richard A. *Wisdom and Spiritual Transcendence at Corinth.* Eugene, OR: Cascade, 2008.

Long, Burke O. *2 Kings.* Forms of the Old Testament Literature 10. Grand Rapids: Eerdmans, 1991.

MacDonald, Nathan. *Not Bread Alone: The Uses of Food in the Old Testament.* Oxford: Oxford University Press, 2008.

Mitchell, Margaret. *Paul and the Rhetoric of Reconciliation.* Tübingen: J. C. B. Mohr, 1991.

———. *Paul, the Corinthians, and the Birth of Christian Hermeneutics.* Cambridge: Cambridge University Press, 2010.

Moberly, R. W. L. *The Bible, Theology, and Faith: A Study of Abraham and Jesus.* Cambridge: Cambridge University Press, 2000.

Murphy-O'Connor, Jerome. *Keys to First Corinthians: Revisiting the Major Issues.* Oxford: Oxford University Press, 2009.

Niebuhr, Reinhold. *Beyond Tragedy: Essays on the Christian Interpretation of History.* New York: Charles Scribner's Sons, 1941.

O'Day, Gail R. *Revelation in the Fourth Gospel: Narrative Mode and Theological Claim.* Philadelphia: Fortress Press, 1986.

Sharp, Carolyn J. *Irony and Meaning in the Hebrew Bible.* Bloomington: Indiana University Press, 2009.

Simon, Uriel. *Reading Prophetic Narratives.* Bloomington: Indiana University Press, 1997.

Sweeney, Marvin A. *I and II Kings: A Commentary.* Louisville, KY: Westminster John Knox Press, 2007.

Waltke, Bruce K. *The Book of Proverbs: Chapters 15–31.* Grand Rapids: Eerdmans, 2005.

Wilson, Walter T. *Philo of Alexandria on Virtues: Introduction, Translation, and Commentary.* Leiden: Brill, 2011.

CHAPTER 8

"Good and Faithful Servant"

Matthew Reads Isaiah
on Prophetic Discipleship

> *I will again pour out teaching like prophecy*
> *and give it as an inheritance for future generations.*
> —Sirach 24:33

As the title of this volume suggests, prophetic traditions should be seen as a primary scriptural resource for the lifelong vocation of Christian discipleship, yet it seems that the connection is often missed. In planning the present volume, I have frequently encountered the question, "Why would a book on biblical prophecy include a chapter on discipleship?" The beginning of an answer comes from the apostle Paul, who, as we have seen, represents prophecy, not as the special vocation of a few, but rather as a spiritual gift that any and every member of the church might exercise on an occasional basis (see pp. 197–205). Therefore some exploration of the connection between prophecy and discipleship would seem to be not just warranted, but necessary for the health of Christian congregations.

In this chapter I focus on the Sermon on the Mount, and especially Matthew's versions of the Beatitudes and the Lord's Prayer, texts that surely merit a central place in any treatment of Christian discipleship. In these texts we hear Matthew's Jesus interpreting Israel's scriptural traditions, with particular emphasis on Isaiah, bringing those traditions to bear on the challenges facing disciples

207

in the first century and in subsequent generations, even up to our own time. Before turning to the Gospel, however, I begin by considering briefly how the nature of prophetic discourse in the Bible invites attention to discipleship as its necessary component.

One of the presuppositions of this study is that the "prophetic perspective" as it is expressed throughout the Bible is radically concrete (see pp. 7–10). Prophetic speech is addressed to identifiable social groups within known historical situations. It treats the political, military, economic, and religious dimensions of experience in the present and the projected future for those addressed, provided they heed God's call for a change of heart and also for large-scale social change—two things that are not clearly distinguishable. So, for example, Amos's clarion call, "Let justice roll down like waters . . ." (Amos 5:24) served as the motto for one of the greatest social-change movements of modern times, but its essential content is closely aligned with that of Micah's call, framed in more personal terms, for "doing justice, loving covenant-fellowship (ḥesed), and walking humbly with your God" (6:8). South African theologian and ethicist Piet Naudé characterizes the strength of prophetic discourse as "its ability to unambiguously denounce a specific situation of injustice, and at the same time announce a God-willed alternative future" ("Prophetic Discourse," 105).

Yet Naudé also identifies a lack or lacuna in so-called prophetic speech, both biblical and contemporary. Its rhetorical power may disguise the fact that it often fails to bridge the gap between the declaration of divine judgment and the proposed future. "Ironically, denouncing and dreaming in the name of God can easily stay disconnected to realising God's will" (103). Therefore, he suggests, prophetic speech needs to be supplemented by "identity-sustaining narratives" (100), moral analysis, and other kinds of discourse that may provide "clues about action and discipleship" (103).

In several key texts, the biblical canon itself shows an awareness of the need to address the gap between present failure and the hoped-for future through cultivating discipleship. Within the prophetic corpus itself, the Servant Songs of Isaiah (42:1–9; 49:1–7; 50:4–9; 52:13–53:12) are powerful poetic expressions or portraits of discipleship: "Lord YHWH has given me a disciple's tongue [literally, 'a tongue of those who are instructed']" (50:4). This faithful disciple or servant (42:1; 49:3; 50:10; 52:13) who suffers greatly in God's service is Israel (49:3) and at the same time should probably

208

also be seen as an individual, or a remnant of the faithful within Israel. As I have argued elsewhere (Davis, "Christians Hearing Isaiah"), the book of Isaiah is distinctive among the prophetic books, and probably in the Bible altogether, in giving extensive attention to the question of what constitutes the unique vocation of Israel "as a covenant-people, as a light of nations" (42:6). While that formulation comes from Second Isaiah, all three major parts of the book may be read as constituting an extended reflection, developed over a period of more than two centuries, on aspects of these questions: What does it mean for Israel to be called into the exclusive service of YHWH, for its own sake and ultimately, for the sake of all the peoples of the world? How is it possible for Israel to fulfill that vocation to service, despite its own weakness and the intense opposition it faces—in other words, in the face of threats both internal and external?

Some six centuries later, the prophetically oriented disciple of Jesus who wrote the Gospel of Matthew would return to these same questions, looking to the book of Isaiah as a major source of guidance. A striking visual expression of Matthew's dependence on Isaiah appears in a thirteenth-century stained-glass lancet, prominently located below the south rose window at Chartres Cathedral: the evangelist is portrayed sitting astride the prophet's shoulders, holding onto his head and neck as a small child might do. As we shall see, Matthew's understanding of discipleship grows directly out of his reading of Israel's Scripture. For Matthew, being the light of the world (Matt. 5:14) means reading Scripture and the present moment of history together, and reading both by the light of Christ (4:16). That Source of illumination is what distinguishes Matthew's reading of Torah and the Prophets (5:17), including and especially Isaiah, from that of "the scribes and Pharisees," that is, other authoritative interpreters who were dominant in the larger Jewish community near the end of the first century.

In terms proposed by this study, Matthew was a prophetic interpreter of Scripture; in his own terms, a "scribe 'discipled' [*mathēteutheis*] for the kingdom of heaven" (13:52). He was presumably a Jewish male, learned in Israel's sacred traditions, which he reads as a follower of Jesus. He names Jesus as the Messiah (*Christos*, 1:1, 16, etc.), the one of whom Isaiah and the other prophets spoke (1:22–23; 2:5–6, 15, 18; 3:3; 4:14–16; 12:17–21), God's "beloved Son" (3:17; 17:5; cf. 27:54), the fulfillment of Torah and the Prophets (5:17). Matthew is a teacher whose goal is to equip others to follow Jesus and thus implement their—our—own scripturally informed and prophetically shaped (see 5:12) vocations to a life of service in the kingdom of heaven (5:3, 10).

Discipling in a Sick Society

I will hold the Christlight for you
in the nighttime of your fear.
(Richard Gillard, "The Servant Song,"
        The Faith We Sing, no. 2222)

The Sermon on the Mount is familiar, even to the point of excess, for many Christians; this is the comfort food of the New Testament. Yet it could hardly have been so for Matthew's original audience; he is, after all, preparing disciples to be reviled, persecuted, and falsely accused, just as the earlier prophets were (5:11–12). He doubtless intends to offer real comfort to disciples in such situations: "Rejoice and be wildly happy!" Nonetheless it should be acknowledged that on the rare occasions when this evangelist speaks of wild joy (cf. 2:10), he is envisioning a situation that is not safe for those who have the spiritual insight and the courage to acclaim Jesus as the Messiah (2:4).

If we are to read Matthew's prophetically informed teaching accurately, then we must begin by recognizing that the Sermon was promulgated in a "sick society," to use an image that the Gospel itself foregrounds. It is no coincidence that Matthew prefaces the sermon with an account of Jesus' extensive healing ministry, famed throughout Galilee, all Syria, and beyond (4:23–25). Jesus heals before he teaches; in this respect, the great teaching upon the mountain recapitulates an important element of Moses' Torah (Teaching) on Sinai, in the first ten "words" (Exod. 20:1) or commandments. The so-called historical prologue to the Decalogue, the statement of what God has already done, precedes any demand: "I am YHWH your God, who brought you out of the land of Egypt, out of the house of slaves; you shall have no other gods in my face" (Exod. 20:2–3). First of all, YHWH must be recognized as both compassionate and powerful, as the Deliverer; only then does the notion of exclusive obedience become coherent. Likewise in the ministry

210

of Jesus the Messiah, the exercise of compassion and release from bondage and suffering precedes instruction and demand.

Most scholars date Matthew's Gospel to approximately the year 80 and suppose that it originated among a small group, consisting mostly of Jews and existing as a beleaguered minority within the larger Jewish matrix in Greater Syria (Luz, *Matthew 1–7*, 87–93). By this widely shared reconstruction, Matthew sees no incompatibility between being a Jew and being a follower of Jesus, nor does he reject the people Israel. On the contrary, "the Gospel of Matthew and its author are Jewish to the core" (Saldarini, *Christian-Jewish Community*, 198). While he is open to the inclusion of "all nations" in the church (28:19), Matthew envisions the church as essentially "a Jesus-centered Israel" (*Christian-Jewish Community*, 202). Such a notion was objectionable to the Jewish majority and short-lived among Jesus-followers; it largely died out within a generation of his writing. Nonetheless, it was not entirely anomalous in the first century, a time when any notion of normative Judaism was itself in flux. Jewish groups were divided against each other in "a fluid social situation with imprecise boundaries, ongoing conflict, and unresolved tensions. . . . Matthew's vitriolic polemics, far from showing that he is anti-Jewish or outside the Jewish community, testify to his engagement in inner-Jewish sectarian politics" (*Christian-Jewish Community*, 9).

In order to understand the pressures under which Matthew is writing, it is essential to recognize that the intra-Jewish conflicts to which the Gospel attests assumed their particular form in a region thoroughly under the domination of the Roman Empire and its representatives—political, military, and administrative. Scholars tend to focus on one threat to the Matthean group—either the Jewish majority or the Romans—to the exclusion of the other. Thus the author of the Gospel is often seen to be engaged either in a polemic over interpretation and observance of Mosaic law, or in shoring up resistance against Rome, by delineating "the alternative world of God's empire" (Carter, *Matthew and the Margins*, 1). The perspective taken here is that the evangelist has in view the pressure and threats his group may experience from both the centers of Jewish power and the empire. Certainly Matthew identifies the "scribes and Pharisees" as the overt threat; after the destruction of the temple (70 CE), these were the leaders of the Jewish community in matters both political and religious. They are evidently the

211

immediate persecutors of Matthew's group, whose members can expect to testify before the local Jewish council (Sanhedrin) and to be flogged in the synagogue (Matt. 10:17). Yet throughout the Gospel, Roman imperial power is constantly glimpsed in the background; it is the current with or against which all Jews—indeed, every resident of territory controlled by Rome—had to swim in order to survive, let alone to prosper.

Prosperity was for the few in the latter part of the first century of the Common Era. The eastern Mediterranean under Roman rule was a world of inequities, of deprivation and precarious existence for the vast majority. Despite strong imperial claims that the gods had chosen Rome to manifest the divine blessings of universal peace, justice, and fertility, there was a huge disproportion and disparity between the small group of the socially and economically secure and the 90 percent who were chronically insecure, with no middle class as we know it. It is estimated that the tiny group of the elite—2 to 3 percent of the population—controlled most of the land and consumed some 65 percent of its production, often from an urban base (Carter, *Roman Empire*, 45–46). They were supported by the somewhat larger group (7 to 8 percent) of retainers: soldiers, merchants, priests, town or village elders, petty officials, and tax collectors. (Bruce Longenecker offers a more differentiated model for reckoning the economy scale for Greco-Roman urbanism; see *Remember the Poor*, 44–59.) These last were powerful agents of empire in a situation in which the empire laid claim to land and all basic foodstuffs: crops, animals, fish; all the essentials of life were heavily taxed. Together, then, the groups of those who exercised more or less power within the society constituted some 10 percent of the population. The remainder, that is, the socially disenfranchised, were field laborers and fishermen, urban artisans and unskilled workers, and day laborers and beggars.

It may be more than an accident of geography that the first disciples of Jesus the Galilean belonged to the low-status rank of fishermen. The summons of Peter and Andrew (Matt. 4:18–22) is a variation on prophetic call accounts such as those of Moses (Exod. 3), Elisha (1 Kgs. 19:19–21), and Amos (Amos 7:15). We might suppose that any one of their three prophetic predecessors was called to leave a reasonably prosperous family business (Elijah was plowing with twelve yoke of oxen!); likely each of them had some standing in their agrarian communities. But for the two fishermen in the world of imperial Rome, this is not so; in Cicero's ranking of the occupations according to social status, fishing takes the very lowest place. Moreover, the empire exercised tight control over the industry; fishermen were required to be licensed, to supply a certain quantity of fish, and to pay taxes on both catch and transport (Carter, *Matthew and the Margins*, 121). "Follow me, and I will make you fishers of people" (Matt. 4:19)—Jesus' call to Peter and Andrew might be heard as a claim that stands in some tension with the regular economic demands of the empire. All the more striking, then, is the emphatic and repeated statement that they and two others, James and John, "immediately" (*eutheōs*, vv. 20, 22) left nets, boat, and family (Zebedee, the father of James and John) to follow this new master.

Roman animosity against Jews would have been acute in Matthew's generation, more indeed than in Jesus' own time. Putting down the lengthy First Jewish Revolt (66–70 CE) had proven unexpectedly costly to Rome and thus caused the deepest outrage and determination to humiliate. Having razed the temple in Jerusalem, the Romans replaced the annual half-shekel temple tax with the *Fiscus Judaicus*, a tax levied only against Jews; the revenue was used to reconstruct another temple, that of Jupiter Capitolinus in Rome. Matthew's account of Jesus' altercation with the Pharisees and the "Herodians" (perhaps a general term for those who collaborated with the government) over the imperial tax (Matt. 22:15–22) likely reflects that insult. Coins were issued bearing the image of a weeping woman, with the legend *Judea Capta,* "captured Judea." Moreover, new cities were constructed (e.g., Neapolis, near Shechem), while Jews were expelled from Caesarea and other established cities, in order to accommodate the increased presence of Roman officials and other Gentiles (Levine, "Visions," 385).

After the Jewish Revolt, Roman military presence was also greatly increased in Syria and Palestine. The Tenth Legion, which had fought in the war, was permanently posted to Jerusalem. Warren Carter notes that in Antioch (one possible provenance for the Gospel), 20,000 Roman soldiers were garrisoned alongside a general population of 150,000—a presence impossible for any citizen to ignore. In addition to direct taxation to support the army, animals were requisitioned for transportation and people for labor; food and lodging were secured at the community's expense, sometimes by evicting people from their homes (Carter, *Matthew and Empire,* 41). Matthew assumes a social world in which tax collectors and centurions are prominent, and anyone might be commandeered on the road and forced to carry a soldier's pack (5:41).

Matthew and his group are pressed on every side by multiple opponents, and those opponents stand in complex relation to each other. Whatever may be the composition of the group(s) he calls "scribes and Pharisees," they should not be seen simply as allies or agents of Rome. The Gospel itself attests to arguments between them and Matthew's group over eating with tax collectors (9:9–13); on this point, Matthew's group is evidently more open than they to Roman collaborators, who may have been Jews or Gentiles. At the same time, the chief priests and the elders are portrayed as conspiring with the Romans in the events leading up to and following Jesus' death. It is a common irony and tragedy of history that threatened religious communities are often bitterly divided among themselves; their hatred of each other mirrors the hatred they see in (and feel toward) their external enemy.

Furthermore, not everything that Matthew writes about his Jewish opponents should be taken as an accurate account of the attitudes and teachings of the Pharisees, the spiritual ancestors and teachers of the rabbis who shaped normative Judaism in late antiquity, whom Matthew consistently represents unfavorably. Sometimes his representation of Torah (or contemporary Torah teaching) amounts to caricature, such as "You shall love your neighbor and hate your enemy" (5:43). No such teaching is found in the Hebrew Bible itself, nor in rabbinic texts; it is found among the sectarian Qumran scrolls (Levine and Brettler, *Jewish Annotated New Testament,* 12), which differ on many counts from what became normative Judaism. Matthew speaks disparagingly of the scribes and Pharisees imposing heavy burdens on others (23:4), and most Christian readers have accepted that as simple fact. Yet followers of the Pharisaic movement, which was gaining in popularity in Matthew's time, may have felt quite differently. Following the destruction of the temple, Pharisaic Judaism, which had been in existence for a couple of centuries, provided a point of religious orientation for many. "From the vantage point of a demoralized and perhaps confused and oppressed populace, they offered clarity, stability, and perhaps most significantly, a plan for securing the ritual purity that had been available in Jerusalem" (Charry, *Renewing,* 63).

Jews now had to find a new mode of access to the God of Abraham and Moses, in the absence of the ancient institutions of temple and priesthood. In this situation, new emphasis was given to a mode of purity practiced by individuals, largely in the context of the household. These purity observances worked "from the outside in" (Charry, *Renewing*, 65); they concerned matters of physical and material practice: food and cooking utensils, clothing and hair, bodily functions and the handling of disease and corpses, Sabbath observance. How that should be handled was a point of contention between the Pharisees and the followers of Jesus, as indicated by the disputes about washing hands before eating (15:1–20) or plucking grain on the Sabbath (12:1–8). In his bitter arguments with the Pharisees, Matthew's Jesus does not condemn outright their notion that ritual practices matter; he even judges it right to tithe mint, dill, and cumin (23:23), as long as "the weightier matters of Torah" are not neglected. In his teaching, purity and righteousness derive from personal character (23:25–28), yet this in itself is fully in accord with rabbinic prayers and teachings, which, like Jesus' own, focus largely on human intentions, moral behavior, and the condition of the heart.

Therefore it is a mistake to dismiss the Pharisees' focus on material practices as mere legalism, as though they imagined that God's favor could be obtained in mechanistic fashion, by the manipulation of externals. Moreover, there is a lively debate among New Testament scholars about whether the Matthean community itself may have observed some purity practices. For example, Matthew's Jesus never declares all foods clean (ritually pure) for Jewish consumption, in contrast to Mark (7:19) and Luke (Acts 10:15). What is certain is that for Matthew's group, religious observance must be practiced—and adjusted—in light of the person, teaching, and authority of Jesus the Messiah, who was himself the offspring of Abraham and indeed, the culmination of Israel's whole history (Matt. 1:1–17). This was a point of sharp disagreement—genuine sibling rivalry—with the Jewish majority. Each group was convinced that the other had chosen a dangerously misleading path and was blocking access to God by those who strove to be faithful (cf. 23:13–15).

The angry rhetoric of Matthew's Gospel is one foundational element in Christian contempt for supposed Jewish legalism, even if it is not always recognized as such. Yet, as Anthony Saldarini observes, "Matthew is an authentic witness both to the shared traditions that unite and to the deep hostilities that divide the Jewish and

215

Christian communities. Most important, though, this gospel forces Christians to confront again and again their Jewish roots and rules out Marcion's expedient of obliterating the Jewish foundations of faith in Jesus as Messiah and Son of God" (*Christian-Jewish Community*, 205). So if gentile Christians are to make good use of this Gospel, then we must reckon honestly with the fact that Matthew's characterizations of his Jewish opponents are one-sided (in the manner of all polemic), and moreover, bitter and sometimes misleading. This Jewish evangelist is trying to move the Jewish majority to become, with him, followers of Jesus. Within the Gospel narrative, that majority is represented by the great crowds of the as-yet-uncommitted, who follow Jesus about (4:25), drawn to his work of healing, listening to him with astonishment, "for he taught them as one having [moral] authority, and not as their scribes" (7:29). Matthew's emotional rhetoric about his opponents is designed to move a crowd, in a way that fair, balanced criticism of the scribes and Pharisees might fail to do.

Contemporary Western Christians may learn something valuable from Matthew, if we recognize that he is struggling mightily, though not always grace-fully, with a problem that belongs to us also, at least to some degree, even if we are not conscious of it. His is the problem of belonging to a despised and sometimes threatened minority. "Christians now need to get used to being a minority," says Christian theologian Ellen Charry, speaking of Western Christians, in a personal communication. "In this, they can learn a lot from Jews." Matthew is part of a tiny minority of Jesus-followers, most of them Jewish, living among other Jews and pagans in a Roman-dominated society; in that challenging situation, he is striving to build a fellowship living in accordance with the Law and the Prophets as interpreted by and around the person of Jesus. In other words, he is committed to the kind of radical discipleship that one modern interpreter of the Sermon on the Mount, Eberhard Arnold, founder of the Bruderhof movement in twentieth-century Germany, suggestively calls "re-becoming" (*Salt and Light*, 57).

Taken from the thought of the German theologian Meister Eckhart, the notion of "re-becoming" might be a good conceptual translation for the biblical concept of *metanoia*, often inadequately rendered "repentance." The call to *metanoia* is the starting point for the preaching of both John the Baptist (Matt. 3:2, 8) and Jesus (4:17); its substance is developed most fully in the Sermon on

216

the Mount. For Matthew, *metanoia* is a complete renewal of the self in response to God's sovereign presence: "You shall therefore be whole [*teleioi*], as your heavenly Father is whole" (5:48). The Gospel makes it clear that for a disciple of Jesus the work of re-becoming entails the relinquishment of fear (10:26–31) and the presumed right to judge the way others "see" (7:1–5). It requires also persistent forgiveness of others (6:12, 14–15), including one's "brother," that is, a member of one's spiritual or biological kinship group (18:21–22). Matthew's harsh judgments upon the scribes and Pharisees show that he falls short of his own understanding of the standard of perfection: "he would condemn himself were he examined for hypocrisy!" (Charry, *Renewing*, 83). The evangelist's own partial failure may caution twenty-first-century disciples of Jesus to seek a deeper humility, as we strive to speak truthfully to and about those with whom we disagree over important religious matters. It might move us also to deeper compassion and respect for Christians who are "not like us," and likewise for religiously committed people of other faiths—all of us living in a dominant society whose values are largely antithetical to the claims of all our religious traditions.

The Privileged Life (Matthew 5)

It is a lost cause to try to follow Christ in only one sphere of life. (Eberhard Arnold, *Salt and Light*, 18)

The Sermon on the Mount is the single fullest statement on discipleship in the Bible. The sermon is addressed in the first instance to the disciples who gather around the seated Jesus (5:1–2)—the customary posture for a teacher. Here for the first time the followers of Jesus are called "disciples" (*mathētai*), a word that among both Jews and Gentiles in the Hellenistic world denoted the adherents of a master teacher of one kind or another: philosopher, musician, rhetorician, religious teacher, or prophet (Wilkins, *Discipleship*, 42, 44, 94). If use of the term here suggests that the teaching is intended primarily for those already committed to Jesus, nonetheless the closing note (7:28) indicates that the crowds overheard, so to speak. The multitudes were astounded at Jesus' display of authority—although not necessarily moved to conviction.

217

The sermon is a carefully crafted piece of poetic prose, composed of short memorable sayings in a terse style devoid of qualifying statements, like the Wisdom literature of the Bible. The sermon also resembles that literature, and especially the books of Proverbs and Sirach (Ecclesiasticus), in that it treats aspects of the daily business of living in community: anger (Matt. 5:22–26), marital fidelity (5:27–32), truthful speaking (5:33–37), greed (6:19–21), and anxiety (6:25–34). Wisdom literature is one of the most important scriptural resources for Christian ethics, and so noting these points of resemblance may counter the tendency to view the Sermon on the Mount as a spiritualizing text that upholds a perfectionist ideal, or one that advances a personal piety rather than offering guidance for the public behavior of Christians.

The sermon also shows the influence of the prophetic literature, especially in its fierce language (Matt. 5:26–30) and its evident intention to unsettle religious expectations through counterintuitive assertions such as the Beatitudes. Ethicist Glen Stassen describes the sermon as expressing a "prophetic realism" (*Thicker Jesus,* 185–86); it delineates "a grace-based practical way of deliverance" (188) from dangerous concentrations of power, through submission to the lordship of Christ. He shows how the prophetic power of the sermon made it a guiding force for the countercultural and dangerous discipleship of modern Christians such as Dietrich Bonhoeffer and Martin Luther King, André Trocmé and other "Righteous Gentiles" of the Nazi period, as well as Muriel Lester, Dorothy Day, and Clarence Jordan, each of whom founded a community and lived with the poor in (respectively) London, New York City, or rural and segregated Georgia.

If many Western Christians are now more comfortable with the sermon than Matthew would have wanted us to be, or if we hear it as a call to an inner piety only, and not to ethical and social change, then that is in part because we do not hear its words in their full scriptural context. We miss some of the echoes that the first, presumably Jewish, hearers would have caught, being more immersed in the thought-world of Israel's Scriptures. Moreover, we may not be listening from the perspective of those whose social situation is precarious, devalued, if not overtly dangerous. If we do nothing to correct those deficits, Matthew might question whether we can hear them as disciples at all—or do we belong more in the category of the crowds who overhear but are not necessarily committed? It

218

is notable in this respect that in Matthew and the other Synoptic Gospels, "persecution and dishonour are associated only with discipleship" (Davies and Allison, *Commentary on Matthew*, 1:544). Maybe it is too much to say that they are *qualifying* conditions for Christian discipleship, but certainly the evangelists lead us to look upon dishonor and persecution as a form of public acknowledgment for those who have most distinguished themselves as disciples. For Matthew, the privileged status of being social outcasts gives a distinctly prophetic character to the lives of disciples (5:11–12) and also links their lives firmly with Jesus' rejection, suffering, and death. Both of these are matters of the greatest ethical significance, as the Beatitudes make clear. The following discussion highlights how the Beatitudes delineate the identity and practices of disciples in terms that are fully coherent only when read against the background of the Old Testament and in relation to particular social contexts, ancient and contemporary, to which the Gospel speaks.

The first word that Jesus utters to his disciples is *makarioi*—conventionally, "blessed." We may better appreciate how startling is his use of the term in light of Ellen Charry's rendering of it as "privileged"; the poor in spirit, the mournful, the meek, and so on, are honored and dignified in that the favor of God rests upon them (*Renewing*, 66–72). Here he echoes the first word in the Greek translation of Psalm 1, a short wisdom poem that depicts the "privileged" life of the one who "murmurs over" the Torah/Teaching of YHWH day and night (Ps. 1:2). That echo of the well-known psalm might well have suggested to Matthew's hearers that Jesus is redefining Torah piety for his disciples and at the same time identifying a new set of conditions for social standing or belonging: "theirs is the kingdom of heaven" (Matt. 5:3, 10). By stating those conditions in terms that both echo Scripture and obliquely confront fundamental social values in Greco-Roman society, Matthew represents participation in God's kingdom as a scripturally framed and prophetically envisioned alternative to seeking privilege or even safety within the power structures of the Roman Empire.

The prophetic character of the Beatitudes is established through Matthew's transparent use of the language and imagery of Isaiah 61, a passage in which the one whom YHWH has "anointed" (Isa. 61:1) proclaims deliverance for the vulnerable, the broken-hearted, the faint of spirit (Isa. 61:1–3; Matt. 5:3), the mournful (Isa. 61:3; Matt. 5:4). The anointed speaker is making a Jubilee proclamation of liberty in "the year of YHWH's favor" (Isa. 61:2; cf. Lev. 25:8–28), the year when the landless poor are to return to their own land, each family to its ancestral inheritance (cf. Isa. 61:5). The lengthy teaching in Leviticus concerning the Jubilee is the most carefully elaborated divine mandate in Torah. Thus it provides crucial background and substance for Jesus' new teaching, most notably in the third beatitude: "They shall inherit the land/ soil/earth [tēn gēn]" (Matt. 5:5). This connection between the Beatitudes and the Jubilee, via Isaiah, is strong evidence that the sermon is not to be read as advancing a program of personal spirituality abstracted from matters of social justice. Regardless of uncertainty about the extent to which it may have been observed in ancient times, the Jubilee stands in Scripture as a social and economic institution, a community-based mode of public action on behalf of the disenfranchised.

The several allusions to Isaiah 61 with which the sermon begins are a signal to Matthew's hearers that the justice for which disciples hunger and thirst (Matt. 5:6) and suffer persecution (5:10) is now "springing up" at the word of God's anointed, just as the prophet proclaimed (Isa. 61:11; Isaiah's metaphor of righteousness springing up like a plant from soil itself evokes the material reality of the Jubilee year). Other Jewish texts from this period (the Dead Sea Scrolls and the Aramaic *targum*, or expansive translation of the Bible) read this Isaiah passage eschatologically, as portraying the anticipated liberation of Israel's captives in their own time (Allison, *Sermon*, 16). Thus Matthew's hearers would have recognized Jesus as the eschatological prophet whose voice and teaching was first heard long ago, the one upon whom God's Spirit rests (Matt. 3:16; cf. Isa. 42:1). That identity between the ancient Scripture and the new teaching constitutes Jesus' "astounding" authority (Matt. 7:28–29).

"Privileged/favored are the poor in spirit [ptōchoi tō pneumati], for theirs is the kingdom of heaven" (Matt. 5:3)—from an ethical perspective, a major question about the first beatitude is the intended force of the qualifying phrase, "in spirit." Many modern readers, and especially those with a strong commitment to social justice, prefer Luke's version (6:20), where the qualifier does not appear. Yet surely that phrase is not a casual inclusion in Matthew's otherwise terse formulations, so we must ask how he is using it to shape disciples' understanding of what it is to be the divinely favored poor. The obvious answer might seem to be that the phrase has a spiritualizing force; Dale Allison (*Sermon*, 45) draws a contrast between the "spiritual" meaning of *ptōchoi* ("the poor") here and its literal usage everywhere else in Matthew (11:5; 19:21; 26:9, 11). However, one might question how firmly such a contrast can be drawn. *Ptōchos* is a word that denotes social status, namely that of a beggar; it is "the strongest available Greek word for social poverty" (Luz, *Matthew 1–7*, 231). Allison himself envisions the immediate hearers of the sermon as "marginal missionaries with few possessions" (*Sermon*, 45–46).

Matthew's social world was in some respects similar to our own, with great economic disparity and recurrent or extreme economic vulnerability for the largest portion of the population. The sermon itself addresses some people who are devoted to mammon, the form of idolatry that we call "materialism" (6:24); it cautions against anxiety about food or drink or clothing (6:25–34). Some of the first hearers might have been anxious about these things from the standpoint of increasing their prestige; that is, they were in a position to make economic choices. However, it would seem that others were worried from a very different perspective; the day laborers, the beggars, the tenant farmers and smallholders contending with high taxes and frequently poor harvests—they were anxious about simply getting through the next few days (6:34). These were the people who, when they prayed for daily bread (6:11), meant it literally.

In the Scriptures familiar to Matthew, several Hebrew words usually rendered "poor, afflicted, needy, humble" (*'ānî, 'ānāw, 'ebyôn*) express poverty, with both literal and spiritual connotations. These words appear frequently, especially in the Prophets and Psalms, and often it is impossible to distinguish between the two senses. Matthew might well have had in mind a text such as Psalm 34, which lets us hear the voice of one who appears to be socially oppressed as well as spiritually humble:

> In YHWH my whole-being glories;
> let the humble [*'ănāwîm*] hear and rejoice.
> . . . .
> I appealed to YHWH and he answered me,
> and from all my terrors he delivered me.
> . . . .

221

> This poor-one ['ānî] called out, and YHWH heard,
> and from all his troubles saved him.
>
> . . . .
>
> YHWH is close to the brokenhearted
> and saves those crushed in spirit.
>
> (vv. 3, 5, 7, 19 [2, 4, 6, 18E])

Here the reference to "spirit" does not exert any mitigating force. On the contrary, the phrase "crushed in spirit" (dakkě'ê rûaḥ) captures the grinding effects of the "terrors and troubles," some of which likely derive from poverty itself, which leaves no part of one's personhood untouched. The standard Hebrew lexicon lists "contrite" as the primary meaning of dakkā' (Brown, Brown-Driver-Briggs, 194), which occurs just twice (cf. Isa. 57:15), but that spiritualizing translation is too narrow; the core meaning of the adjective is "crushed." The related verb, which is common, is used in a metaphorical but not spiritualized sense, to denote the crushing effect of social oppression (e.g., Isa. 3:15). Moreover, in Isaiah the adjectival form occurs specifically in the context where the prophet condemns the greed of the powerful (56:11) and the callous exploitation and destruction of the righteous (57:1)—while those who are "crushed" remain close to God and thus susceptible to being restored to genuine life (57:15). It would seem that the psalmist, Isaiah, and likewise Matthew perceive that social and economic position is a factor related to the disposition of the heart before God.

Among contemporary theologians, perhaps the Brazilian Catholic Leonardo Boff has most fully explored the relation between a social location among the poor, on the one hand, and Christian theology and spirituality, on the other. In many books he writes of the "spiritual shock" of a new revelation of God bursting forth in history in our time, summoning into being a new mode of discipleship, namely, "a spiritual experience of encounter with the Lord of the poor" (Faith, 80). His theological position is based on the strong assertion, derived from Matthew (25:31–46, cited repeatedly) and many other biblical texts, that God maintains an "especially concentrated" presence in the poor, who are themselves the sacrament of God's self-communication. Because this sacrament of divine presence is directly embodied in human beings, the poor are now much more than an object of mercy for the church. Boff's radical, scripturally grounded claim is that they have a "*privileged position* accorded by the God of the Old Testament to the slaves of Egypt and the captives of Babylon, the position defined by Jesus from the very beginning of his proclamation of his Good News. In short, theirs is the place of the poor in the Reign of God" (*When Theology Listens*, 30).

As human sacraments, the poor collectively have a unique spiritual capacity to show forth Christ to the church and the world. "They possess a singular wealth of their own. They are the chosen vessels of the Lord, the prime addressees of the Reign of God, the potential evangelizers of the Church and of the whole human race" (Boff, *Faith*, 85). Recognizing the full force of this mode of divine revelation must provoke a movement of the heart, a commitment "to struggle against the poverty that demeans persons and contravenes the will of God, to struggle against the fruit of a relationship of sin and exploitation. The true faith itself, precisely by virtue of its truth, implies and demands a commitment to liberation: '. . . and you gave me food . . . (Matt. 25:35)' (*Faith*, 86). The poor draw others to themselves and thus to Christ. In arguing for the full integration of spirituality and politics in "evangelical solidarity with the very needy" (*Faith*, 80), Boff opens up the meaning of Matthew's version of the first beatitude and offers an understanding of discipleship that is indispensable for contemporary Christians.

The first and eighth beatitudes (Matt. 5:3, 10) point to the kingdom of heaven as a reality attainable in the present by the poor and those persecuted for justice: "for theirs is [*estin*] the kingdom of heaven." This repeated declaration constitutes a kind of frame around Matthew's picture of the character and experience of the divinely favored. The present-tense verb in the frame contrasts with the future-oriented promises in the other beatitudes; although the full experience of the kingdom of heaven is not yet evident, faithful disciples are already recognized as belonging to God's alternative empire. This sense of belonging is reinforced by the direct address to the persecuted that follows and amplifies the eighth beatitude: "Privileged are you . . ." (5:11–12). With that, the picture of citizenship in the kingdom of heaven pops out of the frame and directly into the life of the reviled and persecuted. At the same time, this final statement allows faithful disciples to situate themselves within the well-developed scriptural picture of the persecuted prophets "who were before you."

Dale Allison comments perceptively on how these two framing references to the kingdom of heaven (Matt. 5:3, 10) establish the perspective for the sermon: "It does not so much look forward, from the present to the consummation, as it looks backwards, from the consummation to the present" (*Sermon*, 12). That perspective is itself of the greatest ethical significance. If we do the reverse— looking forward, with a focus on the consummation—then the present can seem inconsequential; the sooner it is over and done with, the better. But if we adopt the sermon's perspective and view the present in the light of eternity, then we see how much it matters where we place our loyalties, whose experience we share. If we believe that citizenship in the kingdom of heaven is indeed a present possibility, then we may gain courage for living our faith.

This discussion of the Beatitudes emphasizes that Matthew offers his instructions on discipleship against the background of Scripture. Moreover, he does not attempt to abstract the spiritual disposition of disciples from the social and economic conditions in which they labor to be faithful. These two considerations may be related, and both of them together bear on interpretation of the third beatitude: "Privileged are the meek/humble [*praëis*], for they shall inherit the earth" (Matt. 5:5). Several early authorities place this beatitude immediately after the first, in what may be the original order (Allison, *Sermon*, 48). If so, then the reference to heaven in the first is directly complemented by the reference to earth (or "land") here; these are two angles of vision on our experience of and hope for life in this world. Of all the Beatitudes, this is the only one that has (in paraphrase) proverbial status: "The meek shall inherit the earth." Yet despite the seemingly concrete terms of that assurance, many Western Christians do not ascribe much meaning to it; those I have asked typically say, "I don't know what it means to inherit the earth." A further difficulty with this beatitude is that meekness is generally viewed as a negative character trait in our culture, which encourages self-confidence and rewards self-assertion; it is not easy for us to imagine that meekness, which we associate with weakness, receives any concrete reward.

The most important thing about this statement of divine favor is that all its key terms are echoes of scriptural passages that Matthew might have expected his hearers to know. The word that is inadequately translated as "meek" is *praüs*, which in the Greek translation of Torah is the outstanding attribute of Moses: "And

224

the man Moses was exceedingly *praüs*, beyond all the people who were upon the earth" (Num. 12:3). As we have seen (pp. 35–51, sections on Moses, servant of God, and Miriam), in the context of the story in Numbers, Moses is distinguished for being trusted beyond all others in YHWH's "household" (12:7) and for his humble response to God's taking some of his own prophetic spirit and distributing it among seventy (or perhaps seventy-plus-two) elders (11:24–30). Within Matthew's Gospel, the adjective *praüs* appears elsewhere only in Jesus' self-description (Matt. 11:29) and in the prophetically inspired description of his lowly entrance into Jerusalem (21:5).

These evocations of the mature Moses and of Jesus clarify the meaning of what it is for disciples to be *praëis*. Against the background of the wider scriptural use of the word, Clarence Jordan comments memorably:

> People may be called "meek" to the extent that they have surrendered their wills to God and learned to do his bidding. The meek won't attempt to explain away God's Word if it goes contrary to their selfish wills. . . . Through them [God's] will is done on earth as it is in heaven; through them the kingdom of heaven comes to earth. That's why you can't stop them. That's why they "inherit the land," that is, the promised land or the kingdom. Only the meek, "the terrible meek," the totally committed meek, are considered worthy of an inheritance in the new land, the kingdom of God on earth. (*Sermon on the Mount*, 24–25)

The beatitude is a close paraphrase of the Greek version of Psalm 36:11 (37:11 in the Hebrew and most English versions), which reads, "The meek [*praëis*] shall inherit [the] land, and delight in abundant peace." The theme of inheriting land is thematic in this wisdom psalm, which has strong prophetic overtones. The phrase and the assurance occurs five times (vv. 9, 11, 22, 29, 34), and the whole context argues that it is meant to be taken literally. The psalmist/sage seeks to cultivate trust in God, in the face of "the wicked," "evildoers" who bring their weapons against the "poor and vulnerable" (v. 14) and initiate legal proceedings against them (v. 33). The situation envisioned is one of economic hardship, in which people are borrowing money and it is at least conceivable that children will be forced to beg for their daily bread (v. 25). The probable social setting for such a teaching is an agrarian community of small farmers struggling against the combined forces of a crushing tax burden, periodic famine (v. 19), debts and debt slavery, and legalized land grabs by the "successful" (v. 7). This is exactly the sort of situation that all the legal codes in Torah address, and especially the Jubilee legislation (Lev. 25). The agrarian prophets of the eighth century—Amos, Hosea, Isaiah, and Micah—likewise speak to this social threat (Davis, *Scripture, Culture*, 120–38). Even more directly, one might hear echoing behind this psalm the story of Elijah confronting Ahab over the rigged trial and murder of Naboth and the royal takeover of his valuable vineyard—not incidentally, some of the best agricultural land in Israel (1 Kgs. 21; see Davis, *Scripture, Culture*, 111–17). Against such threats, the psalmist/sage encourages the relatively poor to give and lend generously (Ps. 37:21, 26)—that is, without the exorbitant interest rates that were the ancient norm for money-lenders. Through mutual economic support, the whole community may hope to "dwell in the land and feed on faithfulness" (v. 3; cf. v. 27). Such a scenario of chronic need would have changed little for common folk, from Israelite villagers in the Iron Age to Jesus' followers in the Greco-Roman period. This problem, ancient already in Jesus' time, gives substance to his (or Matthew's) own wisdom teaching, directed toward creating a culture of generosity among disciples:

> Give to the one who asks,
> and the one who wants to borrow from you, do not turn away.
> (Matt. 5:42)

It is evident that the sermon is not a call merely to "an amiable virtuousness," as Dietrich Bonhoeffer cautioned (*Cost*, 144), but rather to costly self-surrender to the will of God and the genuine needs of the neighbor. Further, the cost of "perfect wholeness" or "full maturity" (Matt. 5:48) is spiritual, and at the same time social and economic. As we have seen, most of the disciples to whom this call was first addressed were socially marginal. They would have known that practicing spiritual humility would not exempt them from the public humiliation they could still expect—as the poor, as Jews, as followers of Jesus. Rather, spiritual humility was the condition of the heart that might enable them, in the midst of humiliating experience, to perceive and hold fast to God's faithfulness: "Rejoice

226

and be wildly happy, for your reward is great in heaven, for thus they persecuted the prophets who were before you!" (5:12).

For Matthew, Jesus is of course the foremost exemplar of perfect wholeness, of full surrender to the will of God, displayed under pressure of persecution. He embodies the beatitudes of meekness, mercy, purity of heart, thirst for justice, and willing endurance of persecution; Jesus is the sermon made flesh, as the rest of the Gospel will show. So the life of Christ is the template for the disciples' life that Matthew sketches in the sermon, and behind both the disciples and Jesus there stands yet another figure, namely, the Servant of whom Isaiah spoke. Matthew's prophet mentor is not explicitly named in the sermon, but when Jesus instructs the disciples about how they must face "evildoers" (Matt. 5:38–42), he draws directly upon the picture of the faithful sufferer in Isaiah's third Servant Song (Isa. 50:4–9). The charge to offer one's cheek to be struck recalls the Servant's report:

> My back I gave to beatings, and my cheeks to blows;
> my face I did not turn away from the shame of spitting.
> (Isa. 50:6 LXX)

Seven verbal echoes link the passage from the sermon with the Servant Song:

antistēnai, "stand against, resist" (Matt. 5:39; Isa. 50:8)
rapizō, "strike" (Matt. 5:39; Isa. 50:6)
siagon, "cheek" (Matt. 5:39, Isa. 50:6)
krinō, "bring before a court" (Matt. 5:40; Isa. 50:8)
himation, "cloak" (Matt. 5:40; Isa. 50:9)
didōmi, "give" (Matt. 5:42; Isa. 50:4, 6)
apostrephō, "turn away" (Matt. 5:42; Isa. 50:6)

Further, two of these words—"strike" and "cloak"—appear also in Matthew's account of Jesus' torture and stripping at the hands of Roman soldiers (Matt. 26:67; 27:31, 35).

With this complex set of verbal associations, Matthew gives suffering disciples a new perspective on their humiliation. "If his followers then turn the other cheek and let the enemy have their clothes, will they not be remembering their Lord, especially in his passion?" (Davies and Allison, *Commentary on Matthew*, 1:546). If they recognize themselves as imitators of Christ, then the very

227

possibility of the disciples being humiliated by those who presume to have power over them is undercut. The confluence of words and images from the Servant Song, the passion, and the instruction to disciples creates an acute irony: the more contempt persecutors show for the followers of Jesus, the more they honor them as fellow sufferers with their Lord, who is himself the divinely favored Servant of whom Isaiah spoke. Persecution in effect confers upon disciples a noble lineage; they are worthy descendants of Isaiah's Servant, who is described as one of the *limmûdîm* (Isa. 50:4), a term for a favored disciple or teacher (see Wilkins, *Discipleship*, 44, 49–50, 94). One might say that in this way Matthew's Jesus gives disciples a good reason for loving their enemies and praying for those who persecute them (Matt. 5:44). Despite their own intention to destroy, persecutors may actually help disciples to achieve the "perfect wholeness" (5:48), the Christlike offering of self to which they are called.

Thus Matthew completes the strange picture of divinely conferred privilege that begins with the Beatitudes. It is no coincidence that the sermon begins by depicting the life of disciples as honorable—however peculiar the standard of value—for honor was the coin of the realm in the Greco-Roman world. Virtually every aspect of one's life and social interaction was potentially a point of honor or shame in relation to others. The graduated continuum between those two poles was marked with respect to family lineage and birthplace; the social standing of one's friends, patrons, and clients; one's occupation and clothing; religious rituals performed; banquets given and attended; as well as one's place at the table or—as Matthew tells it—in the synagogue (Matt. 23:6). Then, as now, some pews were more prestigious than others. As Mark Finney observes, "Honour . . . was considered part of what was termed 'limited goods'" and hence "always in short supply" (*Honour*, 29). It was a zero-sum game; one person's gain in honor constituted loss for another. For Greeks and Romans, and also for Jews who had accommodated to some degree to the demands of society, the quest for greater honor was relentless. Likewise, there was a perceived need for constant vigilance against any challenge to or diminution of personal or familial honor, which constituted "an attack on the very basis of one's life and well-being" (*Honour*, 48).

The notion of honor as limited goods was not entirely foreign to ancient Israelite society, as is reflected in the story of competition

228

between Esau and Jacob over birthright and paternal blessing (Gen. 25:29–34 and 27:30–45). Yet after years of separation, precipitated by one brother's hatred and the other's fear, the less-blessed Esau himself upends that notion of limited goods. As Jacob advances cautiously with gifts to appease the older brother whose honor he himself had diminished, Esau runs to embrace and kiss him, declaring: "I have an abundance, my brother; keep what is yours" (Gen. 33:9). Similarly, Matthew challenges disciples to love and pray for enemies, to honor with a greeting those outside their community who treat them with little love (Matt. 5:44–47). He acknowledges that one may not expect such behaviors from Gentiles (5:47). It is notable, however, that some early rabbinic traditions offer a close parallel to Matthew's teachings in this matter: "Be first in greeting every person" (*m. 'Abot* 4:15); "It was related of [first-century] Rabban Yohanan ben Zakkai that no one ever gave him greeting first, not even a gentile in the street" (*b. Ber.* 17a).

While such sources as these may have influenced Matthew to some degree, it is likely that for his inverted logic of divinely conferred honor, he is most indebted to Isaiah. Prominently within the prophetic traditions of the Bible, the poet-prophet whom we call Second Isaiah associates God's favor with conditions of existence that are normally considered anything but desirable. Through the prophet, God addresses strong assurance to the "worm Jacob" (Isa. 41:14), a striking term of dishonor (omitted from the Greek version). The assault on our expectations is reinforced by the four so-called Servant Songs that follow shortly thereafter and present a clear record of God's favor to the one whose circumstances appear to be shameful. Matthew took careful note of this record; he quotes or reflects the central themes of each of the Songs:

> The Servant chosen by God who nonetheless does not seek to be widely recognized as a prophet or religious leader (Isa. 42:1). The whole Song is quoted in Matt. 12:18–21, immediately following Jesus' instruction to the crowds "not to make him known"; Jesus' reed scepter (Matt. 27:29–30) may also reflect the "bruised reed" that the Servant does not break (Isa. 42:3).
>
> The one "deeply despised, abhorrent to Gentiles" (Isa. 49:7)   229
> and yet destined to be honored by kings (cf. Matt. 27:29, 37, 39–42, 54).

The favored disciple and teacher who is beaten mercilessly yet steadfastly refuses to be put to shame (Isa. 50:7); as noted above, the passage echoes through Matt. 5:38–42.

The Servant exalted by God, whom people hold to be of no account, willingly wounded and killed for the *shalom* of those who despised him (Isa. 53:3, 5, 12; v. 4 is cited in Matt. 8:17).

Matthew clearly identifies Jesus as the prophesied and prophetic Servant; his ministry, ignominious death, resurrection, and exaltation exemplify the divinely favored life that would have been incomprehensible without the Servant Songs of Isaiah. By reading Isaiah around Jesus, Matthew offers disciples the pattern for life that is "privileged" by God, a model of the genuinely honorable life that is powerful enough to withstand their own society's pretensions, and indeed its assaults.

Praying Prophetically: The Lord's Prayer (Matthew 6:9–13)

The ubiquity of the Lord's Prayer in Christian usage is such that it is hard to recognize that it comes as a novelty in its scriptural context; this is the first overt instruction in prayer in the Bible. While most biblical prayers are located in Psalms and the Prophets, it is primarily in the New Testament that the activity of praying is treated explicitly as a discipline, that is, a learned behavior (cf. Luke 11:1) that must be practiced with regularity by individuals and the gathered community (1 Thess. 5:17; Acts 1:14). Paul writes frequently of his assiduous prayers for the church (Eph. 1:16–17; Phil. 1:9; Col. 1:9–12). He and others describe and prescribe it as the signature activity and responsibility of the church. The tasks of prayer include praise (Luke 24:53) and petitions for healing (Jas. 5:13–16), for deliverance from danger (Acts 12:5–12), for powerful witness to the gospel (Eph. 6:18–20). Dale Allison suggests that the Lord's Prayer may originally have been meant for use by the relatively small group of itinerant missionaries commissioned by Jesus (*Sermon*, 131–32). Having no single set form (cf. the sparer version in Luke 11:2–4), it was probably intended to be adapted for particular circumstances.

230

The opening address in Matthew's version of the prayer, "Our Father in the heavens [plural]" (contrast Luke's simple address: "Father," 11:2), is far from being a standard biblical idiom of prayer. Only about a dozen times is YHWH called "father" in the Hebrew Scriptures, specifically as the Creator of the people Israel (Deut. 32:6), who cares for them tenderly (Jer. 31:9) and deserves to be honored (Mal. 1:6); as the single Father of the whole people (2:10), for whose sake they should keep with each other the "covenant of life and peace" (2:5); as protector of orphans (Ps. 68:6 [5E]); or in relation to David and his royal house (2 Sam. 7:14; Ps. 89:27 [26E]). Further, just one other biblical prayer is clearly addressed to YHWH as "our Father"—not once, but three times (Isa. 63:16 [2x]; 64:7 [8E]; compare the ambiguous instance of 1 Chr. 29:10, where "our father" could refer to either YHWH or Israel/Jacob). It is notable that Matthew's sole model for addressing God as "our Father" is the book of Isaiah, which, as we have seen, was seminal for his understanding of Jesus and of discipleship. The opening words of Matthew's formulation of the Lord's Prayer are one strong indicator that he hears Jesus with the help of Isaiah. Prayers articulated by that "evangelical Prophet" guide Matthew in presenting his version of the prayer that in turn guides the prophetic ministries of Jesus' disciples.

It is especially appropriate for Matthew to follow Isaiah here, since that prophet's repeated use of "our Father" occurs within a bold and memorable prayer that shows several specific points of connection with the situation of Matthew's community. Despite the seven centuries that separated them from the Judeans addressed by Third Isaiah, members of a marginalized Christian Jewish community in the first century might well have heard the following verses as bringing before God their own urgent appeal:

> Look down from the heavens and see, from the eminence of your holiness and splendor!
> Where is your passion and your might, your gut-felt yearning and compassion?
> They are withheld from me!
> Indeed you are our Father,
> although Abraham does not know us, and Israel does not recognize us.
> You, YHWH, are our Father; our Redeemer from long past is your name.

231

Why would you lead us astray from your ways, harden our hearts
against fearing you?
Turn back for the sake of your servants, the tribes that are your
heritage!
For a little while they dispossessed your holy people; our foes
trampled your sanctuary.
We have long been as those whom you do not rule, over whom your
name is not proclaimed—
if only you would tear open the heavens and come down; the
mountains would quake before you!

(Isa. 63:15–19 [63:15–64:1E])

Some time after the destruction of YHWH's sanctuary in Jerusalem in the sixth century, the prophet-poet composed this prayer
on behalf of a group of Judeans (Jews) about whom we know nothing more than what is indicated here. Although they have been
ostracized by the Jewish majority ("Abraham does not know us"), he
encourages them to see themselves as YHWH's ancient "heritage."
These Jews are evidently suffering from theological confusion at
YHWH's apparent unresponsiveness, and the prophet addresses
their confusion by repeatedly naming them as "servants" (cf. Isa.
56:6; 65:8, 13 [3x], 14, 15; 66:14). The implication is that they stand
in the Isaianic tradition of the divinely chosen Servant who suffers, remains faithful, and ultimately serves to proclaim among the
nations God's glory (Isa. 66:19), God's name (Matt. 28:19).

On these several points—destruction of the Jerusalem temple,
rejection by the larger Jewish community, acute suffering for the
sake of the faith, an evangelical vocation—Matthew and his community would have recognized themselves in the ancient prophecy. Matthew, like Isaiah, is an innovative traditionalist engaged in
combat with those who in the name of Abraham reject other Jews
(Matt. 3:9). He asserts his own counterclaim beginning with the first
words of his Gospel: "A [new] book of Genesis of Jesus Christ, son of
David, son of Abraham" (1:1). Having established their lineage and
their right to pray to the God of Abraham, Matthew now instructs
the followers of Jesus to pray to "our Father," as did Isaiah. A further,
oblique link with Isaiah is the additional phrase "in the heavens"
(often a plural noun in Matthew's Greek, a peculiarity that perhaps
reflects the standard Hebrew word šāmayim, which is formally a dual
form), which is absent from Luke. Like the impassioned prophet,
disciples of Jesus now pray that the "heavens" may be opened and

232

God's rule made fully manifest in human lives: "Your kingdom come, your will be done, on earth as it is in heaven!" (Matt. 6:10).

The disciples' prayer is thus a sequel to Isaiah's; it is necessary for bringing to completion the "new Genesis" account that begins with Abraham, the story of God and those "few" (Matt. 22:14)—or rather the many unlikely ones (22:10)—who do in fact accept the invitation to enter into "the kingdom of the heavens" (22:2). The completion of that story involves the dual agency of God and the faithful servants of God, of whom Isaiah spoke and whom Matthew now identifies with the faithful disciples of Jesus. Paul Minear highlights both this dual agency and the significance of the historical moment, as Matthew perceives it: "What God has now done in the heavens opens up the possibility of a transfer to the earth of God's presence and power. The actual transfer of such power, however, remains subject to the convergence of the Father's design in heaven and the praying of his family on earth" (*Good News*, 150).

The appeal to "our Father" is underscored throughout the Gospel by Matthew's distinctive emphasis on the fatherhood of God. His Jesus speaks of and to God as Father some forty-two times (5:16, 45, 48; 11:25–27; 16:17, etc.), far more than in the other Synoptic Gospels (four times in Mark, fifteen times in Luke). Accordingly, Matthew argues against using that honorific for religious leaders, either in the synagogue or in the church: "And you shall call no one your father on earth, for [just] One is your Father— the heavenly one" (23:9)—a phrasing that probably deliberately echoes the most fundamental statement of Jewish faith, the Shema (Deut. 6:4, quoted in Matt. 22:37 and Mark 12:29; see Davies and Allison, *Commentary on Matthew*, 3:277; cf. also the phrasing of Mark 10:18 and Luke 18:19). Matthew's restricted usage of "father" does not clearly align him with other Christians or distinguish him from rabbinic Jews. Matthew might disagree on this point with the apostle Paul, who speaks of himself as a father to his Corinthian "children" through the gospel (1 Cor. 4:15). But he would find little with which to disagree in the rabbinic literature, which rarely used that honorific for religious teachers (Davies and Allison, *Commentary on Matthew*, 3:277). Moreover, God is sometimes named as Father in Jewish prayers and liturgy, as well as in the Mishnah and the Talmud (Allison, *Sermon*, 117).

In the wider social context of the Roman Empire, for disciples to claim Jesus' Father as their own did definitively set them apart

233

from those who named Jupiter/Zeus as Father, or the emperor as *Pater Patriae*, "Father of the Fatherland" (Carter, *Matthew and the Margins*, 164). Implicit in all such assertions of fatherhood, human and divine, are two connotations: first, special regard by the powerful for those who stand in need of protection, instruction, discipline, and sustenance, both physical and spiritual; and reciprocally, the expectation that "children" will render trust, respect if not affection, loyalty, and obedience to the demands of the father. In Matthew's Gospel, the perfect expression of trusting obedience is found in Jesus' appeals to "my Father" in Gethsemane (26:39–42), where Jesus also prays that God's will be done, and urges the disciples to pray that they may not enter into trial or temptation (*peirasmon*, 26:41, cf. 6:13).

That same trust in the Father is the focus of the climactic words of derision spoken against the crucified Jesus by the chief priests, scribes, and elders: "He has confidence in God; let him deliver him now, if he wishes. For he has said, 'I am God's Son'" (27:43). The earthquake and other disturbing events that constitute the Father's vindication of the Son are the occasion for the Roman centurion's awed declaration: "Truly he was God's Son!" (27:54). Likely some of Matthew's first readers and hearers would have recognized that acclamation as an echo and implied refutation of the same claim made on behalf of Roman emperors. Both Augustus (d. 14 CE), whose adoptive father Julius had been posthumously deified by the Senate, and Nero (d. 68 CE) had been proclaimed throughout the empire as "son of [a] god," via the mass media of Latin coins and Greek inscriptions (Schowalter, "Churches," 391, 402). Thus for Matthew and other disciples in the Greco-Roman world, naming God as "our Father" forged indissoluble and potentially dangerous bonds with Jesus and each other. It was an exclusive and comprehensive assertion of allegiance, both religious and political, in an environment in which "father" and "son" were vexed and consequential categories of identity.

Ages-long use of the Lord's Prayer has muted the strangeness of "our Father in the heavens" for many contemporary Christians. It has at the same time profoundly influenced our view of God, and not necessarily in ways that Matthew would approve. To the extent that it seems natural to think of God as our Father (or our heavenly Parent of no gender), we may, however unconsciously, "believe in"

234

a cozy figure who will give us what we want if only we ask nicely. By contrast, Matthew would say that Jesus, the Son of God, is trying to teach us, with his life and in this prayer, to want what God wants to give us, however difficult that may be to learn. The seven spare petitions that constitute the body of the prayer tell us what it is we need to grow into wanting. The following discussion focuses on a few elements of the prophetic shaping of those petitions, so we may appreciate both their challenge and their strangeness.

The first petition, "Hallowed be your name," is probably opaque to many regular pray-ers, if they ever stop to wonder what they are asking for. Since God is by definition holy, then why should it be necessary even to mention this? From the perspective of the Old Testament, this necessity arises from the fact that YHWH's "name"—that is, the element of divine personhood that is accessible to humans and thus subject to honorable treatment or to contempt—is very often profaned by the nations (Ps. 74:7), and even by the people Israel themselves (Ezek. 36:23). Ultimately, God must act for the sake of God's name (Ezek. 20:9, 14, 22), asserting the radical holiness (36:23) that humans so often fail to perceive and honor.

God's holiness is most economically and elegantly evoked by Isaiah of Jerusalem (First Isaiah): it is the glory from which the seraphs veil their eyes, which is itself the very fullness of the earth (Isa. 6:3). That description suggests that God's holiness exists independent of any creature, and yet it is the privilege and responsibility of humans—and from a biblical perspective, of Israel in particular—to make God's holiness manifest in this world. Humans corroborate God's holiness through their own demonstrations of righteousness. That is at least part of what it means when Isaiah says, "YHWH of Hosts towers in justice; and the holy God is hallowed in righteousness" (5:16). Here the hallowing of YHWH stands in contrast to the contempt shown by those who despise YHWH's instruction, presuming to "call evil good and good evil" (5:20). They "acquit the guilty for a bribe" and deprive the innocent of a fair hearing (5:23), all the while daring YHWH to get in the way of their schemes: "Let it draw near and come to pass, the plan of the Holy One of Israel— that we may know it!" (5:19). "The Holy One of Israel/Jacob" is the distinctive divine name belonging to the Isaiah tradition; it appears multiple times in each of the three "Isaiahs" (1:4; 5:19, 24; 12:6;

29:23; 41:14, 16, 20; 60:9, 14, etc.), thus marking that book as the primary scriptural site for reflection on what it means for God's name to be hallowed.

In various contexts in Isaiah, honoring YHWH as holy means heeding God's Torah and observing justice (5:19, 24), eschewing all false forms of security (such as military alliances) and the false worship that attend them (8:13), trusting in YHWH as Redeemer of the people Israel (41:16; cf. 52:4–6), taking full account of YHWH's works of new creation (41:20). The essential religious paradox with which Israel must reckon through the ages is that "the Great One *in [its] very midst* is the Holy One of Israel" (12:6; emphasis added); the "high and lofty One who dwells for eternity, whose name is Holy" is at the same time dwelling "with the crushed and lowly in spirit," to bring them back to life (57:15). In Jesus, the Matthean community would have seen how profoundly true is YHWH's self-revelation through Isaiah as Immanuel, "God with us" (Isa. 7:14; Matt. 1:23).

For disciples instructed by Isaiah, it is evident that hallowing God's name means acting in bold and welcoming response to the unexpected presence, action, or word of God. In Matthew's Gospel, then, God's name is effectively hallowed first through Joseph's acquiescence to the angel's command concerning Mary and her child (1:20–25), and then through the "overwhelming joy" of the magi, who honor Mary's baby and not Herod as "king of the Jews" (2:1–12), and again in the Roman soldier who proclaims Jesus as the Son of God even as he hangs dead on the cross (27:54). Likewise, God's name will continue to be hallowed as disciples become "whole, as [their] heavenly Father is whole" (5:48)—Matthew's transparent paraphrase of the divine injunction that stands at the heart of Torah: "You shall be holy, for I, YHWH your God, am holy" (Lev. 19:2; cf. 20:26). As these examples suggest, hallowing God's name is closely related to the subject of the second petition, "Your kingdom come." Hallowing God's name is the ability to perceive the reality of that alternative empire and live in active anticipation of it.

The world in which disciples are taught to pray is a place of inequities and acute need, literally a hungry place for very many, and so they are to pray for daily bread—and soon enough, they must themselves provide something to eat (Matt. 14:16; 15:36). In the world where prayer takes place, hearts are burdened by guilt

236

and communities are divided by sin and hard-heartedness, and so disciples must pray to be forgiven and to forgive. This world is a place where every human without exception is assailed by temptation and threatened or trapped by evil, and so disciples are to pray for deliverance. None of this would come as a complete surprise to those who have read the Israelite Prophets; it is the world they describe and address. Thus Jesus' prayer for disciples is the outworking of the prophetic perspective on reality. It is a faithful reckoning with what Leonardo Boff describes as "the existential shock" that lies behind all real prayer (*Lord's Prayer*, 10), the recognition that "God's good creation is dominated by the diabolical forces that torment our lives and threaten our hopes" (23). Boff insightfully describes Matthew's account of Jesus' own temptations as "a constantly faithful search for those concrete steps that would make the will of God a part of history" (105). By beginning the story of the baptized Jesus with this detailed account of temptation (Matt. 4:1–11; compare Mark's cursory notice, 1:13), Matthew is addressing the problem posed at the beginning of this essay: how to fill in the gap between the declared judgment of God (represented by John the Baptist, Matt. 3:1–12) and the proposed future, the kingdom of God. In short, this Gospel shows in Jesus' own life what will become the daily work of prophetic discipleship.

As Matthew's temptation account reveals, "Jesus regards as diabolical any temptation to reduce the kingdom to some particular segment of reality, whether political, religious, or miraculous" (Boff, *Lord's Prayer*, 59). Likewise, the prayer for disciples is in its very brevity emphatically nonreductionistic. Its seven petitions refute the abiding temptation to reduce Christian faith to personal spirituality, as is common in North American Protestantism, or a baptized materialism ("the prosperity gospel"), or a bare social and political agenda. Like the books of the Prophets, the Lord's Prayer holds the focus on God, yet without ignoring material need or trivializing interpersonal relationships. Indeed, the structure of the prayer itself—a quick succession of unamplified petitions—implies the inseparability of these three elements: healing interpersonal relationships, meeting material needs, and sustaining a genuine relationship with God. They cannot be separated, because it is *our* Father to whom we pray, *our* bread for which we pray, *our* sins that are forgiven as *we* enter into the ecology of forgiving relationships and learn to live in ways that are not defined or constrained by sin,

237

anger, and guilt. Thus God guides *us* through and away from temptation and the evil that now threatens us from within and without. Nine times the first-person-plural pronouns appear in this prayer. Children of the one heavenly Parent never pray in isolation. As we come before God, our lives can be neither internally compartmentalized nor separated in the slightest degree from the genuine needs of our sisters and brothers.

There is no single better symbol for this shared and integrated life than Matthew's image of "daily" (?) bread. The adjective *epiousios* is unique to this prayer, and its meaning is debated: "daily," "necessary," "for the future," "essential," "supersubstantial" (Jerome). "It may possibly have been coined to express all the secret wealth that is hidden away in the simple reality of bread" (Boff, *Lord's Prayer*, 85). From a prophetic perspective, one could say that the history of God's grace demonstrated to Israel and humankind is largely a history of shared bread: angels eating Abraham's bread (Gen. 18), Moses and the people Israel eating manna in the wilderness (Exod. 16), Elijah eating bread from ravens in the wilderness and sharing bread with the widow and her son in Zarephath (1 Kgs. 17), Obadiah giving bread to YHWH's prophets whom he has hidden from Ahab and Jezebel (1 Kgs. 18), Elisha commanding the king to feed and not kill the Aramean raiding party (2 Kgs. 6), Isaiah's vision of all peoples feasting "on this mountain" (Isa. 25:6–10) and the call for a "fast" of sharing bread with the hungry (58:7). The history of shared bread continues in the story of Jesus' feedings of the multitudes, the Last Supper with the disciples, the revelation at Emmaus. It continues to unfold in the lives of disciples gathered to eat the bread blessed, broken, and given.

That long history should inform our prayers for daily bread, and also our awareness of what the life of discipleship might mean in our contemporary world—a hungry place, no less than was the Roman Empire. Pablo Neruda's "Ode to Bread" is a poem about sharing and hallowing "everyone's daily bread." The Chilean poet, diplomat, and politician, though not himself a Christian, offers an image of victory over suffering and evil that may illumine Jesus' prayer. He envisions Victory, not with wings, but with bread mounted on her shoulders, soaring aloft, "setting the world free, like a baker borne aloft on the wind." Disciples of Jesus might recognize her as an angel who brings prayers for our own needs and those of all people before "our Father in the heavens."

238

Works Cited in Chapter 8

Allison, Dale C. *The Sermon on the Mount: Inspiring the Moral Imagination.* New York: Crossroad, 1999.

Arnold, Eberhard. *Salt and Light: Living the Sermon on the Mount.* Rifton, NY: Plough Publishing House, 1998.

Boff, Leonardo. *Cry of the Earth, Cry of the Poor.* Translated by Phillip Berryman. Maryknoll, NY: Orbis Books, 1997.

————. *Faith on the Edge: Religion and Marginalized Existence.* Translated by Robert E. Barr. San Francisco: Harper & Row, 1989.

————. *The Lord's Prayer: The Prayer of Integral Liberation.* Translated by Theodore Morrow. Maryknoll, NY: Orbis Books, 1983.

————. *When Theology Listens to the Poor.* Translated by Robert E. Barr. San Francisco: Harper & Row, 1988.

Bonhoeffer, Dietrich. *The Cost of Discipleship.* New York: Macmillan, 1959.

Brown, Francis. *The Brown-Driver-Briggs Hebrew and English Lexicon.* Peabody, MA: Hendrickson Publishers, 1999.

Carter, Warren. *Matthew and Empire: Initial Explorations.* Harrisburg, PA: Trinity Press International, 2001.

————. *Matthew and the Margins: A Sociopolitical and Religious Reading.* Journal for the Study of the New Testament Supplement Series 204. Sheffield: Sheffield Academic Press, 2000.

————. *The Roman Empire and the New Testament: An Essential Guide.* Nashville: Abingdon Press, 2006.

Charry, Ellen T. *By the Renewing of Your Minds: The Pastoral Function of Christian Doctrine.* New York: Oxford University Press, 1999.

Davis, Ellen F. "Christians Hearing Isaiah." In *Preaching from Psalms, Oracles, and Parables,* edited by Roger Alling and David J. Schlafer. Harrisburg, PA: Morehouse Publishing, 2006.

————. *Scripture, Culture, and Agriculture: An Agrarian Reading of the Bible.* Cambridge: Cambridge University Press, 2009.

Finney, Mark T. *Honour and Conflict in the Ancient World: 1 Corinthians in Its Greco-Roman Social Setting.* New York: T & T Clark International, 2012.

Hickman, Hoyt L., ed. *The Faith We Sing.* Nashville: Abingdon Press, 2000.

239

Jordan, Clarence. *Sermon on the Mount*. Valley Forge, PA: Judson Press, 1952.

Levine, Amy-Jill. "Visions of Kingdoms, from Pompey to the First Jewish Revolt." In *The Oxford History of the Biblical World*, edited by Michael D. Coogan. Oxford: Oxford University Press, 1998.

Levine, Amy-Jill, and Marc Zvi Brettler, eds. *The Jewish Annotated New Testament: New Revised Standard Version Bible Translation*. Oxford: Oxford University Press, 2011.

Longenecker, Bruce W. *Remember the Poor: Paul, Poverty, and the Greco-Roman World*. Grand Rapids: Eerdmans, 2010.

Luz, Ulrich. *Matthew 1–7: A Commentary*. Edinburgh: T & T Clark, 1989.

Minear, Paul S. *The Good News according to Matthew: A Training Manual for Prophets*. St. Louis: Chalice Press, 2000.

Schowalter, Daniel N. "Churches in Context." In *The Oxford History of the Biblical World*, edited by Michael D. Coogan. Oxford: Oxford University Press, 1998.

Stassen, Glen Harold. *A Thicker Jesus: Incarnational Discipleship in a Secular Age*. Louisville, KY: Westminster John Knox Press, 2012.

Wilkins, Michael J. *Discipleship in the Ancient World and Matthew's Gospel*. Grand Rapids: Baker Books, 1995.

CHAPTER 9

Prophecy in Interfaith Context

Reading Biblical Traditions in Conversation with Islam

Since this study of the prophetic traditions of the Bible highlights their contemporary relevance for Christian theology, I end with a brief reflection on how interfaith study between Christian and Muslims has affected my reading of the prophetic traditions of the Bible. Of all the world faiths, Islam is the one that is most fully grounded in and oriented to the phenomenon of divine revelation through prophetic mediation. To be a Muslim is to confess in faith that "there is no God [Allah] but God [Allah], and Muhammad is his prophet." Muslims affirm the existence and full reliability of the line of prophets from Adam to Jesus and finally to Muhammad, who is regarded as the "Seal of the prophets" (Qur'an 33:40)—that is, the perfect culmination of the line of mediators to and through whom the divine will and word is revealed.

If it is a coincidence, then it is a consequential one nonetheless that during the several years in which I have been working on this book, I have also been teaching a course with Imam Abdullah Antepli, Muslim chaplain at Duke University Divinity School. Almost all the students enrolled in Listening Together: Christians and Muslims Reading Scriptures are Christians (we have also had one Jewish student). The course is designed around biblical and Qur'anic figures (Abraham, Moses, Job, Jesus, Mary) and theological topics that occupy a central place in each tradition (e.g., the unity of God, social justice, attitudes toward the religiously "other").   241

In addition to the two instructors, a number of Muslim scholars and teachers, as well as Christian scholars learned in Islam, have been invited to address the class; two of our class meetings take place in a local mosque.

A primary goal of this course is to enable students to hear biblical texts in a fresh way, through the experience of reading them in the sympathetic and inquiring presence of Muslim neighbors. As the differences between the two scriptures and faith traditions have become clearer to us, we on either side have sometimes been moved to admire the beauty of the other tradition—to feel what Krister Stendahl, a New Testament scholar and pioneer in interfaith work, called a "holy envy." At other times we must in honesty acknowledge a gap in our understanding or appreciation of the other that we do not know how to bridge.

Here I focus on two topics in an effort to show how my own reading of Scripture has been sharpened, as "iron sharpens iron" (Prov. 27:17), through respectful interaction with Islam and the Qur'an, and especially interaction with persons committed to that tradition in faith and love. The first topic, the prophets and their relationship to God, constitutes one of the major areas of commonality between Christians and Muslims—and is at the same time of pronounced theological difference. Both traditions attest to the authority and indispensability of prophets, inspired persons whom God entrusts with a message that is essential for human faithfulness, for right living, for deliverance from present affliction, and ultimately, for sharing life with God on the other side of death. Yet they differ greatly with respect to the element of protest or resistance to God that figures in numerous biblical stories of prophets and others (e.g., Job), an element that is markedly absent from parallel stories in the Qur'an and Islamic literature. (Kenneth Cragg's *The Weight in the Word: Prophethood, Biblical and Quranic* is an illuminating book-length comparative study.)

The second topic treated here, repentance and salvation, is also an area where the core understandings of Christianity and Islam differ considerably. However, as we shall see, the biblical canon itself includes very different understandings of how human repentance may lead to the divine action of salvation. To my own surprise, it seems that the different theological claims of Islam and Christianity can each be correlated to a great extent with different strands of biblical tradition.

242

The Prophets and Their Relationship with God

For some years I participated in the annual Building Bridges seminar, where Muslim and Christian theologians gather to discuss a theological theme of central concern for both faiths. In one of the first years our chair, Rowan Williams, chose the theme of prophecy and the person of the prophet, supposing that this would provide much common ground for discussion. He was right, although not in the way he had anticipated; at the end of the seminar, he admitted that we could hardly have found a subject that would provide more substantial ground for disagreement. We spent several days studying passages from the Qur'an and the Bible, along with excerpts from important theological works in both traditions. In the end, our major fresh discovery was that, although both scriptures place great emphasis on the essential role of prophets in making the divine will and command intelligible to humans, there is an irreducible difference in the ways Muslims and Christians represent the relationship between God and the prophets. That difference concerns the extent to which the prophet may think or speak or act independently from God and even in resistance to God.

As several essays in the present volume highlight, the biblical tradition represents the prophet as standing in close, even intimate relationship with God. God speaks to Moses "face to face, as a person speaks to a friend" (Exod. 33:11; cf. Num. 12:8). Micaiah son of Imlah is privy to what transpires in the heavenly council, when a deluding spirit is sent forth to beguile Ahab (1 Kgs. 22). Prophecy in the biblical tradition is essentially dialogical. If God puts words in the prophet's mouth (Isa. 51:16; 59:21; Jer. 1:9; 5:14), that "dictation model" certainly does not describe every mode of prophetic speech. Beginning already with Abraham, we see the prophet taking on the role of intercessor (Gen. 18), and indeed cast in that role by God (Gen. 20:7). Intercession also entails challenging or questioning God's judgment of humans, beginning with Abraham and continuing, most famously, with Moses. Amos also implicitly questions God's lack of mercy to Israel: "He is so small!" (Amos 7:2, 5). Jeremiah's protests are more strident and more personal: he dares to bring something like an accusation in court against the Deity (Jer. 12:1); he accuses God of having seduced (20:7) and betrayed (15:18) him. Jeremiah regrets, indeed curses, his whole life (15:10; 20:14–18).

243

From the perspective of Islam, it is misleading, even blasphemous, to portray a prophet speaking against God—and to some extent, getting away with it or even making headway by means of it. The biblical story of the negotiation between God and Abraham over the decree of destruction for Sodom and Gomorrah (Gen. 18) may be instructively compared with Qur'anic portrayals of Noah and Abraham, both of whom are reckoned as prophets. In the latter accounts, these two are moved by their own pity for the condemned to challenge God's intended punishment (Qur'an 11:45–49, 74–76); however, in some contrast to the Genesis account, God shows no willingness to relent. To the contrary, God specifically forbids each of them to plead on behalf of evildoers: "It is not fitting for the Prophet and the believers to ask forgiveness for the idolaters—even if they are related to them—after having been shown that they are the inhabitants of the Blaze" (9:113; cf. 11:76; 23:27). Noah and Abraham quickly yield to God's unfathomable wisdom; Noah's statement of submission is reminiscent of Job's response when God speaks from the whirlwind: "My Lord, I take refuge with You from asking for things I know nothing about. If You do not forgive me, and have mercy on me, I shall be one of the losers" (11:47; cf. Job 42:1–6).

The difference between the two perspectives is not the depth and scope of divine mercy, which both traditions strongly affirm; rather, it is the degree to which human opposition to God is viewed not just as a problem but as a genuine tragedy. "A sense of tragedy is much more readily discovered in the Bible than in the Qur'an" (Marshall, *God*, 202). Opposition to God is from a biblical perspective the most far-reaching of all human tragedies. Therefore the prophet, who is intimately bound to the people as well as to God, is necessarily embroiled in the most painful ways, including tension between the prophet and God. Like most family tragedies, this one puts an enormous strain on every relationship.

Altogether, the twenty-five prophets of the Qur'an (including other characters from biblical narrative, such as Lot, Jacob, David, and Solomon) are shown as exemplars of moral perfection and total obedience to God. It is precisely the role of the prophets in Qur'anic tradition to bring people to acknowledge their wrongdoing and wrong thinking before they are destroyed or disgraced on the day of judgment (Qur'an 21:14, 46, 97). Therefore the prophets themselves cannot be guilty of anything more than innocent error

244

or brief resistance, as seen in the story of "the man with the whale," where Jonah cries "in the deep darkness, 'There is no God but You, glory be to You, I was wrong'" (21:87; cf. 37:139–48). Qur'anic Jonah's repentance is a full turning to God, a thoroughgoing and permanent submission of his will. In contrast, the biblical Jonah might have prayed a proper psalm from the belly of the fish (cf. Jonah 2:3–10 [2–9E]), but the last scene in his story shows a highly disgruntled prophet, not yet reconciled to God's intentions for the Ninevites or himself. Abdullah Antepli comments (in a personal communication), "The Gospels' account of the sinless life of Jesus of Nazareth is—apart from the claims for Jesus' status as the Son of God—the biblical portrait closest to the Islamic understanding of the prophet's perfect human life."

While prophetic resistance is greatly muted in Islamic accounts, the suffering of the prophets as a result of their call to speak for God is emphasized. However, the theological meaning of suffering and the questions it raises are not the same for Muslims as for Western Christians. For us, the suffering of the innocent—not to speak of the suffering of the faithful specifically in God's service—makes acute the question of God's justice; the long-suffering Jeremiah speaks for them in this respect (Jer. 12:1). Therefore it is invariably puzzling or even shocking for our divinity students to learn that theodicy—the justification of God's actions—is not a recognized theological topic in Islam, either among professional theologians or among believers. Rather, Muslims often speak of suffering as a test of one's wholeheartedness toward God. Christians might see here a point of contact with Matthew's prophetic view of discipleship (see chap. 8 above), as informed by his account of Jesus' own faithful endurance of temptation (Matt. 4:1–11), his agony in Gethsemane and the charge to the disciples in Gethsemane to pray that they not be tested (26:41), and the petition in the Lord's Prayer to be delivered from temptation or testing (6:13).

Jeremiah does not appear in the Qur'an (although subsequent Islamic tradition treats him as an obedient prophet), but the equally long-suffering Job is counted among its prophets. It is notable, then, that when Qur'anic Job cries out to God, his words are not a protest, as in the Bible, but rather the strongest affirmation of divine mercy: "Suffering has truly afflicted me, but you are the Most Merciful of the merciful" (Qur'an 21:83). Yet here, too, what at first seems contrary to the biblical account might cause us to look more carefully

245

at its witness about the suffering of the faithful. In fact, the issue of theodicy may not be as prevalent in the Bible as we commonly suppose, including in the book of Job. What Job persistently demands is not an explanation of his suffering, and certainly not a theoretical defense of God's justice. His four visitors and volunteer theological consultants—Eliphaz, Bildad, Zophar, and Elihu—all give him more than he needs along those lines. Rather, Job wants God to show up and hear him out; he wants to "see [God] for myself, my own eyes shall see and not [as?] a stranger" (Job 19:27).

The apostle Paul, himself a bearer of the spiritual gift of prophecy (1 Cor. 14), suffers acutely in God's service, yet this does not move him to question God's justice. To the contrary, suffering is for Paul a sign of or an opportunity for intimacy with God in Christ. It is a sharing in the human life of Christ (Rom. 8:17; Phil. 3:10; 2 Cor. 4:7–12; cf. Col. 1:24) and in the fellowship of the gospel (2 Cor. 1:3–14; 2 Tim. 3:12). Far from viewing suffering and imprisonment as an evil, Paul sees them as opportunities for magnifying the gospel message (Phil. 1:12–14) and preparing for "an eternal weight of glory" (2 Cor. 4:16–18). To borrow a term from Islamic thought, the apostle might be called a "muslim" (lowercase *m*) in the general sense, namely, a *devoted* person—completely and selflessly devoted to God, regardless of circumstances. (Here it should be acknowledged that in practice Muslims give little attention to Paul, as he is considered to be the one most responsible for "perverting" the monotheistic character of Jesus' own prophetic message.)

Repentance and Salvation

Both Christianity and Islam have a strong orientation toward what have traditionally been called "the Last Things": repentance, death, salvation, and divine judgment. (This end-time orientation of Christian and Muslim theologies distinguishes them to some extent from Judaism, at least in most of its modern expressions.) As noted here, one of the chief roles of the prophet in Islam, like the biblical prophets, is to bring people to repentance before the day of judgment. Nonetheless, despite these strong points of contact between the two traditions, there is also a deep tension between them with respect to repentance and its relation to salvation. The tension revolves around the different answers that many Muslims

246

and Christians might give to the following question: "Viewed from the human side, is repentance the primary element in the economy of salvation?" To parse that question more carefully, is repentance, *viewed as a human initiative,* possible? Is it the definitive movement with respect to righting a damaged or broken relationship with God, and therefore efficacious for salvation?

As I understand it, Islam would answer a strong yes to this complex question, whereas the basic claims of Christian theology would call for certain qualifications before answering in the affirmative. In order to get some perspective on the tension or disagreement between the two faiths, I begin by looking at how different strands of biblical tradition might themselves respond, for in this matter there is certainly no general agreement within the covers of the Bible.

The strongest biblical affirmation that repentance is the key to salvation comes from the Deuteronomistic tradition, overall the dominant shaper of the prophetic perspective in the Bible. This tradition—or complex of related traditions—is the source of Deuteronomy itself, the "final testament" of the paradigmatic prophet Moses, as well as the Former Prophets (Joshua through Kings). It has put its stamp on Jeremiah and others of the Latter Prophets, and its perspective is reflected in Ezra and Nehemiah. Walter Brueggemann calls the Deuteronomists "the principal carriers of reformist faith in the Old Testament" (*Like Fire in My Bones,* 154). The reformist tendency, expressed already in the earliest of the classical prophets, is evident in repeated strong appeals to Israel to turn back to God (e.g., Jer. 3:12–14, 22; Amos 4:6, 8; Hos. 3:5; 6:1), to turn away from sin (1 Kgs. 8:35) and experience complete renewal—spiritual, social, and political—in the presence of YHWH (Jer. 3:15–18). Brueggemann's further comment is instructive: "The repentance urged by the prophets is both theological-covenantal, urging Israel to return to YHWH, and socioeconomic-political, urging Israel to enact the radical public claims of Yahwism. The convergence of covenantal theology and public policy is at the heart of prophetic faith" (154).

It is intriguing to consider whether there might be some similarity between Islam and these Deuteronomistic strands of the Bible, precisely in the convergence of theology and public policy. Widely though those traditions differ in many respects, the following characteristics of the Deuteronomistic traditions might offer points of comparison with classical Muslim texts:

247

1. They set forth *a program of public theology*, in which socio-economic and other humanitarian concerns (e.g., for the poor, the widow, and the orphan) are central.

2. This theological program is *moral rather than mystical* in character and tone; there is throughout a strong appeal to rationality and the human will. Deuteronomy assumes the voice of Moses the preacher, the scrupulous teacher, and admonisher and exhorter: "Hear, O Israel" (Deut. 6:4); "Be careful" (2:4); "Be on guard against evil" (4:15–16; 23:10 [9E]). Within Torah, such moral appeals contrast starkly with the reticent style of the Priestly tradition, where the only "rationale" is the bare assertion, "I am YHWH your God" (Lev. 11:44; 18:2, 4, 30; 19:3, 4, 10, etc.).

3. There is a kind of *spiritual optimism* in Deuteronomy and the Deuteronomistic History, even though they reckon squarely with the threat or reality of exile. God's Instruction (Torah) is rigorous but "not too baffling for [Israel], nor beyond reach" (Deut. 30:11). Even the disaster of exile will not *in the end* prevent the people from turning back to God in obedience, with all their heart and soul (30:2, 10). "Israel can—after all!" might be the motto of the Deuteronomists. Humans, and Israel in particular, are constitutionally capable of what God commands: "For the word/matter is exceedingly close to you, in your mouth and in your heart, to do it. . . . And you shall choose life!" (30:14, 19).

However, the Bible also includes another very different theological strain, one that emphasizes it is not repentance in the first instance, but rather the unilateral initiative of God that changes hearts and lives. "Only God can!" maintains this alternative tradition. Within the prophetic corpus, this interpretation of Israel's situation (or the human situation) is represented by a vivid image such as Jeremiah's new covenant written directly on the heart, with no (fallible or potentially corrupt) teacher serving as an intermediary (Jer. 31:31–34). Similarly, Ezekiel speaks of the divine renewal of Israel, putting YHWH's own spirit within them, and a new heart of flesh rather than stone (Ezek. 36:26–27). Notably, it is only after this dramatic (if metaphorical) act of organ replacement that Israel becomes capable of genuine repentance: "And [then] you will remember your evil deeds and no-good ways, and you will loathe yourselves on account of your iniquities and your abominable acts" (36:31). The message here is that Israel can be restored to a life-giving covenantal dynamic of repentance and forgiveness, but only

248

if God acts first, changing them in a way so fundamental that it must be seen as something like a new creation or a second Sinai.

It is no coincidence that these heart images are among the prophetic passages best known to and most beloved by Christians, for Christian theology likewise affirms that God will do anything to transform human character and our situation in relation to God, even to the point of entering fully into human flesh. As the very first Christian theologian saw clearly, the incarnation of God in Christ is the ultimate—and divinely willed—undoing of divine dignity in this world. Paradoxically, God's dignity is restored only through Jesus' fully human submission to the most humiliating of deaths (Phil. 2:6–11).

Although Islam honors Jesus as a prophet, it denies categorically that God did or ever would take on human flesh. The Christian doctrine of the incarnation is from the perspective of Islam a category mistake, for it violates the total transcendence of God. This is an irreconcilable theological difference between the two faiths, and our class experience of "listening together" to our scriptures did nothing to diminish the difference. However, it did help us to set that difference in a larger theological context, and to see that the two positions of Christianity and Islam align with two different strands or complexes of the biblical prophetic traditions.

As in the Deuteronomistic traditions, Islam's thoroughly transcendent view of God is associated with an "optimistic" theological anthropology; for all their failings, humans are fundamentally capable of doing what God demands of them. For the Deuteronomists and for Islam, the prophetic word and the exemplary lives of the prophets may succeed in bridging the gap between the Creator and creatures. By calling humans to repentance, they make salvation possible for those who can hear. By contrast, Christianity aligns with elements of the Hebrew Scriptures, and especially the prophetic traditions, that are less hopeful about our capacity for turning fully and forever back to God, at least on human initiative. Therefore they stress God's unilateral action of entering directly into history in radically new ways, making a new covenant, remaking the human heart, ultimately making "new heavens and a new earth" (Isa. 65:17; 66:22; cf. 2 Pet. 3:13 and Rev. 21:1).

The difference between Islam and Christianity with respect to repentance and salvation is very great. Lest we think it is so great as to preclude meaningful conversation between Muslims and Christians about these most basic matters of human life in the presence

249

of God, it is important to recognize that the Bible at different moments and in many places affirms both the "optimistic" anthropology and the need for dramatic divine intervention. Sometimes they appear close together, even within a single prophetic book: Jeremiah articulates both the strong, repeated call to return to covenantal obedience and God's announcement of something drastically new, a covenant written on Israel's heart. Perhaps that biblical example of theological difference and tension, with neither position discrediting the other, may encourage Muslims and Christians to continue theological conversation across our differences.

Works Cited in Chapter 9

Brueggemann, Walter. *Like Fire in My Bones: Listening for the Prophetic Word in Jeremiah*. Minneapolis: Fortress Press, 2006.

Cragg, Kenneth. *The Weight in the Word: Prophethood, Biblical and Quranic*. Brighton, UK: Sussex Academic Press, 1999.

Marshall, David E. *God, Muhammad, and the Unbelievers: A Quranic Study*. Richmond, Surrey, UK: Curzon, 1999.

The Qur'an: A New Translation by M. A. S. Abdel Haleem. Oxford: Oxford University Press, 2010.

BIBLIOGRAPHY

Allison, Dale C. *The Sermon on the Mount: Inspiring the Moral Imagination.* New York: Crossroad, 1999.

Alonso Schökel, Luis. "Isaiah." In *The Literary Guide to the Bible,* edited by Robert Alter and Frank Kermode. Cambridge, MA: Belknap/Harvard University Press, 1987.

Aristides, P. Aelius. *The Complete Works.* Translated by Charles A. Behr. Leiden: E. J. Brill, 1981.

Arnold, Eberhard. *Salt and Light: Living the Sermon on the Mount.* Rifton, NY: Plough Publishing House, 1998.

Aubet, Maria Eugenia. *The Phoenicians and the West: Policies, Colonies, and Trade.* Cambridge: Cambridge University Press, 1993.

Aune, David E. *Revelation 17–22.* Word Biblical Commentary 52C. Nashville: Thomas Nelson Publishers, 1998.

Bailey, Kenneth E. *Paul through Mediterranean Eyes: Cultural Studies in 1 Corinthians.* Downers Grove, IL: InterVarsity Press, 2011.

Barker, Margaret. *Creation: A Biblical Vision for the Environment.* London: T & T Clark International, 2010.

Barlow, Maude. *Blue Covenant: The Global Water Crisis and the Coming Battle for the Right to Water.* Toronto: McClelland & Stewart, 2007.

Barth, Karl. *Church Dogmatics.* Peabody, MA: Hendrickson, 2010.

Bauckham, Richard. *The Bible and Ecology: Rediscovering the Community of Creation.* Waco, TX: Baylor University Press, 2010.

———. *The Bible in Politics.* Louisville, KY: Westminster John Knox Press, 1989.

———. *The Climax of Prophecy: Studies on the Book of Revelation.* Edinburgh: T & T Clark, 1993.

———. *The Theology of the Book of Revelation.* Cambridge: Cambridge University Press, 1993.

Beker, J. Christiaan. *Suffering and Hope: The Biblical Vision and the Human Predicament.* Grand Rapids: Eerdmans, 1994.

251

Bellis, Alice Ogden. *Helpmates, Harlots, and Heroes: Women's Stories in the Hebrew Bible.* Louisville, KY: Westminster John Knox Press, 2007.

Benedict XVI. Homily at the First Vespers of the Feast of Saints Peter and Paul, Rome, June 28, 2008. http://www.vatican .va/holy_father/benedict_xvi/homilies/2008/documents/ hf_ben-xvi_hom_20080628_vespri_en.html.

Berkovits, Eliezer. *With God in Hell: Judaism in the Ghettos and Deathcamps.* New York: Sanhedrin Press, 1979.

Berrigan, Daniel. *Daniel Berrigan: Essential Writings.* Selected by John Dear. Maryknoll, NY: Orbis, 2009.

———. *Jeremiah: The World, the Wound of God.* Minneapolis: Fortress Press, 1999.

———. *Testimony: The Word Made Fresh.* Maryknoll, NY: Orbis, 2004.

Berry, Wendell. "The Agrarian Standard." In *The Essential Agrarian Reader,* edited by Norman Wirzba. Lexington: University Press of Kentucky, 2003.

———. *Home Economics.* New York: North Point Press, 1987.

———. *Leavings.* Berkeley, CA: Counterpoint, 2010.

———. *The Long-Legged House.* Washington, DC: Shoemaker & Hoard, 2004. First published 1969 by Harcourt, Brace & World.

Blenkinsopp, Joseph. *A History of Prophecy in Israel: From the Settlement in the Land to the Hellenistic Period.* Philadelphia: Westminster Press, 1983.

Blount, Brian. *Revelation: A Commentary.* New Testament Library. Louisville, KY: Westminster John Knox Press, 2009.

The Book of Common Prayer. . . according to the use of The Episcopal Church. New York: Church Hymnal Corporation, 1979.

Boesak, Allan A. *Comfort and Protest: Reflections on the Apocalypse of John of Patmos.* Philadelphia: Westminster Press, 1987.

Boff, Leonardo. *Cry of the Earth, Cry of the Poor.* Translated by Phillip Berryman. Maryknoll, NY: Orbis Books, 1997.

———. *Faith on the Edge: Religion and Marginalized Existence.* Translated by Robert E. Barr. San Francisco: Harper & Row, 1989.

———. *The Lord's Prayer: The Prayer of Integral Liberation.* Translated by Theodore Morrow. Maryknoll, NY: Orbis Books, 1983.

———. *When Theology Listens to the Poor*. Translated by Robert E. Barr. San Francisco: Harper & Row, 1988.

Bonhoeffer, Dietrich. *The Cost of Discipleship*. New York: Macmillan, 1959.

———. *No Rusty Swords: Letters, Lectures and Notes, 1928–1936*. New York: Harper & Row, 1965.

Boyle, Gregory. *Tattoos on the Heart: The Power of Endless Compassion*. New York: Free Press, 2010.

Braaten, Laurie. "Earth Community in Hosea 2." In *The Earth Story in the Psalms and the Prophets*, edited by Norman C. Habel. The Earth Bible 4. Sheffield, UK: Sheffield Academic Press; Cleveland: Pilgrim Press, 2001.

Brichto, Herbert Chanan. *Toward a Grammar of Biblical Poetics: Tales of the Prophets*. New York: Oxford University Press, 1992.

Brodie, Thomas L. *The Crucial Bridge: The Elijah-Elisha Narrative as an Interpretive Synthesis of Genesis-Kings and a Literary Model for the Gospels*. Collegeville, MN: Liturgical Press, 2000.

Brown, Francis. *The Brown-Driver-Briggs Hebrew and English Lexicon*. Peabody, MA: Hendrickson Publishers, 1999.

Brown, Raymond E. "Jesus and Elisha." *Perspectives* 12 (1971): 85–104.

Brueggemann, Walter. *Inscribing the Text: Sermons and Prayers of Walter Brueggemann*. Edited by Anna Carter Florence. Minneapolis: Fortress, 2004.

———. *Like Fire in My Bones: Listening for the Prophetic Word in Jeremiah*. Minneapolis: Fortress Press, 2006.

———. *The Practice of Prophetic Imagination: Preaching an Emancipating Word*. Minneapolis: Fortress Press, 2012.

———. *The Prophetic Imagination*. Minneapolis: Fortress, 2001.

———. *Texts that Linger, Words that Explode*. Edited by Patrick Miller. Minneapolis: Fortress Press, 2000.

Buber, Martin. *The Prophetic Faith*. New York: Harper & Row, 1949.

Carter, Warren. *Matthew and Empire: Initial Explorations*. Harrisburg, PA: Trinity Press International, 2001.

———. *Matthew and the Margins: A Sociopolitical and Religious Reading*. Journal for the Study of the New Testament Supplement Series 204. Sheffield: Sheffield Academic Press, 2000.

————. *The Roman Empire and the New Testament: An Essential Guide*. Nashville: Abingdon Press, 2006.

Cavanaugh, William T. *Being Consumed: Economics and Christian Desire*. Grand Rapids: Eerdmans, 2008.

Charry, Ellen T. *By the Renewing of Your Minds: The Pastoral Function of Christian Doctrine*. New York: Oxford University Press, 1999.

Conrad, Edgar W. *Fear Not Warrior: A Study of 'al tîrā' Pericopes in the Hebrew Scriptures*. Brown Judaic Studies 75. Chico, CA: Scholars Press, 1985.

Cragg, Kenneth. *The Weight in the Word: Prophethood, Biblical and Quranic*. Brighton, UK: Sussex Academic Press, 1999.

Davies, W. D., and Dale Allison. *A Critical and Exegetical Commentary on the Gospel according to Saint Matthew*. International Critical Commentary. 3 vols. Edinburgh: T & T Clark, 1988–97.

Davis, Ellen F. "Christians Hearing Isaiah." In *Preaching from Psalms, Oracles, and Parables*, edited by Roger Alling and David J. Schlafer. Harrisburg, PA: Morehouse Publishing, 2006.

————. *Scripture, Culture, and Agriculture: An Agrarian Reading of the Bible*. Cambridge: Cambridge University Press, 2009.

DeVries, Simon. *1 Kings*. Word Biblical Commentary. Nashville: Thomas Nelson Publishers, 2003.

Domeris, William Robert. *Touching the Heart of God: The Social Construction of Poverty among Biblical Peasants*. New York: T & T Clark, 2007.

Evans, Christopher F. *Saint Luke*. TPI New Testament Commentaries. Philadelphia: Trinity Press International, 1990.

Finney, Mark T. *Honour and Conflict in the Ancient World: 1 Corinthians in Its Greco-Roman Social Setting*. New York: T & T Clark International, 2012.

Ford, David. *Self and Salvation: Being Transformed*. Cambridge: Cambridge University Press, 1999.

Fretheim, Terence E. "The Earth Story in Jeremiah 12." In *Readings from the Perspective of Earth*, edited by Norman C. Habel. The Earth Bible 1. Cleveland: Pilgrim Press, 2000.

————. *God and World in the Old Testament: A Relational Theology of Creation*. Nashville: Abingdon Press, 2005.

Friedman, Richard Elliott. *Commentary on the Torah.* New York: HarperCollins, 2001.

Fujimura, Makoto. "Beauty in Culture." Video of a talk by Makoto Fujimura, available at Q: Ideas for the Common Good. http:// www.qideas.org/video/beauty-in-culture.aspx.

———. Makoto Fujimura Web page. http://www.makotofujimura .com/works/.

———. *Refractions: A Journey of Faith, Art, and Culture.* Colorado Springs: NavPress, 2009.

Gafney, Wilda C. *Daughters of Miriam: Women Prophets in Ancient Israel.* Minneapolis: Fortress Press, 2008.

Gleick, Peter H. "Facing Down the Hydro-Crisis." *World Policy Journal* 26:4 (Winter 2009/10): 17–23.

Goldingay, John. *Israel's Gospel.* Old Testament Theology 1. Downers Grove, IL: InterVarsity Press, 2003.

González, Justo. *Luke.* Louisville, KY: Westminster John Knox Press, 2010.

Green, Joel B. *The Gospel of Luke.* New International Commentary on the New Testament. Grand Rapids: Eerdmans, 1997.

———. *The Theology of the Gospel of Luke.* Cambridge: Cambridge University Press, 1995.

Greenberg, Moshe. *Ezekiel 21–37.* Anchor Bible 22A. New York: Doubleday, 1997.

Halpern, Baruch, and André Lemaire. "The Composition of Kings." In *The Books of Kings: Sources, Composition, Historiography and Reception,* edited by André Lemaire and Baruch Halpern. Supplements to Vetus Testamentum 129. Leiden: Brill, 2010.

Hardt, Michael, and Antonio Negri. *Empire.* Cambridge, MA: Harvard University Press, 2000.

Hauerwas, Stanley. *Without Apology: Sermons for Christ's Church.* New York: Seabury Books, 2013.

Hauser, Alan J., and Russell Gregory. *From Carmel to Horeb: Elijah in Crisis.* Sheffield: Almond Press, 1990.

Hays, Richard B. *First Corinthians.* Interpretation series. Louisville, KY: John Knox Press, 1997.

Hens-Piazza, Gina. *1–2 Kings.* Abingdon Old Testament Commentaries. Nashville: Abingdon Press, 2006.

Heschel, Abraham Joshua. *The Prophets: An Introduction.* 2 vols. New York: Harper & Row, 1962.

Hickman, Hoyt L., ed. *The Faith We Sing*. Nashville: Abingdon Press, 2000.

Holt-Giménez, Eric. "Land Grabs Versus Land Sovereignty." *Foodfirst Backgrounder* 18:4 (Winter 2012–13): 1–3.

Homer. *The Complete Works of Homer*. New York: Random House, 1950.

Hopkins, Gerard Manley. "As Kingfishers Catch Fire." http://www.poetryfoundation.org/poem/173654.

Horsley, Richard A. *Wisdom and Spiritual Transcendence at Corinth*. Eugene, OR: Cascade, 2008.

Institute for Food and Development Policy (Food First). http://www.foodfirst.org.

Jidejian, Nina. *Tyre through the Ages*. Beirut: Dar el-Mashreq Publishers, 1969.

Johnson, Luke Timothy. *Prophetic Jesus, Prophetic Church*. Grand Rapids: Eerdmans, 2011.

Jordan, Clarence. *Sermon on the Mount*. Valley Forge, PA: Judson Press, 1952.

Karris, Robert J. *Luke, Artist and Theologian*. Eugene, OR: Wipf & Stock, 2008.

Katho, Bungishabaku. "The New Covenant and the Challenge of Building a New and Transformed Community in DR Congo: A Contextual Reading of Jeremiah 31:31–34." *Old Testament Essays* 18:1 (2005): 109–23.

Keller, Catherine. "No More Sea: The Lost Chaos of the Eschaton." In *Christianity and Ecology*, edited by Dieter Hessel and Rosemary Radford Ruether. Cambridge, MA: Harvard University Press, 2000.

King, Philip J., and Lawrence E. Stager. *Life in Biblical Israel*. Louisville, KY: Westminster John Knox Press, 2001.

Kraybill, J. Nelson. *Imperial Cult and Commerce in John's Apocalypse*. Journal for the Study of the New Testament Supplement Series 132. Sheffield: Sheffield Academic Press, 1996.

Lang, Bernhard. *Monotheism and the Prophetic Minority*. Sheffield: Almond Press, 1983.

Lefebvre, Henri. *The Production of Space*. Oxford: Blackwell, 1991.

Levenson, Jon D. *Creation and the Persistence of Evil: The Jewish Drama of Divine Omnipotence*. New York: HarperCollins, 1988.

————. *Resurrection and the Restoration of Israel: The Ultimate Victory of the God of Life*. New Haven, CT: Yale University Press, 2006.

Lévinas, Emmanuel. *The Levinas Reader.* Edited by Seán Hand. Oxford: Blackwell, 1989.

Levine, Amy-Jill. "Visions of Kingdoms, from Pompey to the First Jewish Revolt." In *The Oxford History of the Biblical World*, edited by Michael D. Coogan. Oxford: Oxford University Press, 1998.

Levine, Amy-Jill, and Marc Zvi Brettler, eds. *The Jewish Annotated New Testament: New Revised Standard Version Bible Translation*. Oxford: Oxford University Press, 2011.

Lipton, Diana. *Longing for Egypt and Other Unexpected Biblical Tales*. Sheffield: Sheffield Phoenix Press, 2008.

Long, Burke O. *2 Kings*. Forms of the Old Testament Literature 10. Grand Rapids: Eerdmans, 1991.

Longenecker, Bruce W. *Remember the Poor: Paul, Poverty, and the Greco-Roman World*. Grand Rapids: Eerdmans, 2010.

Lundbom, Jack R. *Jeremiah Closer Up: The Prophet and the Book*. Hebrew Bible Monographs 31. Sheffield: Phoenix Press, 2010.

————. *Jeremiah 1–20*. Anchor Bible 21A. New York: Doubleday, 1999.

————. *Jeremiah 21–36*. Anchor Bible 21B. New York: Doubleday, 2004.

Luz, Ulrich. *Matthew 1–7: A Commentary*. Edinburgh: T & T Clark, 1989.

MacDonald, Nathan. "Listening to Abraham, Listening to YHWH: Divine Justice and Mercy in Genesis 18.16–33." *Catholic Biblical Quarterly* 66 (2004): 25–43.

————. *Not Bread Alone: The Uses of Food in the Old Testament*. Oxford: Oxford University Press, 2008.

————. *What Did the Ancient Israelites Eat? Diet in Biblical Times*. Grand Rapids: Eerdmans, 2008.

Mariani, Paul. *God and the Imagination: On Poets, Poetry, and the Ineffable*. Athens: University of Georgia Press, 2002.

Marlow, Hilary. *Biblical Prophets and Contemporary Environmental Ethics*. New York: Oxford University Press, 2009.

————. "Justice for All the Earth: Society, Ecology and the Biblical Prophets." In *Creation in Crisis: Christian Perspectives on*

Sustainability, edited by Robert S. White. London: Society for Promoting Christian Knowledge, 2009.

Marshall, David E. *God, Muhammad, and the Unbelievers: A Quranic Study*. Richmond, Surrey, UK: Curzon, 1999.

Martin, Clarice. "Polishing the Unclouded Mirror: A Womanist Reading of Revelation 18:13." In *From Every People and Nation: The Book of Revelation in Intercultural Perspective*, edited by David Rhoads. Minneapolis: Fortress Press, 2005.

Masefield, John. *Salt-Water Poems and Ballads*. New York: Macmillan, 1944.

Master, Daniel M. "Institutions of Trade in 1 and 2 Kings." In *The Books of Kings: Sources, Composition, Historiography and Reception*, edited by André Lemaire and Baruch Halpern. Supplements to Vetus Testamentum 129. Leiden: Brill, 2010.

Mays, James Luther. *Amos*. Old Testament Library. Philadelphia: Westminster Press, 1969.

McFague, Sallie. *The Body of God: An Ecological Theology*. Minneapolis: Fortress Press, 1993.

McMurtry, Megan. "The Cosmos in Jonah." Dissertation proposal, Vanderbilt University, May 14, 2010.

McNeill, J. R. *The Mountains of the Mediterranean World: An Environmental History*. Cambridge: Cambridge University Press, 1992.

Milgrom, Jacob. *Numbers*. JPS Torah Commentary. Philadelphia: Jewish Publication Society, 1990.

Miller, Patrick D., Jr. "'Moses My Servant': The Deuteronomic Portrait of Moses." *Interpretation* 41:1 (January 1987): 245–55.

Milman, Henry Hart. "Ride On! Ride On in Majesty." In *Hymnal 1982: according to the use of the Episcopal Church*. New York: Church Hymnal Corporation, 1982.

Minear, Paul S. *The Good News according to Matthew: A Training Manual for Prophets*. St. Louis: Chalice Press, 2000.

———. *I Saw a New Earth: An Introduction to the Visions of the Apocalypse*. Washington, DC: Corpus Books, 1968.

Mitchell, Margaret. *Paul and the Rhetoric of Reconciliation*. Tübingen: J. C. B. Mohr, 1991.

———. *Paul, the Corinthians and the Birth of Christian Hermeneutics*. Cambridge: Cambridge University Press, 2010.

Moberly, R. W. L. *The Bible, Theology, and Faith: A Study of Abraham and Jesus*. Cambridge: Cambridge University Press, 2000.

————. *Prophecy and Discernment.* Cambridge: Cambridge University Press, 2006.

Moore, Tara. "Beating the Coming Water Shortage." *Fortune,* October 17, 2011.

Muffs, Yochanan. *Love and Joy: Law, Language and Religion in Ancient Israel.* New York: Jewish Theological Seminary of America, 1992.

Murphy-O'Connor, Jerome. *Keys to First Corinthians: Revisiting the Major Issues.* Oxford: Oxford University Press, 2009.

Naudé, Piet. "Is Prophetic Discourse Adequate to Address Global Injustice?" In *Prophetic Witness: An Appropriate Contemporary Mode of Public Discourse?,* edited by Heinrich Bedford-Strohm and Etienne de Villiers. Münster: Lit, 2011.

Nelson, Richard D. *First and Second Kings.* Interpretation series. Atlanta: John Knox Press, 1987.

Neusner, Jacob. *Genesis Rabbah: The Judaic Commentary to the Book of Genesis: A New American Translation.* Atlanta: Scholars Press, 1985.

Niebuhr, Reinhold. *Beyond Tragedy: Essays on the Christian Interpretation of History.* New York: Charles Scribner's Sons, 1941.

O'Connor, Kathleen M. *Jeremiah: Pain and Promise.* Minneapolis: Fortress Press, 2011.

————. "Jeremiah's 'Prophetic Imagination': Pastoral Intervention for a Shattered World." In *Shaking Heaven and Earth,* edited by Christine Roy Yoder et al. Louisville, KY: Westminster John Knox Press, 2005.

O'Day, Gail R. *Revelation in the Fourth Gospel: Narrative Mode and Theological Claim.* Philadelphia: Fortress Press, 1986.

Odell, Margaret S. *Ezekiel.* Macon, GA: Smyth & Helwys, 2005.

Olson, Dennis T. *Numbers.* Interpretation series. Louisville, KY: John Knox Press, 1996.

Parker, Simon B. *Ugaritic Narrative Poetry.* Society of Biblical Literature Writings from the Ancient World. Atlanta: Scholars Press, 1997.

Pritchard, James B. *Ancient Near Eastern Texts Relating to the Old Testament.* Princeton, NJ: Princeton University Press, 1969.

The Qur'an: A New Translation by M. A. S. Abdel Haleem. Oxford: Oxford University Press, 2010.

Rad, Gerhard von. *Old Testament Theology.* 2 vols. New York: Harper & Row, 1965.

Rice, Chris, and Emmanuel Katongole. "A Christian Vision of Reconciliation." *Divinity* (Duke University), Spring 2012.

Ross, J. F. "The Prophet as Yahweh's Messenger." In *Israel's Prophetic Heritage*, edited by Bernhard W. Anderson and Walter Harrelson. New York: Harper, 1962.

Rossing, Barbara R. "Alas for Earth! Lament and Resistance in Revelation 12." In *The Earth Story in the New Testament*, edited by Norman Habel and Vicky Balabanski. Earth Bible 5. London: Sheffield Academic Press, 2002.

———. "River of Life in God's New Jerusalem." In *Christianity and Ecology*, edited by Dieter Hessel and Rosemary Radford Ruether. Cambridge, MA: Harvard University Press, 2000.

Rowe, C. Kavin. *Early Narrative Christology: The Lord in the Gospel of Luke*. Grand Rapids: Baker Academic, 2006.

Royalty, Robert M., Jr. *The Streets of Heaven: The Ideology of Wealth in the Apocalypse of John*. Macon, GA: Mercer University Press, 1998.

Russell, Letty M. *Just Hospitality: God's Welcome in a World of Difference*. Louisville, KY: Westminster John Knox Press, 2009.

Saldarini, Anthony J. *Matthew's Christian-Jewish Community*. Chicago: University of Chicago Press, 1994.

Sarna, Nahum. *Exodus*. JPS Torah Commentary. Philadelphia: Jewish Publication Society, 1991.

Schaefer, Steve. "How to Make Money Off the Drought: Fertilizers and Food." *Forbes*, September 10, 2012. Online: http://www.forbes.com/sites/steveschaefer/2012/08/22/how-to-make-money-off-the-drought-fertilizers-and-food/.

Schowalter, Daniel N. "Churches in Context." In *The Oxford History of the Biblical World*, edited by Michael D. Coogan. Oxford: Oxford University Press, 1998.

Sharp, Carolyn J. *Irony and Meaning in the Hebrew Bible*. Bloomington: Indiana University Press, 2009.

Simon, Uriel. *Reading Prophetic Narratives*. Bloomington: Indiana University Press, 1997.

Smith, Mark S. *The Early History of God: Yahweh and the Other Deities in Ancient Israel*. Grand Rapids: Eerdmans, 2002.

Smith, Morton. *Palestinian Parties and Politics That Shaped the Old Testament*. New York: Columbia University Press, 1972.

Sommer, Benjamin D. *The Bodies of God and the World of Ancient Israel*. New York: Cambridge University Press, 2009.

Stassen, Glen Harold. *A Thicker Jesus: Incarnational Discipleship in a Secular Age*. Louisville, KY: Westminster John Knox Press, 2012.

Stavroulakis, Nikos. *The Book of Jeremiah: A New Translation*. Philadelphia: Jewish Publication Society, 1973.

Stockitt, Robin. *Restoring the Shamed: Towards a Theology of Shame*. Eugene, OR: Cascade Books, 2012.

Strawn, Brent A. "On Vomiting: Leviticus, Jonah, Ea(a)rth." *Catholic Biblical Quarterly* 74:3 (2012): 445–64.

Stulman, Louis, and Hyun Chul Paul Kim. *You Are My People: An Introduction to Prophetic Literature*. Nashville: Abingdon Press, 2010.

Sweeney, Marvin A. *I and II Kings: A Commentary*. Louisville, KY: Westminster John Knox Press, 2007.

The Sibylline Oracles, Thesaurus Linguae Graecae. Irvine, CA: Thesaurus Linguae Graecae, 1996–.

Tuan, Yi-Fu. *Space and Place: The Perspective of Experience*. Minneapolis: University of Minnesota Press, 1977.

Vincent, Janet. "The Worst of Times: Sharing Faith through Tragedy." *Virginia Seminary Journal*, Fall 2012.

Waltke, Bruce K. *The Book of Proverbs: Chapters 15–31*. Grand Rapids: Eerdmans, 2005.

Weil, Simone. "The *Iliad*, Poem of Might." In *The Simone Weil Reader*, edited by George Panichas. New York: McKay, 1977.

Wilbur, Richard. "Advice to a Prophet." http://www.poets.org/view media.php/prmMID/15485.

Wilkins, Michael J. *Discipleship in the Ancient World and Matthew's Gospel*. Grand Rapids: Baker Books, 1995.

Wilson, Walter T. *Philo of Alexandria on Virtues: Introduction, Translation, and Commentary*. Leiden: Brill, 2011.

Wirzba, Norman. *The Essential Agrarian Reader: The Future of Culture, Community, and the Land*. Lexington: University Press of Kentucky, 2003.

Wright, Christopher J. H. *God's People in God's Land: Family, Land, and Property in the Old Testament*. Grand Rapids: Eerdmans, 1990.

261

————. *Old Testament Ethics for the People of God*. Leicester: InterVarsity Press, 2004.

Zornberg, Avivah Gottlieb. *Genesis: The Beginning of Desire*. Philadelphia: Jewish Publication Society, 1995.

————. *The Particulars of Rapture: Reflections on Exodus*. New York: Doubleday, 2001.

INDEX OF SCRIPTURE AND OTHER
ANCIENT SOURCES

263

270

INDEX OF SUBJECTS

273